About the author

Eddi Fiegel is a freelance journalist and broadcaster, working for the *Guardian*, the *Sunday Times* and BBC Radio. She is well known for her interviews with artists across the musical spectrum from Paul McCartney to kd Lang, David Bowie and Philip Glass. She has been especially enthralled by the music of the 1960s from an early age and has been collecting John Barry's work in particular ever since.

JOHN BARRY
A SIXTIES THEME

FROM JAMES BOND
TO MIDNIGHT COWBOY

Eddi Fiegel

BOXTREE

First published 1998 by Constable and Company Limited

This paperback edition published 2001 by
Boxtree
an imprint of Pan Macmillan Ltd
Pan Macmillan, 20 New Wharf Road, London N1 9RR
Basingstoke and Oxford
Associated companies throughout the world
www.panmacmillan.com

ISBN 0 7522 2033 0

1 3 5 7 9 8 6 4 2

A CIP catalogue record for this book is available from
the British Library

Typeset in Monotype Bembo 11½pt by
Rowland Phototypesetting Ltd
Printed and bound in Great Britain by
Mackays of Chatham plc

CONTENTS

ACKNOWLEDGEMENTS

Top of the list, a major Thank You is due to Lloyd Bradley for epic encouragement and advice from the very beginning, and in whose case the 'without whom' cliché fully applies.

Inevitably, during the course of nearly three years' research, there have been a vast number of other people who have helped in various ways. Of these, thanks must go to: Robert Wood at Movie Boulevard in Leeds and Phil Richmond for their time and for allowing me access to their unofficial John Barry archives; to Alan Field, Debra Geddes at EMI; Fred Dellar, John Coxon; Pru at Rough Trade; Sister Gregory at the Bar Convent Museum, York; Paul Mitchell at St Peter's School, York; Elaine Woods at the Musicians Union North, Eddie Levey, Alan Rowett, John Repsch, Laura Parfitt, Tony Phillips, Chris Kimber, Marla Ludwig, Richard Jolley and Claire Evans; to Tara Lawrence and all at Constable; to Joan Deitch, Andrea Rosenberg and Stephanie Rushton. My special thanks also to my friends: Andrea, Tamzin and Marcelle and to my family, particularly my parents, Ruth-Eva and Gideon for their support.

Thanks are obviously also due in no small part to all the people who gave up their time to be interviewed. Of these I would particularly like to thank the following: Bryan Forbes, Leslie Bricusse, Michael Caine, Anthony Harvey, Trevor Peacock, Richard Lester, Peter Hunt, Bob Kingston, Sid Margo, Doug Wright and Pete Varley for not only taking time to cast their minds back thirty years, but also in some cases to delve into their archives and attics for photographs, press cuttings and phone numbers. Other interviewees were: Jane Birkin, Anthony Newley, Guy Hamilton, John Schlesinger, Sidney J. Furie, Lewis Gilbert, John Dankworth, Adam Faith, John Burgess, Jack Parnell, Don Lusher, Gered Mankowitz, Gene Gutowski, Jeremy Clyde, Les Reed, David Jacobs, Brian Matthew, Don Black, Brian Kershaw, Ric Kennedy, Vic Flick, Ken Golder, Mike Cox, Lillie Taylor, Eric Tomlinson, Ron Heffernan, Dr Francis Jackson, Hugh Murray, Richard Polak, John Leach, Rodney Oxtoby, Terry Snowdon, Malcolm Addey, David Picker, Geoffrey Heath, George Ciancimino, Jarvis Cocker, David Arnold, Barry Adamson, Paul Hartnoll and Adrian Utley.

Finally, of course, my heartfelt thanks must go to John Barry, firstly for giving me so much to write about, but equally for his unfailing commitment to this book, as well as his invaluable recollections, insights and ideas.

LIST OF ILLUSTRATIONS

Section 1

The Prendergast family (*courtesy of John Barry*)
Doris Prendergast (*courtesy of John Barry*)
Jack Prendergast (*courtesy of John Barry*)
Doris and Jack with Louis Armstrong at the Casino Theatre, York (*courtesy of John Barry*)
John outside his army tent in Egypt (*courtesy of Pete Varley*)
The Green Howards at Liverpool Station (*courtesy of Pete Varley*)
The John Barry Seven (*The Harry Hammond Archive, V & A Picture Library*)
John, Blackpool Sands (*EMI Music Archives*)
John with Adam Faith (*EMI Music Archives*)
John at home in Cadogan Square (*Cliff Jones*)
John and Shirley Bassey (*courtesy of Pete Varley*)
Saltzman, Fleming and Broccoli (*PIC Photos*)
John conducting a Bond session (*PIC Photos*)

Section 2

Michael Caine in *The Ipcress File* (*United Artists. All rights reserved*)
The girls from *Passion Flower Hotel* (*From a collection in the Theatre Museum, V & A*)

John and Jane at the premiere of *Born Free* (*PIC Photos*)

John with Bryan Forbes and his wife Nanette Newman (*courtesy of Bryan Forbes*)

Renata Tarrago and Bryan Forbes (*courtesy of Bryan Forbes*)

John at work (*PIC Photos*)

John, 1969 (*Richard Polak*)

With Louis Armstrong and Hal David (*United Artists. All rights reserved*)

With Jane Sidey, 1969 (*Express Newspapers*)

John, taken by Kate Barry, 1997 (*courtesy of John Barry*)

INTRODUCTION

John Barry fans lurk in the most unexpected places. Fellini once said that *Goldfinger* was his favourite film score, Alice Cooper claimed that the *Goldfinger* title song inspired him to become a performer, and the Pope apparently listens to *Dances with Wolves*.

Since the beginning of Barry's career, there have been fans encompassing the full spectrum of devotion, from the casual enthusiast to the lifelong obsessive. Among musicians, his influence has always been enormous, but recently there has been an upsurge in recognisably Barry-inspired work. Listen to the music of contemporary artists from Portishead, Orbital and Morcheeba to Barry Adamson, Pulp and Mono, and film composer David Arnold, and you'll hear the unmistakable sound of John Barry.

The term 'Barryesque' has become standard music terminology to describe a soaring but plaintive string-style, and its impact has been widespread. 'Seeing *You Only Live Twice* tainted me for life,' says David Arnold. 'Apart from the opening sequence, there was that incredible string melody, and the music completely blew my head off. It was a fairly substantial event for me that just got me hooked, and I knew that was what I wanted to do for a living.'

The music John Barry created for Bond and his other scores was unique. Musicians invariably comment on the originality of his chord structure, the sparse perfection of his melody lines and the emotion which comes through it all. 'There's something about the way he puts melodies and chords together,' says Pulp's Jarvis Cocker. 'It conjures up an atmosphere. Sometimes when you first listen to one of his songs you'll think that it's playing bum notes. It'll always go somewhere a bit weird. That's what I like about it. It never really goes where you think it's gonna go.'

Barry Adamson is another fan. 'The way he does things – the strings up top, the trombones at the bottom, there's an accessibility there, a simplicity and succinctness in the discovery of a chord. It's so graceful in terms of that. Listening to him I've learned to just happen upon things musically myself, just to listen to where the hands fall on the piano. Even the way he puts a line together is original. Suspense is suspense, sadness is sadness and joy is joy. But what's remarkable is to convey those emotions and have your identity in there as well. The access to darkness is another thing I really admire. To convey darkness in a way that doesn't frighten people away, but just does enough to get at you. That's really something.'

Another aspect of Barry's work which has been drawn on is the Eastern European-style Cold War sound which he created for *The Ipcress File*, and later evolved in his landmark theme for *The Persuaders*. You can hear it on Pulp's 'I Spy', and more overtly on Portishead's 'Sour Times'. 'That John Barry spy sound,' says Portishead's Adrian Utley, 'was the main Barry element I tried to put into our music. I wanted to capture that sound of the Cold War. For me, *The Ipcress File* was just perfection. It's one of my favourite films ever.' Orbital's Paul Hartnoll is also a confirmed Barry fan and 'The Box' is equally resonant of *The Persuaders*. 'I just love his melody and harmony,' says Hartnoll. 'His music always had catchy tunes, and that made it more accessible than the dirge of pretend classical music that most film music sounds like now. With "The Box", I went to quite a lot of lengths to get that dulcimer sound and manipulate it, because I'd always loved that whole Barry concept.'

The Persuaders was a hit in 1972, *The Ipcress File* in 1965, so why should there be such a huge burst of interest now? There are various possible answers to this question. The increasingly corporate, finance-driven nature of the music industry has divested rock and pop of its magic and mystery, and people have begun to look further afield for their music. From the musician's point of view meanwhile, pop, in terms of style, has always appropriated and plundered its own past, and so thirty years since its birth, it is only natural that it may need to look beyond itself for inspiration. The emergence of instrumental dance music over the last decade has also created a generation who are more naturally attuned to the concept of instrumental music than the three-minute vocal pop tradition of previous years.

Dance music and specifically ecstasy culture have also spawned the 'chill-out' concept – the cossetted approach to communal drug come-down. There was a new need for string-soaked sounds, easy on the helter-skeltering ear. Suddenly long-forgotten Barry classics were being played in 'chill-out' rooms at clubs across Britain and another generation of fans was born.

The so-called 'easy-listening' boom of the Nineties was another factor in the renewed interest in the soundtrack genre, but although Barry's work is frequently included in the category, it is a misnomer. The predominant feature of 'easy' is its martini-swigging, breezing-down-a-freeway trouble-free luxuriance. Some Barry music may occasionally fulfil these requisite criteria – lush, sweeping strings, twanging guitars – but there are always darker elements which cannot be ignored.

On a more general level, the thirtysomething generation's fascination with the Sixties can easily be attributed to a basic psychological attraction to the decade of one's infancy, to the time of one's earliest memories. As a decade the Sixties also resonate in our cultural memory as a time of optimism, of social upheaval and freedom, and phenomenal creative energy. Particularly now, as we face an altogether more prosaic, aggress-ively cut-throat world, the contrast is even more evident. Much of the music John Barry created in the Sixties has become synonymous with that era. As much as The Beatles and Carnaby Street, the soundtracks to *Goldfinger*, *The Ipcress File* and *The Knack* abound with the exuberance of 'swinging London', but their real appeal lies in the music itself.

I personally discovered the John Barry sound as a teenager when I was given The John Barry Seven's album *Stringbeat*. At around the same time I also chanced upon the theme to *The Persuaders* and the *Goldfinger* soundtrack. They were monumentally exciting events. In the lacklustre pop environment of the mid Eighties, their music punched you in the stomach and made your heart break. It was unlike anything else around. And it wasn't just the emotional appeal of their melodies. The strangeness and the originality of their intrinsic sound gave them a fascination way beyond the norm. As I became familiar with more of the Barry catalogue over the years, I also naturally became interested in the music's origin, and the end result has been this book. What I wanted to do was to present the stories of the music and the films that had meant something to me. To investigate how they had come about and why. Over extensive interviews with John Barry, I therefore tried to explore not only the circumstances of his work but the thoughts, motivations and ideas behind it.

During the course of nearly three years' research and over fifty interviews with colleagues, collaborators and friends, I have also tried to reach as deep an understanding as possible of the social and professional environment in which he lived and worked. What follows is therefore not a cataloguing of dates, events and line-ups – a full discography and filmography is provided at the back of the book – but rather an examination and appreciation of John Barry's career through the Sixties in the context of the changing world around him.

GOLDEN WORDS

September, 1964. Cadogan Square, Chelsea, London. It's 4 a.m. Michael Caine is staying in John Barry's spare room, desperately trying to get some sleep while John pounds away at the piano, night after night, after night. Suddenly, the music stops and Caine is jolted out of semi-sleep by the shock of the silence. Bleary-eyed, he staggers into John's bachelor-pad drawing room and finds the composer slumped over the piano. 'I've cracked it,' he says. And as the sun comes up and fills the room, he plays the lingering melody which will lodge in Caine's head for the next six months. 'What's it called?' says Caine. ' "Goldfinger",' says John, before he falls asleep over the keyboard.

Michael Caine was the first person to hear 'Goldfinger'. The second was Trevor Peacock, John's regular lyricist, whom he'd commissioned to write the words. However, a week later, Peacock was still struggling. It was a tough task. John had already had a nightmare sorting out the music; now he urgently needed a lyric. And it had to be perfect. John had been hounding the Bond producers to let him write a title song for months, and they'd finally given him the go-ahead with *Goldfinger*. He couldn't afford to let them down. After all, he could have written the best melody in the world, but if the lyric didn't work, he'd be in trouble.

So he took it to Leslie Bricusse and Anthony Newley, the hot song-writing pair about town, who'd just had a huge hit with their musical *Stop the World, I Want To Get Off*. If anyone could sort this out, John thought, they could.

So they came to Cadogan Square and John sat down at the piano and played them what he'd written.

'But what's it all about, John? What the hell do we do with it?' they asked.

'It's "Mack the Knife",' he told them.

'What I meant was,' John explains, 'it's a song about a bad guy, and there aren't that many songs about bad guys. "Mack the Knife" was the greatest one, set in that German period in the 1930s. So I said to them: "This is a guy – a villain – who paints women gold. It's pretty mad." And then they knew.'

Bricusse and Newley had never worked so hard in their lives. 'It nearly drove us crazy,' admits Newley. 'It took us weeks, because it wasn't a very long song, and you had to get all this information into a very short musical timespan. But in the end I think it was one of the strongest lyrics we did. It's quite hard and informative, and it seems to hit right on the money as to who Goldfinger was.'

What the pair came up with captured the spirit of Bond perfectly. 'The same way the films had those throwaway Bond one-liners with those puns,' says Leslie Bricusse, 'the songs all needed to have equally tongue-in-cheek lyrics, so that's what we did. I thought it was the silliest lyric I ever wrote!'

As well as matching the Bond humour, Bricusse and Newley's lyrics also worked perfectly with John's music. John had built 'Goldfinger' around a song structure that dated back to the 1930s – the Broadway musical song tradition that he'd grown up with – and Bricusse and Newley were part of the same school. The result brought us rhymes like the wonderfully louche, ironic pairing of 'Midas touch' and 'spider's touch'. 'Bricusse was very heavily into inside rhymes,' says Newley, 'and it nearly drove me crazy, 'cause most people don't give a rat's. Most singers and songwriters don't even try and do inside rhymes any more because it's not important to the young listeners, but to the old craftsmen it's a thing of pride really.' John, Bricusse, Newley and also, importantly, Shirley Bassey had one foot in showbiz in the old sense of the word, and one foot in the very swinging present, and it was that combination which made 'Goldfinger' work.

The song wasn't quite perfect yet, however. Even after John's weeks at the piano, when it came to the session, there was still something missing; it was only during the run-through for the title sequence that the final arrangement came to him.

'We went into the studio initially,' says John, 'because Robert Brownjohn who was designing the title sequence was desperate to hear something.' Brownjohn was a crazy, strung-out New Yorker whose drug-raddled mind created the gloriously lurid fantasies for the title sequences of both *From Russia With Love* and *Goldfinger*. And it was only once John put his music to those opening images, that the whole thing really started to come together.

'The main brass idea only came to me that day on the session,' he recalls. 'I realised it was too down, and it needed something else, so at the break everyone went off and I went back to the piano.' What John came back with was the sleazy *wah wah wah wah wah* brass line that follows the opening chords, and it was the final magic ingredient in the mix. 'It was like a common scream,' says John, 'but it worked like a bitch. And Brownjohn just said, "Yeah, it's perfect. It's vulgar, it's wonderful."'

What John and Brownjohn ended up creating became probably the most famous Bond title sequence of all, and the story goes that what's at the start of the film is not even half of what was originally planned. 'They edited things out you wouldn't believe,' says John, 'but I still look at that opening title and think, Yeah, it works. I remember the first time I saw the finished sequence with the music and I thought, Jesus! Those images: the hand coming up and the golfball between the breasts and the Aston Martin. It was like two minutes of total entertainment. Audiences went crazy. They applauded at the end of it and just went nuts. It was *the* most effective title sequence and it hasn't dated at all. It still sends shivers down you.'

Even without Brownjohn's images, 'Goldfinger' still sends shivers down most people, but it wasn't just the drama, sex and sleaze of it all that made the song so special. Bassey's hard-as-nails vocal was perfect for the villain whose 'heart is cold', but if John's melody had been equally chilled, the song would never have had the impact it did. What made it work was the combination of that icy, razor-sharp vocal with the poignancy at the melody's core. That was what made you care. There was ruthlessness in this song, but there was also the enticement of a dangerously slow seduction. The combination of menacing drive and aching lyricism was key to 'Goldfinger'. It was also key to the sound of John Barry.

I

BLACK AND WHITE MICE

Most film composers end up writing for film by accident. They're usually either classical composers or rock musicians who fall into it as a means of branching out. For John Barry it was neither of those things. For him it was what he had always wanted to do.

'One of my very earliest memories is as a small child being carried through big double doors to the cinema by my dad, and seeing this enormous black and white Mickey Mouse on the screen – and just being hugely excited about it,' says John. 'I thought to myself – my daddy works in a place where there are big black and white mice on a screen. I think I like it here.'

And he did – he liked it a lot. The place where Daddy worked was like a magic carpet ride to some other, brighter universe. And John knew that somehow or other he wanted to be part of that.

How that would happen soon became clear. The big screen was one kind of escape from real life, but there was another – music. 'Apart from the movies, there was only one other thing that got to me as a child, and that was music. I remember being off school sick, and lying in bed listening to classical music on the radio in the afternoons – and it just got to me. I thought, This is another world, and it's better than this one. That and the movies. Movies and music were always the two things I loved.'

By the time John was nine years old he knew he wanted to be a musician, and by the time he was sixteen, he knew he wanted to make music for films. It was the perfect way to bring together his two favourite things.

The great Hollywood composers – Korngold, Steiner and Rozsa – had enchanted him with their scores for Hollywood classics like *The Adventures of Robin Hood* and *Gone With the Wind*, but for most young boys growing up in Yorkshire in the 1930s and 1940s, the world of Hollywood film composing would have been very far off in every sense. While Britain did have its own film-composing tradition with classical composers like William Walton and Ralph Vaughan Williams writing for the cinema, the profession was still in its infancy and there were no schools or university courses which taught it, nor published scores or soundtrack records to study. But for John this didn't really matter, as he had a natural school of his own. And it was right on his own doorstep. 'I grew up with movies,' he says, 'and that's the best school a film composer could ever have.'

John Barry Prendergast was born in York on 3 November 1933, into a family that was far from obscure. His father, Jack Xavier Prendergast – or 'JX' as he was often called – was known throughout the North of England as an enormously successful showbusiness entrepreneur; he owned eight cinemas and theatres across Yorkshire, including the flag-ship Rialto in York.

Often dubbed 'the Lew Grade of the North', JX Prendergast played host to the most prestigious performers of the day. Orchestras, conductors and artists from all over the world performed at his venues, including The Hallé and Sir Thomas Beecham, and Victoria de los Angeles. JX was not only a success professionally, he was also a larger-than-life personality: a character in the truest sense of the word. He was a tall, big, charismatic man who was always immaculately tailored, wore his trademark trilby cocked to one side and never left the house without his snuff box. 'You don't know what's good for you!' he would holler if anyone tried refusing an offer of snuff.

JX also loved a good party and never missed an excuse to throw one. No performance at the Rialto was ever complete without some kind of a drinks reception afterwards, and these often led to friendships with the artists. While John was growing up, it was not unusual for him to find someone like Sir John Barbirolli in the living room at home, or to meet and chat with the stars of the day in an informal atmosphere.

But although his children were born into showbusiness, Jack Prendergast himself was not. His success was entirely self-made and his own start in life had been much more humble. The Prendergasts were Irish Catholics and Jack was born in 1898 near Cork, coming over to Liverpool with his family when he was still a child.

Jack started his career in showbusiness as stage manager in a theatre in Liverpool, but soon realised that the future of entertainment lay with that stunning new invention from America – motion pictures. So he got himself a job as a cinema projectionist and from there worked his way up to managing the Palladium Cinema in Lancaster. Prendergast had the knack of recognising a market and an audience almost before it existed. He had drive and he was also a supremely charismatic hustler – two qualities that were later inherited by his son John Barry.

Alongside the Palladium, on the main town square in Lancaster, was the local repertory theatre which had recently been bought by Henry Wilkinson, a retired sea-captain. There Jack met Mr Wilkinson's willowy young daughter Doris – a frail, gentle young Lancashirewoman who had trained as a classical pianist. Doris was immediately captivated by their dynamic new neighbour.

The couple were soon married and in 1923 their son Patrick was born, followed by daughter June in 1928 and then, after another five-year gap, by John Barry – named after the film actor John Barrymore. By this time, Jack Prendergast had seen the Casino Theatre and Ballroom in Fishergate up for sale in York and decided to buy it. Within a few years, after the original theatre had burned down in a fire, he had built a new, state-of-the-art theatre and cinema – the Rialto – on the same site. Shrewdly, he reasoned that as York was a major railway link and also the last big station before the Scottish border, any performing troupe heading North would play York as the perfect stopover. And they did.

Meanwhile he had bought a small family house at 167 Hull Road on the outskirts of the city. York is one of England's oldest, most historic cities, famous for its medieval Minster, Roman heritage, Georgian architecture and narrow cobbled streets, but it's also one of England's smaller cities and in the 1930s still only had a population of about 90,000. This meant that you could easily get out to the green surrounding countryside, and Doris Prendergast often used to take her children for outings to nearby Helmsley and other areas. But generally, as a youngster, John found the atmosphere in York less than uplifting.

'York is the most beautiful city in the world,' he says, 'the most extraordinary place. But it's sad as well, and to live there – that's something else. One of my earliest childhood memories is of the sun going down, and it was as if the whole town had gone to sleep. You could hear footsteps on the streets, and I used to think to myself, Surely the rest of the world can't be like this! At the bottom of it all, I guess I also wanted to get away from my father. He was a very dominating gentleman.'

The family led a comfortable life. Jack Prendergast was one of the few people in town to possess his own motor car, the couple employed a full-time nanny for their children and by the time John was a teenager they were living in the beautiful, Georgian Fulford House. However, JX was a strict authoritarian, whose word was law in his household, despite his wife's softer influence.

'He was a very bright gentleman and very knowledgeable about living, but he didn't have a gentleness towards us,' says John. Rodney Oxtoby, John's closest friend at secondary school, remembers JX as a rather daunting figure. 'We used to keep white mice in the outbuildings in their garden, but if his father suddenly came back, it would always be a case of, Look out! Here comes Mr Prendergast!'

Jack and Doris were themselves the products of a strict Victorian upbringing, so in their house, as in many other households in Britain in the 1930s, particularly in the North of England, you got on with things and you didn't 'make a fuss'. Emotions were something you kept to yourself; displays of them were certainly not encouraged. 'I would never say I was a deprived child,' John comments. 'I wasn't. I was an extremely *lucky* child – but there was an emotional level that just wasn't acknowledged.' The atmosphere of emotional repression was to have a strong impact on John's life and his music, because pent-up feelings eventually need an outlet. And John made sure they found one.

Like most intelligent children, he grew up questioning everything. 'I remember looking at the mottled wallpaper in my bedroom from my cot, and I used to see faces and clouds in it. Then when traffic went by I'd see the light coming back reflected in the wardrobe mirror and I used to go to sleep wondering why the car was going one way and the light was going another.'

The young John – or Barry as he was known until his twenties – also had plenty of time alone to indulge his imagination. Jack Prendergast was usually busy taking care of the eight theatres and his mother had a household to run. 'My dad used to be in the theatres every night till late. Then by the time he was up in the morning, my mum would make him bacon and eggs or whatever, and then he'd be back in the theatre. So he wasn't there an awful lot.'

Instead of getting bored with so much time to himself though, as some children might have done, John loved his private time. What he had seen in his father's cinema had inspired him to create his own fantasy world with his toys, and once alone in his room he would put on his favourite records by Sibelius or Ravel, and act out adventures with his Dinky toys. All the feelings he had that you weren't supposed to show went into these dramas. And the music determined the plot. Instinctively he was developing a fundamental understanding of the relationship between music and drama. If you'd tried inventing a 'learn to be a film composer' children's game, this was probably what you'd come up with. 'Young composers sometimes ask me today,' says John, 'how you work out writing music that isn't just good music, but that fits the drama of a scene as well. And I say, "If you haven't got that in-built sense of it to start with, you're lost".' John himself clearly did have it, but for the moment it was secret – and it was important that his private world be kept that way.

'I was being private, thinking my own thoughts,' John recalls 'I was also shy about other people seeing, so it was like – "Don't interrupt". When you're in the middle of a good play – with Sibelius going and all these Dinky toys, the last thing you want is somebody walking in the room, disturbing those thoughts.'

When John was only six years old, it was announced that Britain was at war with Germany; although he was too young to understand the full significance of this, he could sense the foreboding among the adults around him.

'I remember so clearly being in the sitting room of our house in Hull Road, and it being late morning when Chamberlain came on the radio, the BBC. He said "As of now, we are at war", and I was sat in the bay window and I knew something was up. I didn't understand what "a state of war" really meant, but I remember my mother going up to my father and saying, "At the end of all this, if you and I and the three kids are stood in a field – that's all I want". And I thought, Oh my God. Something must be really wrong here.'

The war was to have an immeasurable impact on John's life, but at first this only filtered through his childhood reality. 'Before the war I had had traditional English military tin soldiers with red uniforms,' he remembers. 'When war happened, suddenly we had grey battleships. War became our toy. I had a Dinky model of HMS *Hood*, and I remember listening to the one o'clock news on the BBC one day and hearing that it had been sunk in the North Sea, with only one survivor. It was as if my Dinky toy had been sunk.'

By this time John had become a pupil at the Bar Convent Catholic Junior School just outside the centre of York. The school was one of the oldest in the town and had a reputation for sound academic teaching. But it was also strong on discipline. John was used to discipline at home, and now he had to face a new set of rules and regulations at school.

'It was the most severe Catholic teaching ever, and I hated it,' John recalls with a shudder. 'You were surrounded by nuns who asked you questions like, "Who do you love more – God or your mother and father?" And I used to say, "My mother and father," and they'd say, "Oh, if that's the case you're sure to go to hell".'

But in spite of these far from gentle applications of the Catholic faith, the religion was to stay with John for life. 'I hated it,' he says, 'but you know it gets so ingrained in you, that kind of thing. I'm still a very strong Catholic. There's something awful about the faith, but there's something terribly good about it as well.'

By 1942, World War Two was at its height, and much of it was being fought in the air. Night-time raids were a reality for anyone living in Britain's cities, and everyone, including the children, had to learn how to deal with them. John, however, showed a stoicism and courage remarkable in a child. When he was nine years old, his mother had led him down into the air-raid shelter during a particularly bad raid. 'Mummy, are we all going to be killed now?' he asked matter-of-factly. Years later she would say to him, 'You were so practical, you seemed to have no fear.'

The whole atmosphere of unspoken fear and anxiety that the war engendered was traumatic enough for a sensitive young child, but the air raids were to have an even more lasting impact. One particular set of raids caused huge amounts of damage, both to the historic fabric of England's cities and to the country's morale. The 'Baedeker Raids' as they came to be known were so called because the Germans targeted the towns most cherished by Britain's famous guidebooks – the medieval city centres. Between April and June of 1942, the cathedral cities of Exeter, Bath, Norwich, Canterbury, Ipswich and York were attacked at least once, causing varying degrees of damage.

By the time of the attack on York, nightly air raids had become such a regular part of life that most major buildings had their own shelter. The Bar Convent School had one of the largest in the city – a catacomb-like space seven flights of stairs below the old school building that was considered one of the safest places in York. On the afternoon of 28 April 1942 John was at school when the air-raid sirens went off, signalling the start of a raid.

'It was very unusual,' he explains, 'because the raids were always at night. But you only had to have one plane go over for the sirens to go off, and I remember that was one of the first times the nuns read us *Gulliver's Travels*. Then in the late afternoon the All Clear sounded and my mother and father came in the car to pick up my sister and me. The nuns were very against us going home, though, and urged my parents to leave us there in the shelter. "Leave them here, Mr Prendergast" I remember them saying. "This is the safest place on earth." But for some reason my parents were determined to take us home. So I got home and it was all very peaceful and I went to bed. The air raids usually started about eight o'clock at night, but that night there was no sign of anything. It was all quiet. Then at about eleven o'clock it started. And they blitzed York.'

That night's raid proved devastating. Seventy-nine people were killed and ninety people seriously injured. York's narrow medieval winding streets with their tall timbered buildings were the perfect firetrap, and the blaze raced through the town. The famous Minster remained unscathed, but there was severe damage throughout the rest of the city.

In the Prendergast household, Jack as head of the York Fire Service had been called out for most of the night. At one point he came home though, and John remembers him staggering in soaking wet and black. '"I'm going to take you out there, Barry," he said. "I want to show you something." And my mother said, "No, Jack, no." But he dragged me out into the garden and all you could see was the whole city burning. The sky was bright red.

'The next morning when I woke up they said, "You don't have to go to school today." My first reaction was that I was thrilled, 'cause I hated it so much there anyway. Then it turned out that the school had been hit and the bomb had gone right through the building. The so-called safest place in York had been hit: five of the nuns had been killed, and a whole wing of the school was destroyed.'

The atmosphere of devastation was all the more traumatic for John as it remained unaddressed. 'Nobody ever talked about it,' he says solemnly. 'It was just never mentioned. It was as if everyone knew something terrible had happened, but you didn't speak about it.'

The impact of having so narrowly missed death himself and seeing the town in flames went very deep. Many years later, John would draw on the events of the raid and express the sense of tragedy in 'Memories of Childhood' on his 1998 *Beyondness of Things* album, poignantly quoting the children of the Convent singing, 'Nick, nack, paddywack'. But at the time, as a nine-year-old, it was only the day-to-day effects that he was consciously aware of.

The centre of York was closed off for two days after the raid but because of Jack Prendergast's role in the Fire Service he and his family were allowed in. 'I remember I had a favourite pair of shoes that we'd left to be mended at the Saxone shoe shop – which was suddenly no longer there. And the whole of the tar on Coney Street had melted with the heat of the burning buildings, and the blast had blown diamond watches from the jewellers' shops. I thought, My shoes are in there somewhere, melted. The worst thing was the stench, though. It's a strange smell, the stench of burning buildings and burning bodies. It's something you never forget.'

Two weeks later, John was allowed back to the Bar Convent, where the teachers tried to carry on as normal. 'I remember going back to school and seeing that the whole left wing of the building where the bomb had gone through just wasn't there any more. There was all this rubble everywhere, but there was also this huge veil of secrecy which you kind of went along with. You said your prayers and you never asked anything, and the teachers would just come in and say, "The lesson for today is . . ." and that was it. The really strange part of it is that my parents never talked about any of it either. It was that Yorkshire thing of being very closed off.'

When he was eleven, John left the Bar Convent and started at St Peter's public school in York. Dubbed 'the Eton of the North', the school was one of the oldest and best in England, with a list of past pupils which included Guy Fawkes and captain of the England cricket team Norman Yardley, as well as numerous heads of industry. Its emphasis was firmly on academic prowess, and its punishingly strict regime left little time for the hours of freedom that John was used to.

'I hated school,' John says bluntly. 'Hated it beyond belief. There were one or two masters whom I really liked – Mr Le Tocq who taught Physics and Collier who taught Art. They were terrific, but the rest I hated. I just loathed the whole process.'

Although John was only a day pupil at St Peter's, school was six days a week: Monday to Saturday from nine in the morning to nine at night. John felt the wrench from his old home-life keenly. 'I used to get on my bicycle at nine o'clock at night, go home, go to bed, get up and get on my bicycle at eight-thirty in the morning and go back to school. Not much of a life, was it?'

Apart from missing his home-life, John also experienced the sting of prejudice, aimed at him by the rigorously academic and conservative schoolmasters. 'There were about twelve students there who were Catholics, and we were treated differently from everyone else,' he says with a touch of bitterness. 'We didn't go to school prayers, and they just didn't like us – it was as simple as that. I was picked on the whole time.'

He also suspected that the teachers looked down on his father. JX was of course a well-respected and obviously wealthy local businessman, but he was involved in the world of showbusiness, which was still considered with disdain by the so-called professional classes.

But the main thing John disliked about St Peter's was the regimented atmosphere and lack of spontaneity and imagination. 'There was no warmth, no kindness, no individuality,' he explains. 'Nobody saw anybody who shone and helped them, lifted them through the loop into something else. It was horrendously cold. It was worse than the Convent. I had hated it there, God knows, but the Protestants were even worse than the bloody Convent!'

In response to the stultifying atmosphere, John found small ways in which to rebel and indulge in some time-honoured schoolboy mischief. 'We used to fart in class when the teacher wasn't looking, and I must say, I was pretty good at it. The teacher would turn round and say, in that terribly terribly clipped English accent: "Who has made that *frightful* sound?" Sometimes I'd own up, and then it would be, "Go and stand out in the corridor, Prendergast".'

In his school reports they said: *Is a dreamer, looks out of the window and doesn't apply himself.* But when he did apply himself there was no stopping him. He was top of the class in Art, Physics and Chemistry. With those subjects he had the chance to do something practical, something that wasn't all in-the-air theories. 'My friend John Mason and I always made the best crystals in chemistry lessons,' says John. 'When it came down to actually doing something, I functioned very well.'

What he really wanted to do though was to study music. By the time he was about nine years old he knew without a doubt that he wanted to become a musician. As a small child, his Dinky-toy dramas had been acted out to Sibelius and Ravel, but what had really moved him were the sounds of Chopin and Beethoven. Music, he learned from these two composers, had the power to be more than just a pleasurable escape and diversion. In them he discovered two elements which were to become crucial to his own writing later on: romanticism and drama. He saw that it was possible for music to be achingly beautiful and yet quite tragic. It could take you on a journey of emotions, yet leave you uplifted at the end. And none of these lessons were forgotten.

He was also struck by the sheer physicality of Beethoven. 'If you listen to Beethoven,' he says, 'never a note flags. Everything pours out alive with the energy of the moment of creation. That's what it's really all about – energy.'

Music was not something that the worthy St Peter's encouraged, but it did offer piano lessons as an extra-curricular option and so John persuaded his father to let him learn. However, in the highly macho atmosphere of Yorkshire in the 1940s, piano lessons were never really considered something that a serious young boy should be occupying himself with, and John was made to feel it. Because they were not part of the normal timetable, he had to be called out of regular classes for each lesson. The music-teacher's runner would come knocking on the door in the middle of ordinary lessons, causing embarrassment to John and no end of sarcasm from the teacher whose class was being interrupted.

'The runner would come in and say, "Can Prendergast come to his music lesson now?" remembers John. 'And the geography teacher or whoever would say, "All right, Prendergast, off you go. You don't know a thing about geography, but you go off and study your music."

[19]

It was always interrupting something, so everybody developed this absolute hatred for you.'

The music lessons themselves were far from inspiring, and John was subjected to a rap of the teacher's ruler over his knuckles every time he played a wrong note. But it wasn't enough to dissuade him. He loved the idea of becoming a professional pianist and accompanying the world's great orchestras, but at the same time he was self-critical enough to realise that he lacked one of the major requirements for the job – a superb memory. He had been told that he had excellent technique, and very good touch, but as he says himself, 'You can't sit down and play a piano concerto with someone turning the pages.'

Performing also terrified the wits out of him. 'I became a composer out of sheer fright,' he jokes. 'Stage-fright was the worst thing I'd ever known.' And so the idea began to crystallise of pursuing the more private side of music – composing. And not just any composing. John knew he wanted to compose for film.

At fifteen John had to decide whether to stay on in the sixth form at St Peter's or leave. He was now clear in his mind about his vocation, and as the school offered no substantial music programme, he persuaded his parents that the best thing for him would be to leave and study music seriously elsewhere.

This turned out to be a fortuitous choice for John. The search for a music teacher led Jack Prendergast to Dr Francis Jackson, Master of Music at York Minster, and it was this association that would form a crucial part of John's musical education. Twenty years later, when John was writing a medieval choral score for *The Lion in Winter*, it was to this same musical heritage that he would turn.

As York is a cathedral city dominated by its famous medieval Minster, the town has a strong tradition of religious music, and Dr Jackson was widely revered as one of the foremost musical teachers of the day. He still remembers being approached by Jack Prendergast and being asked if he would teach his son.

'I knew Mr Prendergast anyway,' says Dr Jackson, 'because The Hallé Orchestra used to play at the Rialto quite regularly and there was always a drinks reception afterwards to which I was invited. So we knew each other from those. I had quite a few pupils at that time, and so I was glad to take John on.'

Each afternoon John would go to Dr Jackson's house in the quadrant behind the Minster, sit at the piano in his drawing room and study the basics of music theory. Dr Jackson remembers John being a very serious, rather reserved young man; unfortunately, he never got to know him well enough 'to work out what made him tick'. He does, however, remember him ardently wanting to compose for film, and he thought that if that was what he was going to do, then he ought to know harmony and counterpoint. So he set about teaching him the rudiments of both.

The lessons with Dr Jackson concluded the first phase of John's musical education. The grounding that Jackson gave him in the workings of melodies and counter-melodies and the understanding of choral and religious music proved invaluable to his later writing.

His studies at the Minster had consolidated his love of classical music and allowed him to understand some of its structure. The next phase of John's musical education would be of a different nature altogether. It involved the discovery of something new: something which would have an enormous impact on John's entire musical career. That something was called jazz.

2

MUSIC BY MATHS

In the 1940s, the arrival of swing jazz turned John's musical world upside down. Up until then, he had been a classical-music snob, turning his nose up at anything considered popular or contemporary, but the explosion of jazz into his life changed all that, affecting his whole approach to music.

Inspired by the swing sounds of Benny Goodman and Harry James, John set about learning jazz trumpet – and that in itself was the first stage in his understanding of brass. Having realised that composing was his eventual goal though, he also started a correspondence course in an avant-garde style of composition used by jazz arrangers, known as 'Music by Maths'. Just as his schooling with Dr Jackson had cemented his understanding of classical music, John's teenage studies marked the first step towards his eventual mastery of the jazz idiom.

John had been helping out in his father's cinemas since he was a small boy. It was a family business, after all, and it was not only he, but his brother Patrick and sister June who would all muck in and help run the show, with their mother Doris in charge of the booking office in the foyer. And so now that John no longer had full-time school to attend, he began spending more and more time learning the ropes. He knew how to work the limelights, the projector and run the box office, and to the staff he was literally part of the family.

'By the time I was fourteen I knew everything about the projection room. If my father said: "Projectionist's ill today, he's off," I'd just get up there, and I could run the whole thing. That meant lacing up two machines, changing over and putting my hand through the reel. It was wonderful and I just loved doing it all.'

John was also beginning to learn more about the business side of things, the basic principles of management, advertising and marketing – all of which were to stand him in good stead in years to come. But although he loved working in the 'theatres' – as the cinemas continued to be known – and brought new, successful ideas to the running of them, these times were not particularly happy ones for John.

'My father would never give anybody a compliment or praise anyone,' says John. 'I used to complain to my mother and say, "Isn't he pleased with anything I do? I've been working my butt off and made loads of changes in the theatres." Then I'd come home at night and my father would say, "I understand you're not happy because I'm not giving you any compliments." "I'm all right, I can cope with it," I'd tell him. Then he'd say, "If you do the right thing, it's logical. If you do the wrong thing, I'm going to beat the hell out of you," which he never did. He wasn't a violent man, but he really believed that the right thing was logical and the wrong thing wasn't. So he never ever said, "You're really terrific, that's wonderful." My mother used to tell us, "He's really quite nice, you know, he's really quite lovely," and I think he actually was, but he just couldn't get it together to say those things. I expect his father had been like that to him, so that's where it came from.'

Understanding the psychology behind his father's attitude didn't necessarily make it any easier to deal with, though. Over the next twenty years, Jack Prendergast would never miss a chance to tell people about his talented son, and show his fatherly pride, but the one person he couldn't show it to was John himself. He never managed to make John feel that he'd quite made the grade . . . and the absence of that approval perhaps fuelled John's later striving towards ever-greater musical achievements.

Jack Prendergast's brusqueness wasn't just restricted to his family either, and the staff in his theatres soon came to look to John as a sympathetic ally. He may have been the boss's son but he more than understood what it was like to be on the receiving end of his father's wrath, and often ended up covering up for this projectionist's mistake or that attendant's lateness. John was by now also at an age where girls had started to become an interesting concept, and his friendship with his father's staff certainly extended to at least one young cinema usherette.

Musically, meanwhile, John was about to discover a whole new world. Up to this time there had been plenty of music in his life: he had had music on his doorstep. Not only were there the regular classical concerts by major orchestras in his father's theatres, but the family living room was also frequently the scene of informal recitals by musical luminaries. And if there were no live performances there were always gramophone records and classical music on the wireless.

He had grown up enchanted by the music of Sibelius and Beethoven, and it had been his love of Chopin that had originally made him want to become a professional pianist, but now there was a new kind of music. His elder brother Patrick had come home one day with a bunch of records under his arm. 'Barry,' he said urgently, 'you've got to hear this new stuff. It's fantastic! It's American and it's jazz, but it's not like the old-style traditional jazz. This is something new!'

The sounds of Benny Goodman, Harry James, Duke Ellington, Artie Shaw and Louis Armstrong were like nothing John had ever heard. They were the rock and roll of their time. To a generation brought up on classical music, with the likes of Vera Lynn and George Formby as the only 'popular' alternatives, this was as anarchic as anything Elvis Presley would come up with ten years later. Structurally and rhythmically it broke all the rules. It was faster than anything else around. It was loose, it was fun and it was sexy. What really got to John, though, was the brass. Brass was at the core of it all, and he began thinking: If I can't be a pianist, maybe I can do something else after all. I'll be a trumpet-player.

He idolised Harry James and George Swift. Swift was living in London at the time – 1951 – so John said to his father, 'George Swift is the best trumpeter in the world. I want to study with him.' To his credit, JX was willing to indulge his son and take on board the idea that he was really serious about music. 'OK,' he told him, 'you've got two weeks.' And so John set off to London.

The lessons with Swift were instructive, although it seemed early on that John was not a complete natural with the instrument. 'You've got the wrong *embouchure*,' Swift complained, referring to the way John was holding the trumpet to his mouth.

Learning the trumpet was hugely important for John, and although he may not have become the world's best trumpeter, that wasn't the point. Knowing how brass worked, what made it tick and how it could sound was to inform almost everything he wrote.

That fortnight in London was to prove significant for John in another way. As soon as he arrived in the capital, his first move was to check out what films were showing, and that particular week happened to be the opening of Vincente Minnelli's classic Hollywood musical *An American in Paris*.

Based around George Gershwin's orchestral ballet suite of the same name, the film starred Gene Kelly and introduced the still unknown Leslie Caron. It was a gloriously exuberant romance featuring some of the most thrilling dream-dance sequences ever made, and the teenage John was captivated. If swing jazz was an important influence on him, Gershwin's innovative mix of jazz and orchestra was almost equally so, and the way he used strings would later on become a central element to the Barry sound.

But it wasn't just the music in the film that entranced John. The fact that the music came wrapped up in Hollywood's charmed, technicolour vision didn't hurt either. 'The first thing I did was fall in love with Leslie Caron and all Gershwin's music and Alan Jay Lerner's screenplay,' says John. 'I saw the movie five nights in a row and each day I fell more in love with Leslie Caron, the humour, Gershwin's music, Paris, the dancing . . . everything. That movie took me out of my everyday reality and made me think, That's the life I want to lead – *that's* what I want.

'George Swift lived in Stansted and every day after I'd first seen it,

I'd finish my lesson with him and say, "I've got to go. I have to get back to London." And he used to ask me what I was doing there every night, but I was always too embarrassed to say, "I'm going to see *An American In Paris* yet again".'

Once John got back to York, he lost no time getting an audition with semi-professional local dance band The Modernaires. He may have known the trumpet wasn't necessarily the be-all and end-all of his life, but for now, it was his meal-ticket to the world of professional music. And John was not one to hang about. He knew what he wanted, and he was going to get on and do it.

His sister June was a regular at the local De Grey Rooms dance hall where The Modernaires played and she knew the leader Johnny Sutton. 'I understand Barry's playing the trumpet,' Sutton said to her. 'Why doesn't he come down and play for me?' So after a brief audition, John joined The Modernaires on third trumpet and was soon playing gigs on Wednesday, Friday and Saturday nights.

By this time John had already begun writing his own compositions, both for the pit orchestra in his father's cinemas – at that time, all cinemas still had a pit from which either a pianist or a live orchestra would play music before the start of the film – and also for The Modernaires. Vocalist Keith Kelly – who was later to join The John Barry Seven – sang John's first composition, with lyrics written by his sister June, and the band were not unimpressed.

Encouraged by the reactions to his first efforts, John decided to make a demo of his songs and take it down to London to a music publishers. Jack Prendergast had an old friend, Eddie Standring, who now worked at Campbell Connelly music publishers. He called him up and said, 'My son's trying to get into professional music and he's written a few pieces. Would you see him?' 'Absolutely,' said Standring.

So John headed hopefully down to London, floating on dreams of stardom and fortune, but they were not to be realised quite that easily. Eddie Standring was indeed a good friend of Jack Prendergast's, but he was also a straight-talking Lancashireman. After hearing one blast of John's demo he said, 'It's terrible, lad. Basically it's just an absolutely terrible song. But I will give you one bit of advice. In this business, you have to get a good title.' And in a spirit indicative of the Tin Pan Alley humour of the day he added, 'I'll tell you a great title. It's spot on – but you'll never be able to use it.' 'What is it?' asked John eagerly. '"It Gets Harder When I Think of You",' chuckled the older man.

John didn't let the disappointment in London bring him down. On the contrary, he became determined to improve his writing. So when he saw an advertisement for a correspondence course in 'The Schillinger Method' or 'Music by Maths', he was immediately interested. The Schillinger Method was a composition system which had been used by Gershwin on *Porgy and Bess* and his variations on 'I Got Rhythm'; it was the brainchild of Joseph Schillinger, a Ukranian musician, composer and mathematician.

The whole thing seemed ideal to John. Firstly, a correspondence course appealed because he hated teachers and so he reckoned the distance could only be a good thing. Secondly, a system which could give him further insight into the mechanics of composition was exactly what he needed. 'What I liked about it was that instead of learning all the scales, they just said to you, "This is the maths behind it all. A major scale is built up of this mathematical formula, a minor scale of this one, and a twelve-tone one of that one",' says John.

'I can look at a chord sequence and know immediately which tones are similar to one another, and which chords are sympathetic or harsh to each other. So when people say, "How do you write counter-melodies? Do you know the effect they'll have?" I say, "Yes," because it's all maths; you can work it all out. On *The Persuaders*, I found this wacky Egyptian instrument, but you could only play certain notes on it. You were very restricted and had far fewer notes than usual to use, but because of the maths you could work it out. You knew exactly how far you could go.'

Completing the course gave John new confidence in his writing and soon, having successfully written more material for The Modernaires he began to think to himself, If I can write properly for this band, surely my compositions should be good enough for professional bands. Never one to hide his light under the proverbial bushel and spurred on by his father, John began sending compositions to the biggest name bands of the day – Jack Parnell, Ted Heath and John Dankworth.

The fact that these band-leaders knew his name and would have recognised him from casual meetings when they had played at the Rialto certainly did John no harm. Brian Kershaw, trombonist with The Ted Heath Band, recalls occasions at the Rialto when Heath would say, 'Look, guys, there's going to be a young kid coming along with his own composition, but whatever it's like, don't say anything, 'cause his father owns the theatre.' But his fears were to prove unfounded as John's compositions were immediately considered perfectly adequate and actually rather impressive, given his youth.

John Dankworth certainly thought so. At the time he was one of the country's most successful band-leaders, and had his own Wednesday-night radio show – *Johnny Come Lately* – on the BBC's Light Service. Dankworth remembers meeting the teenage John in York: 'We always used to play the Rialto in York and on one occasion Jack Prendergast had Jack Buchanan there – he was one of the biggest musical variety stars of the day. He always had people like that up for the weekend, and it was on one of those occasions that I'd met John and established enough contact for him to approach me himself and say, "Would you mind if I sent you some music I've written?" and so I said, "No, sure".

'At that time on my show we used to have a spot each week where the band would play something unusual that wasn't one of the standard pieces of the time. And so when Barry's piece sounded interesting and quite good, I introduced it and said, "Here's a surprising score from a young writer called Barry Prendergast" and we played it on air.

'It was actually quite an ambitious piece of writing in the style of Stan Kenton, who at the time was seen as rather avant-garde and pushing back the boundaries of traditional arranging. It wasn't the most accessible piece of music you've ever heard – you needed to know a bit about jazz to appreciate it – but it was big-band jazz style of the time and it certainly gave no indication as to what he was going to go on to do.

'The Schillinger Method was also quite controversial at the time,' continues Dankworth. 'It was kind of like a musical equivalent to

Scientology – something you either became completely devoted to, or viewed with scorn, but it was used by Stan Kenton's arrangers and his was definitely the number one band of the time. I think essentially that for someone of eighteen to write a piece as a result of a correspondence course, which was playable and presentable enough to be broadcast by a famous band of the day, was definitely quite an achievement for a young writer.'

Of the three band-leaders John had sent arrangements to, not one had rejected him. Jack Parnell had also been encouraging, and had suggested that John might perhaps think about forming his own band; this piece of advice would indirectly set John on his way to pop success. But first of all, there were other obstacles John was going to have to overcome.

3

JAZZ IN THE DESERT

Imagine any Bond score without the brass, and what you're left with might be all sorts of things, but it wouldn't be Bond. And it definitely wouldn't be John Barry. The sound of brass and the sound of swing give John's scores verve, excitement and drama; it became a vital part of their identity.

John had discovered swing as a teenager, and he'd learned to play the trumpet, but where he really found out how brass worked was during the three years he spent in Egypt and Cyprus doing his National Service. Three years in the Army, playing in a military band, might not immediately seem the most relevant training for an aspiring film composer, but John found a way of making it so. Listen to his '007 Theme', or 'Teasing The Korean' from *Goldfinger*, or 'Journey to Blofeld's Hideaway' from *On Her Majesty's Secret Service*, and you'll hear the ghost of an Army band, albeit spruced up in couture musical clothing.

But it wasn't just John's ability to adapt and appropriate styles that made his time in the Army useful. The most important thing National Service gave John was the time to study and the chance to experiment. It was here that he learned the art of arranging – by long-distance correspondence with that maestro of swing, The Stan Kenton Band's Bill Russo. The Army also gave John invaluable opportunities to improvise and practise different writing techniques, and not a moment of it was wasted.

Most young men faced with two or three years of Army service would resign themselves to putting their life on hold for a while and just enjoy what they could of this time out. For John, however, the whole idea of wasting any valuable time when he could be pursuing his musical goal was completely alien. If he was going to be stuck in the Army he would use every moment he could to his best advantage.

'Of all the people I've met in my life since,' says Army friend Terry Snowdon, 'none has ever been on a path of success at such an early age. It was obvious right from the start that he was going to make something of himself. John was very forceful in his approach to life; at a very early age, he knew what he wanted – and he went out to get it.'

In 1952, when John was called up, National Service was still compulsory for all 'able-bodied' men. You might think that your average, reasonably sensitive young man would be filled with horror by the idea, but the general feeling towards military service at that time was considerably less hostile than it might be today. John was part of a generation who had grown up through World War Two and subsequently felt a powerful sense of national pride and patriotism. His own brother Patrick had volunteered for service in the navy during the war. 'You didn't think about getting out of it,' John explains. 'There was something very British about it. It was part of the culture. You went in and you did your stuff, much as you hated it.'

The standard deal was that everybody had to do two years, but the Army had cunning ways of wrestling more time out of you. If you wanted to continue with your own profession or choose what you did during your Army time, you had to sign on for an extra year. John considered this, and finally decided that if he spent the next two years doing whatever the Army wanted, he might as well kiss those years goodbye. On the other hand, if he signed up for the extra year, he could be a bandsman, and would at least be playing music. And so three years it was, and he never regretted his decision. Those years proved to be far from uneventful, either musically or personally.

Having signed on to be a bandsman, you were told which military bands had vacancies and given a choice of which you wanted to apply for. John's first option was The Coldstream Guards – by far the best band in the country. So, feeling cripplingly nervous, he came down to the King's Road Barracks in London for an audition. But as he blew away at the required Gilbert and Sullivan, either the trembling must have got to his fingers or the band-master didn't consider him up to standard for he was told he hadn't passed. The band-master did however suggest that he might like to try his luck with a new regimental band – The Green Howards – who were based in Richmond, Yorkshire and who were apparently desperate for musicians.

The audition for The Green Howards was held in the basement of a large music shop in Leeds, and this time it was more a case of 'he can walk, he can blow – we'll take him'. Having passed the audition, John began to feel that the situation wasn't actually too bad. Richmond was a beautiful town only forty-five minutes away from York, and as The Green Howards were a new band he reckoned they wouldn't get sent abroad. Great, he thought. He'd spend the next few years there and probably be home every weekend. Life would be just terrific.

The first ten weeks of Army life, however, consisted of training, and this applied to everyone. So off John went to Richmond to begin his new life. There he met Terry Snowdon or 'Snowie' – who would become his closest friend over the next three years.

'The first time I saw him,' remembers Snowdon, 'we were all in this great long, stone-built barrack room, and he was sitting on his bed playing his trumpet, just having a blow. There were all these rough and ready Geordie lads thinking to themselves: What the bloody hell's *he* doing? and John was just blowing away by the side of his bed, playing "Don't Worry 'Bout Me". I thought he looked just like Harry James. He had no inhibitions, did John, even at that age. Today a lot of young people are quite uninhibited, but in those days people were a bit more reserved. John never gave a damn about anybody, though. He always just got on with what *he* wanted to do.'

Five weeks later, John was beginning to settle in, although the gruelling regime and freezing cold were far from ideal. Suddenly, he was sent for by the commanding officer. In the characteristically clipped English tones that were still ubiquitous among Army officers, he was informed: 'We're going abroad.' 'Where to?' asked John incredulously. 'Egypt,' the officer said.

At this time, in the period before the Suez crisis, the British were still an occupying force in Egypt, guarding Britain's access to the strategically crucial Suez Canal; consequently, there was considerable local hostility towards the troops. As Egypt was therefore considered an active zone, this meant that soldiers couldn't be sent there automatically, so what was being offered was another of the Army's incentive-orientated schemes. If you volunteered to go to Egypt, you were spared the remaining five weeks of training, so long as you were ready to sail from Southampton the following week. As the weather in Richmond in November was more than a fraction chilly, and hotter climes seemed increasingly attractive, John willingly signed up.

'Despite my original plan to stay in Richmond for the whole three years, within five or six weeks I was on this goddamn boat headed for Egypt,' he laughs. 'And the next thing I knew, we were landing in Suez in Port Said.'

Hotter climes Egypt may have boasted, but they were dustier ones too. 'The whole aim of the British presence there in Egypt was to guard the canal,' explains fellow Army bandsman and future John Barry Seven member Mike Cox. 'So we were in the middle of nowhere, just in the desert really. The canal's a hundred miles long and we were just at the side of it in a barbed-wire enclosure – one Army camp adjacent to the other. It was a hundred miles of Army camps – pretty awful really, and all that with very basic living conditions as well.'

The atmosphere inside the camp was far from carefree. In 1957 the Cold War was just beginning and the supposed Russian quest for world domination was seen as a major threat to be instilled in the minds of the force's young recruits. Military history lessons were given monthly, but they were often more geographical than historical. Pointing at a map the officer would explain: 'This is Egypt where we are – here – and that's where the Russians are – there. They could cut through Iraq with tanks and if they encounter no resistance, we could be annihilated. They could be here in no time at all!' The message was: the British were there for a purpose. Although John and his fellow recruits were aware that with something in the region of 10,000 Allied troops to protect them, the whole prospect of a Russian advance seemed rather unlikely, they were at the same time persuaded that they were important and necessary.

The new recruits now supposedly knew why they were there, but this still didn't prepare them for the atmosphere in the camps. 'When I went to Egypt, it was like going onto the set of *Gunga Din*: guys polishing everything, military types in loads of straps – all terribly terribly,' says John. 'And nobody ever called the local people Egyptians, it was always "the wogs". That was the dialogue – totally racist.' But although he, Terry Snowdon and some other close friends would have questioned it, they accepted it in the light of the gruesome murders of British soldiers which the Egyptians were carrying out.

In protest at the British presence, local Egyptian activists had got into the habit of decapitating any stray British soldiers they happened to come across, and posting their heads on poles; an atmosphere of fear had understandably built up. It also meant that the soldiers had no freedom to explore anywhere beyond the immediate vicinity of the camp.

'We were so restricted,' remembers Snowdon, 'that in the whole nine months we were there we never saw a pyramid, a sphinx, the Nile – nothing. We didn't even get to see the Suez Canal, 'cause we were three and a half miles away from it! It was the most miserable place you could ever imagine. It was dreadful! People think it was like *Lawrence of Arabia* or something but I tell you, even the sand was gravelly. It wasn't a patch on Blackpool sand!'

The daily routine in the camp itself was far from strenuous, despite an early start to the day. 'You'd get up at five,' says John, 'shower, have breakfast, shave and then by seven-thirty you were playing music and rehearsing with the band-master. Every Thursday night we used to play in the officers' mess. It was what they called "mess night", so the officers'd have this big piss-up and we used to sit there and play selections from popular standards like *Guys and Dolls*, Gilbert and Sullivan and light classics. Sometimes you'd get a few nurses, so that was always big news once we got back to camp. You can imagine, there were only seven of us there so we just used to play on the other men's fantasies. It was like, "Did you see that red-head or did you see that blonde?"'

But although John – or 'Pren' as his fellow soldiers called him – would be one of the lads on a Thursday night in the officers' mess, the rest of the week was a different story. He got on perfectly well with everyone, but being stuck in the middle of the desert with nowhere to go and nothing to do, he decided his evenings would be much better spent working on exercises from the Schillinger Course. And so that was what he did, every evening without fail.

'Immediately we came back from evening meal,' says Terry Snowdon, 'if we didn't have any duties, John was straight into bed. Where some of the fellas were going over to the NAAFI and having a few beers, you could guarantee John'd be straight into bed, and not laid on his bed, but sat up actually inside it, with the blankets covered in papers, sheet music, books and pens and all sorts, doing this course.'

John's Army colleagues soon got used to his evening routine, and pretty soon gave up any attempts at conversation. It was obvious that socialising was not a priority. 'Most of the guys in the Army thought John was a bit of a recluse really,' says Mike Cox. 'He didn't smoke, didn't drink – none of that. And he was a bit quiet. He'd never go out and get rat-assed like the rest of us. He was sensible and he'd got other priorities.' 'He had such strict principles,' agrees Terry Snowdon, 'and every moment was precious to John. He couldn't have afforded to feel a bit slack with a hangover the next day, because the next day was so important to him. He was dedicated.'

There was sometimes the odd occasion though when John would be forced to join in extra-curricular activities. Snowdon remembers one particular afternoon when a football match had been organised. John was apparently far from keen to get involved. 'He was a bit ungainly on his feet, John, and although he was tall and slim, he wasn't particularly well-built. He wouldn't let anybody push him around, though. He could stand his corner anywhere, could John, either verbally or physically.' And when it came to being dragged away from his music to play football in the heat, John was particularly keen to 'stand his corner'. 'I'm not going out to play football, I'm busy,' he told the guys.

'Usually he was very good-natured,' says Snowdon, 'but at times like that he could be a bit aloof.' And on this particular occasion his determination was over-ridden. 'This senior soldier decided to pull rank on him,' says Snowdon. 'He just said, "Get out there and get your kit on, Prendergast. You're playing football." I always remember that game because John just stood there for about eighty-seven minutes doing absolutely nothing, hardly running around at all, and then suddenly in the last three minutes of the game, the ball came his way and he scarcely touched it, but somehow he managed to score a goal. It was like he'd done nothing the whole game, and then he'd got the distinction of scoring a goal. You should have seen the smile on his face.'

After about three months, there was a vacancy for the position of 'storeman' and as John had made a favourable impression as an organised, reliable type, he was offered the job. Being storeman was somewhere between being the band librarian and a roadie. Your duties included taking care of the instruments, making sure they were all clean, and looking after the sheet music. But rather than viewing it as a chore, John saw it as a means of gaining freedom, for the upside of the job meant that you got your own little Nissan-type hut, complete with a bed, a table, and most importantly – a piano. After sleeping in a communal tent for three months, it was a definite improvement. It would give him the privacy and freedom he had been desperately wanting, to get on and study.

'We never saw much of him after that,' says Snowdon. 'Every evening, after dinner, I remember you could always guarantee seeing him walking past our tents with his little green washing-up bowl to get water, so he'd have it ready to wash and shave in the morning. 'Cause otherwise there was always this massive queue for the taps in the morning. It wasn't that he was stuck-up, he just planned everything out very meticulously. Everything he did had a reason and a meaning. And 'cause he had to have all the music on the stands well before seven each day, he didn't want to be delayed in the morning.'

And so eight months passed, and eventually John and the others were given four weeks' leave; having spent the whole time in Egypt without even a weekend off, the idea was more than welcome. So John, Snowdon and their friend Brian Harwood got on a plane back to England to enjoy their short burst of freedom. 'We landed at Stansted,' says Snowdon, 'which was still a tiny little place at that time, just one little reception room when you came off the Tarmac – and we decided that we'd spend a few days in London before heading back home to Yorkshire.'

They spent that night at the Union Jack Club for Servicemen, which offered accommodation at cheap, subsidised rates. 'But you could only stay there one night,' recalls Snowdon, 'so the next night we had to find somewhere else. I was very green at that age. I'd never been around and John was already quite worldly-wise compared to me, so he took the lead. We tried two or three different places, but couldn't get in anywhere. Then suddenly John said, "I'm bloody sick of this. Come on," and hailed a taxi. "Russell Square," he told the driver. And John, cool as anything, just marched into the Hotel Russell and booked the three of us in. The Hotel Russell was one of the smartest places in London – I'd never seen anything like it! The way that John marched in there, full of confidence . . . I'll never forget that. It impressed me so much.'

Over the next couple of days John lost no time in making sure they made the most of the capital's attractions. They managed to cram in two musicals: *Kismet* and *The King and I*, and an opera. 'We saw *La Bohème* at Covent Garden,' smiles Snowdon, 'and it was a magical experience. We were sat upstairs, right at the top and the sound was so wonderful even up there. We all just loved it.'

After hitting the town in London, it was back to Yorkshire for the rest of the leave, and John was glad to be home. For those four weeks, instead of playing military band music, he could get back to playing the usual Wednesdays, Fridays and Saturdays with The Modernaires.

This was a whole lot better. He was also busy reading the music magazine *Downbeat*, which at that time – alongside *Metronome* – was the
biggest music paper there was; it covered all the West Coast American
dance bands that John loved so much. In one edition, he noticed in
the small ads that Bill Russo, who was the orchestrator and arranger for
the number one Stan Kenton Band, had left the band and was giving
a correspondence course from his home in Chicago. The course was
called 'Composition and Orchestration for the Jazz Orchestra', and John
resolved to use his spare time in the Army to investigate. But first it
was back to Egypt.

When he arrived, however, all was not quite as he had left it. 'They're
not here any more,' an officer curtly informed him. 'Your lot have
gone off to Cyprus.' Marvellous, thought John, while he set off to
spend the next two weeks in a hot, dusty transit camp waiting for a
plane to get him out of there.

John was to stay in Cyprus for the next sixteen months. Once again
he had his own little hut and his daily duties. Each day the band-master
would say, 'Today we're going to rehearse so and so,' and John would
go and put the music on the stands and at the end of each day, he'd
take it back. He was also beginning to delegate some of his more basic
duties. The Army at that time had boys who would volunteer to help
out, and John made full use of them, getting into the swing of the 'do
this, do that' commanding role. He had been told at school that he
was a born leader, and the Army soon recognised this and made him
a Corporal.

Meanwhile John hadn't forgotten the correspondence course he'd
seen advertised in London. But how would he pay for it? 'Can I send
money to America?' he asked at Barclays Bank in Larnaca.

'Afraid not,' they said, as at that time in the early 1950s there were
enormous restrictions on currency, and you weren't allowed to send
money anywhere. It was going to be difficult doing a correspondence
course if you couldn't find a way to pay for it, John thought. Then
one night, a solution miraculously arrived. He'd gone out in Larnaca
and was in a tourist shop surrounded by the usual fayre of tasteful
ashtrays featuring maps of Cyprus, when a tall genial-looking Armenian

who was working behind the counter approached him out of the blue and said, 'Have you just arrived?'

'Yes,' John replied, wondering what he wanted.

'Are you looking for dollars?' he said, as if by psychic divination. 'If you like, I can get you some,' and he promptly opened a drawer and took out a huge wad of American notes.

John couldn't believe his luck. His problem was solved, and his course was on. So from then on, each week, he would set out on his bicycle and head off down the dusty ten-mile road into Larnaca, where a regular scenario of *Casablanca*-style black-market dealings would take place. First he'd exchange his Army pay for American dollars, then – following a ruse that he'd seen in a film – he'd wrap them in carbon paper to disguise the money from security X-rays, put them in an envelope and surreptitiously send them off to America.

The course itself proved to be a far cry from the mass-produced impersonal courses you might get today. It was literally a personal correspondence and was to prove a godsend to John's musical development. The Kenton Band were like The Velvet Underground of the swing-jazz scene. They were seen as an experimental, avant-garde and above all intelligent band. 'I loved The Kenton Band,' enthuses John. 'I just thought it was a whole different musical sound from anything that existed in America. A lot of people were critical that they weren't pure jazz, but they had a great sense of form and shape, which I loved as a composer. The music had structure and they were all young, highly educated students. The guys in that band were a different calibre from the usual lot. Most jazz musicians would be reading *Playboy* but they'd be reading Proust. They were just in a different league of intelligence.'

The same would later be said of John's approach to music and composition. His music had emotion aplenty, but there was always a core element of intelligence, thought and analysis behind every project John took on, and so The Kenton Band were a natural source of inspiration. And, as the mastermind behind the Kenton sound, Bill Russo was the perfect teacher.

Each week Russo would give John an arrangement to do and a structure to work to, and then the following week he'd send him back constructive criticism and comments on the results. He took a particular interest in John, as out of the ten students on his course John was the only non-American, and he was fascinated by what his mind would produce, as opposed to an American one.

Significantly for John, Army life in Cyprus provided ample time for study and experimentation. Daily band rehearsals finished at midday as the heat would by this time be in the nineties and hundreds. Then there was lunch, followed by compulsory rest, but after that the afternoons and evenings were free. And as John explains: 'There was nothing to do except go to a local village and get drunk, so I sat in the storehouse with a piano for sixteen months and taught myself arranging.'

Later on, during the 1960s, John would gain a firm reputation as a bon viveur, but whilst in the Army his primary aim was to study. He knew that in order to get where he wanted he needed to study hard, and that was what he did. The fact that most of the other band members were sitting around bored, reading magazines and playing records, also meant that John had a full military band at his disposal. So he would do a Russo lesson, write a short piece, take it to the band and say, 'Can you play this?' and usually they were more than willing. 'I remember him experimenting with really weird chords, and peculiar chord progressions,' says Snowdon, 'but he was always really keen for us to play all this stuff, 'cause it was his only opportunity to hear what he'd written.'

This was one of the best learning experiences a budding composer and arranger could hope for. It gave John an invaluable opportunity to experiment with different structures and styles, and see what worked and what didn't. Sometimes though, their sessions were interrupted by more practical concerns such as security alerts if someone had been shot. The Union of Greece guerrilla group wanted Cyprus to be reunited with Greece and so there were often shootings. Usually the band didn't get sent on guard, but if there was an alert and the battalion was already out, as a last resort they would call the band out, thrust a gun into their less than eager hands, and send them out to walk around the perimeter of the camp.

But even taking into account security alerts and John's musical exercises, the band were still left with an awful lot of free time on their hands. While in England, John had also noticed that *Downbeat* magazine was selling orchestrations from the major big bands of the day: Count Basie, Ray Anthony, Glen Miller and Ted Heath. What's more, they were selling them cheaply. For three dollars you could buy five arrangements – and this sent John's mind racing. Why didn't they form a proper band of their own? he thought. So he approached the guys once more. 'Look,' he said, 'I'm getting all these arrangements, so why don't we form the non-official Army band – a big band where we can play all this new stuff instead of Gilbert and Sullivan?' The guys needed little persuading.

And so with four trumpets, four trombones, five saxophones, a rhythm section and a euphonium, a band was formed. They rehearsed every day in the free time between four and six, and not only did the guys in the band love it, but so did everybody else who used to hear the music wafting through the camp. Within a few weeks they had reached a reasonable standard. 'Why don't we talk to the people at the NAAFI and see if we can do a concert there?' John suggested. The NAAFI was the soldiers' canteen-cum-social-club – a huge, metal-domed place where the soldiers generally smoked and drank themselves silly out of sheer boredom and so the idea was welcomed immediately.

Word spread rapidly through the camp, and the NAAFI was packed out. On a makeshift stage created from bedsteads, the band played a forty-five minute set and the place went mad. Everyone loved it. The next morning, however, John was called in by the officer in charge. 'Prendergast,' he said forbiddingly. 'What's all this about a band?'

'Well, we're a little bit bored, sir, and we've been rehearsing this stuff, you see,' said John, anxiously anticipating a reprimand at the very least.

'I understand everybody rather loved it,' the officer suddenly beamed. 'There was even cheering, I'm told. I'd like to hear what you were doing. Can you play me something?'

So the band got together and played him a sample selection. 'Super,' he said. 'I'd like you to continue doing this every week.' And so they did, and as time passed, John, never one to rest on his laurels, began to smuggle his own compositions into the sets, trying them out and learning what worked with an audience and what didn't.

Socially meanwhile, John's life had also become more interesting. As a soldier, when it came to sex you had one of two choices: you could either brace yourself for three years of monastic purity or you could enlist the services of the local 'dance-hall girls'. Most soldiers, including John, opted for the latter, as the chances of meeting any local talent socially were about as strong as catching salmon in the Sahara.

Every Saturday night he and his friends used to go into Larnaca, which at that time was still a simple, small Mediterranean town, full of quaint little winding streets and whitewashed houses with courtyard fountains and plants. Family life was also very traditional, and down the main streets young girls would chastely promenade with their chaperones.

On one of these evening visits John had met Kyriacos – a local Cypriot shopkeeper, with a swirling moustache – and he and his wife had got into the habit of inviting him for dinner at their home. But one day as he walked into the shop, his attention was caught by the girl behind the counter. She was about sixteen years old and, according to John, the most beautiful thing you've ever seen: big brown eyes and dark straw-blonde hair. Enchanted by all of that, her simple black dress and sandals and a whole lot more, John soon found out that her name was Christella and his visits to the shop suddenly became more frequent.

He would go into the shop, and although she didn't speak any English and he couldn't speak any Greek, she would smile and hold out her hand. Kyriacos soon gave up wondering whether John was ever going to buy anything, and asked him if he liked her. He then told him that her father lived in America, was the owner of many nightclubs and that she had several brothers – and by the way, would he like to have dinner with her? The question hardly needed asking, and an arrangement was made for dinner at Christella's mother's house, with Kyriacos offering to accompany him. This was not exactly what John had had in mind, but it was certainly better than nothing.

The evening turned out to be a success, in spite of John being offered a seemingly never-ending stream of bizarre but delicious Cypriot food, and a second dinner was planned. A serious courtship was now becoming established, and this meant that the couple were allowed to be alone for a full half-hour after dinner. But as verbal communication was a non-starter due to the language problem, the time was taken up with holding hands and the exchange of many meaningful looks and smiles. John was euphoric, but his happiness was shortlived.

Crisis struck in the Army barracks when the police station in Larnaca was blown up. This was the first major terrorist attack on the island, and the Army was immediately put on alert. An unsuspecting John was meanwhile sent for by the battalion's Commanding Officer Roberts.

'Sit down,' said Roberts. 'Have you been seeing someone called Christella?'

'Yes,' said John, mystified. What did his recent courtship have to do with anything?

'What's that been like? Give me the history.'

John duly explained about the dinners and reassured the CO that he'd hardly ever been alone with her.

'And have you met any of her brothers, or any of the rest of the family?' demanded Roberts.

'Well, sir, I know that she's got two brothers, a father in America, and there may be an aunt somewhere. But I've only met her mother. Why, sir? Is there a problem?'

'Well, you could say that,' said Roberts. 'Did you know that the police station at Larnaca was blown up last night?'

'Yes, I did, sir,' said John.

'Well, it's Christella's brother who is responsible. We've got him and he's in gaol. But I'm telling you right now that this is trouble, and it's something we've been anticipating for some time. So on no account try to see her or her family again. If you do, the chances are you'll end up down an alley with your throat slit.'

John was devastated. He had really fallen for this girl and thought of their relationship as something pure and romantic; now a bombshell had literally destroyed it. He never saw Christella again, although her name would crop up some years later as the title of a lush, romantic John Barry Seven B-side. He was, he says, 'madly in love with her', but at the same time, he was practical enough to realise that getting his throat cut was not an ideal scenario. Shortly afterwards, the battalion left the island with the still heartbroken John gazing back towards the shore and the girl he was leaving behind.

John's Army years had given him invaluable time and opportunity to experiment with band arrangements, styles and techniques, and by the time he was demobbed, he was well on the way to becoming a master of that craft. His teenage years of training with Dr Francis Jackson had been the first important stage of his musical development. His Army time had been the second. What was waiting for him back in England would provide the third and most unexpected stage, but it was one which would prove just as significant to his future career. While John had been away in the Army, music had moved on from jazz, and the words 'popular music' suddenly had a whole new meaning.

4

THE TWANG'S THE THANG

Go anywhere in the Westernised world and you'll be hard pushed to find someone who doesn't recognise the opening guitar riff of 'The James Bond Theme'. If the sound of one instrument ever defined a character, it was that guitar's rumbling twang, expertly played by Vic Flick, guitarist with The John Barry Seven. And that same twang played an important part in the establishment of John's career, springboarding him into film-writing big time.

In the late 1950s and early 1960s the Seven were second only to The Shadows as Britain's top instrumental band. John had started writing instrumentals mainly because he couldn't sing and he hated the whole notion of fronting a band: 'I used to sing and I'd get so petrified going out onstage that in the end, the easiest way out of it was to write instrumentals.' These instrumentals proved the perfect training ground for his entry into the world of film-writing.

The Seven had started off as a rock and roll outfit, for in spite of John's jazz background, he had recognised almost as soon as he was out of the Army that big bands were no longer where things were at.

'When we all got demobbed, John started talking about getting something together,' remembers Mike Cox. 'I didn't expect it to be a rock and roll band, though. I thought it might be something more sympathetic to our calling. We were more into the jazz thing, so I was quite surprised when he said it was going to be a rock and roll band. But rock and roll was really exploding at that time, so in a way it made sense.'

It certainly did make sense. John needed to make a name for himself in the music business, and the quickest way to do that was to go with the flow.

The England John came home to after his National Service was a very different place to the one he'd left. The old England had been a grey, earnest and staunchly conservative place – preoccupied with getting the country back on its economic feet after the war. Food rationing had continued until as late as 1954, but now, suddenly, there was change in the air. Economic recovery was in sight, and it was clear already that this didn't mean a return to the life people had known before the war.

New technology was heralding a 'modern' age of jet aeroplanes, long-playing records and transistor radios. But there were two other factors which were changing the nature of everyone's lives. The first was the number of people who now had motor cars and could therefore travel further than their backyard without public transport. The second was the arrival of commercial television and the end of the BBC's broadcasting monopoly. Many more people now had televisions, and suddenly American-style advertising with its shiny new consumerism was being beamed into homes across the country. Britain was changing for good.

There was a new mood on the streets as well. York was filled with 'Teddy boys', and there were sounds coming out of the radio at night that were like nothing John had heard before. Something big had happened to music while he'd been away – and it was called rock and roll.

For the previous three decades economic depression, war and ration-ing had meant that young people had been united with their parents in the common goal to outwit the enemy and survive the austerity of food shortages. But by the mid-1950s, with the war long over, these values no longer applied and the emerging generation were keen to assert their own identity. If you were young and your family wasn't on the breadline, chances were you had money in your pocket and time on your hands. The only hitch was there was nothing to buy and not much more to do. And this was where music stepped in.

In 1954 Bill Haley, an American ex-Country singer released 'Shake Rattle and Roll' and 'Rock Around the Clock'. Both were massive hits in America and Britain, and although no one realised it at the time, musically and socially things were never going to be quite the same again. The records were essentially a white, cleaned-up version of the black R&B which artists like Louis Jordan and LaVern Baker had been recording, and drew on the Southern blues traditions of Muddy Waters and Howlin' Wolf.

With their innocuous lyrics, Haley's records were bland enough to get past the censor, but still raw enough to make an impact. Bill Haley may not really have been able to sing, but compared to the 'moon in June'-style crooners of the day, this was positively belting. Most people in Britain had never heard the original American blues artists – their records were only available as imports, so unless you knew about them you were unlikely to ever hear them – and compared to the anodyne romance that was the norm, this had energy, a much stronger beat, and apart from anything else, it was a lot louder than most records anyone had ever heard.

If you were into music you couldn't possibly avoid it. So while John got back into his old pre-Army life, playing with The Modernaires and sending his big-band arrangements to Jack Parnell and John Dankworth, it quickly became obvious that rock and roll was the future.

Jack Parnell had told John that if he really wanted to get on, he should start a band of his own – and make it a commercial one at that. 'There's no point struggling away for years playing what *you* want while you starve and no one pays any attention. What you need is a small compact unit with an out-and-out one hundred per cent commercial policy,' he insisted. 'That way, you'll be able to afford to play the type of music *you* want as well.'

Never slow to recognise sound practical advice when it was offered, John immediately saw the wisdom in this. So he started approaching musicians who might be right for a small combo. Army-bandsman Mike

Cox was an obvious choice, alongside his fellow Leeds saxophonist Derek Myers. Keith Kelly from The Modernaires was another, but John still needed a drummer, a guitarist and a bass-player. Help was to come in the form of a girl he'd met while playing with The Modernaires in York.

One night while onstage at the De Grey Rooms, he'd noticed a particularly pretty, tall, slim blonde girl dancing in the crowd. She was a regular there, and John soon found out that her name was Barbara Pickard. She had a kind of English Rose beauty and always looked very glamorous. She was classier-looking than most of the girls around York and John lost no time in asking her out. As it turned out she lived in Scarborough, but luckily for John, she worked in York, at Cussen's Electrical Stores, and they were soon seeing each other on a regular basis. By the time John came to be setting up a band, Barbara mentioned that she knew some musicians in The Jeff Laycock Orchestra, the house band at the Spa Ballroom in Scarborough. She'd already heard them playing the latest Stan Kenton numbers and thought they might be just what John was looking for.

So in the interval one night, Barbara approached guitarist Ken Richards, drummer Ken Golder and bass-player Freddy Kirk. 'Barbara came up to us,' says Ken Golder, 'and said, "Barry'd like a word with you."

'"I'm thinking of starting a little group," he said, "about seven musicians – would you be interested?" We said we would, and he was really delighted. So we went for a drink afterwards and all got on pretty well. We'd all just come out of the Army and played in military bands so we all had the same background and spoke the same language.'

'"We can use the Rialto in York for a rehearsal on Sunday," he said. "Can you make that?" and we said, "Yes." And so that was how it started.'

Once John had found his band members, it was a question of sitting down and working out what they were going to play. The obvious thing if they were going to be a rock and roll band was to copy the records that they knew and start from there.

'We sat down with a bunch of Bill Haley records,' says John, 'and copied them note for note. All the group were basically jazz musicians, so we knew how to do that, but it was a whole new style for us.'

It worked though, as drummer Ken Golder remembers: 'We spent nearly a full day that first Sunday trying to get a sound together, and by four o'clock we were getting there. By four o'clock the following Sunday it was even better, and so we stuck at it and within a few weeks we were sounding pretty good.'

John always reckoned if you were going to do something, it was worth doing properly. If he was going to have a rock and roll band, they needed to sound like one. So with the help of a major loan from his father, he headed off to Leeds where there was a music shop which sold up-to-the-minute instruments and equipment and for what seemed like an absolute fortune, he bought two of the latest imported amplifiers, complete with maroon fake-leather Rexine covers. He also purchased a German imported Hofner bass guitar – something which would be noticed a year later at the Cavern Club in Liverpool by a keen young musician called Paul McCartney.

This was to make the Seven the first rock band in Britain to have a bass guitar. Audiences had seen them being played by visiting American bands, but no one had actually got one and used it – mainly because they didn't know how. And this was no less of a problem for The John Barry Seven.

'Here – that's a guitar,' said double-bass-player Fred Kirk when he turned up for rehearsal. 'I thought I was playing the bass.'

'You are,' said John. 'This is a bass *guitar*. It's only got four strings.'

'Blimey, this is bloody difficult, ain't it!' continued the bewildered Fred.

'Fred,' said John calmly but firmly. 'Why don't you take it home for a week and see how it goes?'

Within a few days Fred reckoned he'd cracked it. The only thing they needed now was a singer. Guitarist Keith Kelly had a good voice, but big-band tradition dictated that it was always the leader who sang, and so, even though this was a rock and roll band, John followed tradition.

'John wasn't a singer, of course,' chuckles Cox. 'He was a trumpet-player – and he was the worst singer in the world, but somebody had said, "You're the band-leader, you've got to sing," and so he did.'

Adding his halfpenny's worth at most rehearsals was also the indomitable JX.

'He used to come to all the rehearsals and criticise us to death,' remembers Mike Cox, 'and of course JB – as we called him – was doing the singing. JX was always complaining about the way people sang, and he used to demonstrate how they should do it, even though he must have been sixty or seventy odd at the time. We were all kids doing this rock and roll thing, and there he was nagging John about projecting, and filling the stalls from beyond the footlights. He used to give him a terrible time: "You're not *projecting*," he'd be saying. Or "You're singing out of tune. We can't hear you" – ooh, it was awful. And then he'd throw these tantrums 'cause his son wasn't measuring up. He'd shout and bawl and basically give him a bollocking for not getting it right, but he didn't really mean it. JB perhaps was a bit embarrassed, but we lapped it up. His dad was just this larger-than-life, totally outrageous character and it was tremendous entertainment.'

In spite of Mr Prendergast's reservations, after a few more practice sessions The John Barry Seven decided they were ready to brave a live audience. The fact that Jack Prendergast ran a string of concert halls made getting their first gig rather less problematic than it might have been otherwise, and so on 17 March 1957, John Barry and the Seven made their professional début at the Rialto in York, supporting Mitchell Torok and Cy Laurie's jazz band – both long since relegated to the graveyard of showbiz obscurity. However, although the Seven had improved since their first rehearsal, when it came to performing live, they still had a few things to learn.

'It was hilarious,' smiles John. 'We'd be in the middle of a show and Fred would hit a wrong note, and I used to look round and he'd go, "Oh, sorry!" out loud and on mike, in the middle of a song. Forget *The Full Monty* – we were just finding out what the hell it was all about.'

They may not have sounded like the most professional band ever, but John at least made sure they looked the part. He himself had always dressed impeccably, and while working for his father in the cinemas, had learned the importance of professional presentation. He applied everything he knew to the Seven. The whole band were kitted out in smart, matching grey suits, bow ties, black shoes and black socks. But it wasn't enough just to look smart.

Instead of woodenly standing onstage, playing their instruments like dummies, John got the band doing choreographed steps, in the style The Shadows would later make famous. John knew about showbusiness – he'd grown up with it – and was aware that if the band went out onstage, they needed to look like an act, not just a bunch of musicians huddled together.

Most bands formed around that time usually stumbled on for a few gigs and then either gave up completely or at best settled for a career gigging round local dance halls. But not so John Barry and his Seven. From the start John had always seen the group as his passport to the professional music world, and within weeks of forming the band he had brought them all down to London, cut a demo tape and sent it off to Jack Good – producer of BBC TV's 6.5 *Special* – the hippest and only pop-music show on television.

Jack Good was one of the few people in the media at the time who recognised rock and roll for what it was – a major new phenomenon, that was here to stay. Most people who had any say in the music industry were still convinced that it was just another passing fad, that in a few months' time it would be replaced by the next 'new sound'.

Good was different. He was young, dynamic, and bursting with enthusiasm for rock and roll. An Oxbridge graduate who'd been President of the Oxford Dramatic Society, everybody imagined he would go on to prominence in the arts. 'He was always larger than life. One expected him take over the National Theatre or something,' says Trevor Peacock, his colleague on 6.5 *Special* and later lyricist for John. Instead of that, however, Good had been captivated by the energy of rock and roll.

'I've found what we're going to do,' he told Peacock. 'What?' his friend asked, expecting him to say 'Greek theatre', or something similar. 'Meet me at Finsbury Park Empire at seven o'clock and I'll show you,' smiled Good. Top of the bill that night was Tommy Steele. 'That's the future,' he told an unconvinced Peacock – and he was right.

Steele had been discovered singing in the now legendary 21s coffee bar in London's Soho – the epicentre of what had become the new Fifties' British pop scene. Coffee bars were where you went if you were remotely hip. Rock and roll was on the jukebox and coffee was the 'in' thing to drink, since having 'a nice cup of tea' was as much a part of the older generation and the national psyche as 'Land of Hope and Glory'. Until this point, British pop had remained stuck in the crooning doldrums of the big-band era, while stars like Joan Regan and Dickie Valentine churned out records that sounded like fifth-rate Sinatra but without the flair. This had all changed now though, and the old guard was being swept away by a new generation of young artists, managers and hustlers in an atmosphere of excitement and upheaval similar to what would happen twenty years later with Punk.

Chief of the new hustlers was the original rock svengali Larry Parnes, who was to make stars of Tommy Steele, Billy Fury, Marty Wilde, Joe Brown and Georgie Fame. His tactic, which is still alive and well today, was to find a pretty boy, change his name and groom him as closely as possible to the current singing idol. And in the late 1950s that was Elvis Presley.

Bill Haley's records had made an enormous impact, but he was essentially no more than an overweight, ageing Country singer with about as much sex appeal as a garden gnome. Elvis on the other hand was as far as you could go in the opposite direction. He was drop-dead handsome, wore a gold suit, gold shoes and his pelvic gyrations got him banned in cities across America on obscenity charges. His 'Heart-break Hotel' sold eight million copies in 1956 alone, and so it was little wonder that in England the record companies were keen to find a homegrown version of their own.

With Tommy Steele and the others, Larry Parnes did just that, with varying degrees of success. Initially Tommy Steele rose to the challenge, gave it his best shot and duly became Britain's first rock and roll teen idol. Teenage girls were screaming, fainting and generally getting hys-

terical on a scale never seen before, and it was this atmosphere of
hysteria which had captivated Good.

The BBC meanwhile had met Good and been impressed by his
dynamism, but television scheduling was still in the Dark Ages and they
didn't know where to use him. Children's programmes were on from
five till six in the afternoons, and then adult programming would begin
at seven, but the hour in between was dead time and the screen just
went blank.

'It was all very new,' Trevor Peacock explains. 'Not that many people
had television sets and the BBC just hadn't got the organisation to fill
up all those hours. Then suddenly they said, "We're going to fill six
till seven and on Saturday nights it should be for young people." The
programme they came up with was called 6.5 Special and Jack Good
was the pefect candidate to produce it.'

With 6.5 Special Jack Good created an unpredictable, chaotic live
studio show which featured bands and 'real-life' teenage interviews.
The style of presentation was a mix of old-fashioned showbiz slickness
and what now seem hilarious attempts at informality and slapstick,
although it was to prove an enduring blueprint for TV music shows.
6.5 Special's position as the only pop show on TV gave it unparalleled
power to introduce new acts, and band managers would frequently
approach the production team saying, 'If you can get my band on 6.5
Special, just name your price.' Cutting a demo tape for Good was therefore
an obvious move for John and the Seven: John lost no time in making it.

Despite the barrage of tapes he received, Good listened to The John
Barry Seven, but deemed their Haley-by-numbers style rock and roll
too similar to that of the programme's house band – Don Lang and his
Frantic Five. The trouble was that John and the Seven, Lang and his
Five and any other band of the time had all been copying the same
records – and had consequently come up with exactly the same repetitive formula. All their songs were based around a lyric catchphrase and
were heavily weighed down with saxophones. In a way, it was only to
be expected; they had all come from the same jazz background, and
although they had picked up the new rock and roll style straight off,
they hadn't yet managed to put their own edge on it.

The Seven had also failed the BBC audition which was compulsory for any act wanting to appear on the network – either on radio or television. At that time the BBC still hadn't changed much from the wartime days when radio announcers wore evening dress to read the news, and auditions were held at the Albert Hall. Unless you spoke 'the Queen's English' with the Queen's accent they wouldn't let you anywhere near a microphone, and so consequently the arrival of John's band was greeted with cries of, 'Good Lord – they speak with *Yorkshire accents!*' Nor were the combo's musical talents considered to be up to BBC standards.

This kind of prejudice towards anyone with a provincial or working-class accent was still very much part of the British social structure, present in all areas of the Establishment. 'It was often a bit intimidating,' admits Malcolm Addey, later John's sound engineer at EMI, and himself a Yorkshireman. 'The people who ran EMI, for instance, were always from London and spoke terribly properly. For lads from the provinces it was a hard climb, and you needed to be tough.' John would eventually develop a reputation for being both tough and pushy, but as Addey puts it: 'It was an armour that you developed around yourself. You needed it because you had to prove yourself twice as hard as everyone else.'

Unabashed by their failure with the BBC, the Seven soldiered on, steadily improving and doing more gigs at the Rialto, with John all the while confident that somehow, somewhere along the line, their luck would change. And it did. In the audience one night was London agent Harold Fielding, who was sufficiently impressed to offer them a summer season at Blackpool supporting Tommy Steele.

John and his Seven were thrilled; the season would give them much-needed exposure and experience. Harold Fielding had realised that although Britain was overrun with wannabe rock and rollers, there weren't actually that many bands who could do the thing properly, and by general standards John Barry and the Seven really weren't bad. And so, eager to make the most of this opportunity, John egged the band on to endless rehearsals.

By the time they came to play Blackpool, The John Barry Seven were so well received that the BBC changed their mind about allowing them on *6.5 Special*. And so, by September 1957, only six months after their first gig, they were on the nation's coolest TV show.

Their first taste of live TV went very well, and The John Barry Seven were soon regulars on the *6.5 Special* TV show. It was hard work but fun, and the fact that the show went out live, in front of a live audience, meant there was a real buzz in the studio. 'Onto camera one,' the director would shout. 'Now onto four!' and everybody would have to make sure they were still in shot.

'It was crazy,' says Peacock. 'Sometimes if there was a crisis, everyone had to muck in, so it'd be like, "Trev, camera three's broken down, can you change the shot?" and somehow you had to work out how to change a shot, and there'd be fire officers standing there and then they'd suddenly appear on screen.'

'It was hard work,' agrees Doug Wright, who would later take over as the Seven's drummer. 'Jack Good would have us there from four in the afternoon rehearsing and getting ready, so by the time we finished later on that night, we all used to pile into the pub and it was like, "Thank goodness for that!"'

On the back of their TV success, the band were offered more gigs. They were soon on the road on a regular basis, touring with the likes of Tommy Steele, Paul Anka and Gerry Dorsey (who would later become Engelbert Humperdinck). For their early gigs the band made their own transport arrangements. John's first car was an old Triumph which was not always that reliable. 'We were always seeing John stranded on the hard shoulder of an A road going to Birmingham or somewhere,' says Ric Kennedy, trombonist with Bob Miller and the Millermen, 'and so we used to stop and give him a lift in our tour bus.'

After a while, though, as the Seven's tours became more professional, John accepted the need for some more reliable form of transport. What he came up with was an 'airways observation coach' – essentially a large, single-decker sightseeing bus which had started life taking visitors around Heathrow.

'John bought this thing second-hand,' says Mike Cox, 'and had it painted up jungle green, with *The John Barry Seven* in really outrageous 1960s' lettering on the side. It was like a record cover, with the letters all higgledy piggledy pointing in different directions.'

The bus may have been a sound idea in theory, but the reality didn't quite work out that way. 'It wasn't very comfortable inside at all,' reveals Cox. 'There was a heater at the front and John used to sit next to the driver, so he was the only one who benefited from it. The rest of us freezed our asses off.'

What's more, the bus cost a fortune to run, because it used petrol rather than diesel. 'It was all right when we had other people on the tour – dancing girls and all that,' explains Cox, ''cause you could get maybe thirty or forty people on there, and then it was a going concern. But with only seven of us, it cost an absolute arm and a leg, so we often went on the train.'

The tours themselves were decidedly different from the rock tours of today. They were still a hangover from the days of music hall and variety, where families went out together for their night's entertainment and would expect to see musicians, comedians and all-round entertainers on one bill. Consequently the Seven often found themselves on tour with the likes of Dave Allen, Larry Grayson and Max Bygraves, as well as the other pop acts, and the clash of styles, not to mention volume, was decidedly noticeable.

This soon began to cause problems, with the blue-rinse brigade complaining about the new bands playing too loud. 'There'd be us and all these other bands,' remembers John, 'and then on the first half of the bill there'd be all these old comedy acts with dancers and jugglers. So when we'd go on it was all, "Oy, you, turn it down" – and we were like, "Yeah, well, the point is it's supposed to be loud." And it wasn't just the audience. The management were saying, "If you don't turn those amplifiers down, you won't work in our theatres again. We don't want that kind of thing here." And if you had problems with the management in a theatre there wasn't really anywhere you could go, as one company – Moss Empires – had a monopoly on most venues in the country. They owned five thousand theatres across England and the reality was that although the London music business was beginning to catch on to the idea of a new music, concert promoters still hadn't got it at all.'

Teenagers were now coming to see the bands, alongside the old dears who had turned up to see their comedy acts. The result was chaos, but within a year the youth audience had entirely taken over and the theatres didn't know what to do with the thousands of screaming teenagers causing havoc in their seats. Eventually the Seven started getting offers from ballrooms to play there instead – usually for about three times as much money.

It may seem strange now, but at the time ballrooms were still associated with the old-style dance bands that had long since died out, and it hadn't occurred to anyone that this could be the way forward. 'I never thought that playing ballrooms could work,' says John. 'But then I reflected back: Benny Goodman played Carnegie Hall and then, when he went back into the ballrooms everything just took off. And this was what was happening to us. Suddenly people didn't want to be stuck in stuffy theatres with pit orchestras – they wanted to dance, and that meant they needed space.'

John's experiences on the road with the Seven were to stand him in good stead in the years to come. You might wonder how playing on a rock and roll package tour could benefit the intricate process of writing for film, but what John learned was highly valuable, not least for his work on the Bond scores. During those tours with the Seven, he was exposed night after night to different audiences and got to know what made them tick. He learned how you built up tension, how you developed an atmosphere to create different moods ... and where people got bored. It was a tough apprenticeship, but none of the lessons were wasted.

The John Barry Seven were doing well for themselves, their leader reckoned. They had played prestigious seasons with major stars, and been featured on TV. All they needed now was a record deal, and he was confident that on the strength of their TV appearances, this would not be long in coming. And it wasn't. Harold Fielding had agreed to continue as their agent and almost immediately began negotiations with both Philips and Decca. As it happened, EMI's Parlophone label was the first to come up with a concrete offer, and so John Barry and the Seven signed on the dotted line.

A month later, in October 1957, Parlophone released 'Zip Zip', the first single by John Barry and the Seven featuring John himself on vocal. 'Zip Zip' had been a hit in America for Canadian group The Diamonds, and it was standard practice at the time for British artists to cover tracks which had been recent hits across the Atlantic. The record was not one of John's most memorable, however, and apart from the fact that it was his first ever record release, it probably wouldn't warrant a mention at all.

'One reviewer wrote that I sang like a 45 rpm playing at thirty-three and a third,' laughs John, 'so that gives you some idea. I've tried to destroy as many as I can find!' Imagine a lame version of 'Rock Around the Clock' sung in a very bassy Yorkshire-gone-transatlantic baritone, then substitute the lyrics for the memorable 'Zip zip/ oh she's my zip zip gal/ she makes me flip flip/she's my zip zip' and you get the picture.

By the standards of the day though, 'Zip Zip' was not dramatically worse than the majority of rock and roll imitations of the time. Released both on seven-inch 45 rpm and the old 78 format – as all records still were, the single was not exactly a runaway hit, although it did manage to do quite well in York. After all, if you've got seven people in the band and they've all got families, you're probably not that far from a local hit to start with. But the follow-up 'Every Which Way' which again featured John's vocal talents, also flopped, and unsurprisingly the band decided to concentrate on instrumentals from then on, both onstage and in the studio.

'Being the leader of the band,' John says, 'I thought I had to sing because no one was interested in instrumental music, but I was a terrible singer. The true pitch of my voice is bass, so to be a rock and roll singer when there's all this "ooh bop a lula" stuff going on wasn't such a good idea. So as soon as we could, I started writing instrumental things and it was a good move.'

It was to prove a very good move indeed. Although John didn't know it, the shift towards instrumentals was on its way – and this would provide John not only with hits, but would become the basis of his entry into the film world. The instrumental sound he created with the Seven would also establish the band as one of the country's leading pop acts.

1958 was 'the year of the twang'. In America, Link Wray and Duane Eddy had started making instrumental records like 'Rumble' and 'Rebel Rouser' which focused on the guitar more than ever before. Instead of the weak brass-led sound which most rock and roll bands were still pursuing and which was a throw-back to the big bands, the melody on these new records was driven by the bass strings of the electric guitar – heavily amplified, echoed, vibratoed and tremeloed – to dramatic effect. John was immediately struck by this new sound as were fellow instrumentalists The Shadows in Britain and The Ventures in America, and they all duly set about getting it.

For The John Barry Seven the twang arrived in the form of guitarist Vic Flick. Flick was Britain's answer to Duane Eddy, although Flick himself says he'd been playing his edgy guitar that way for years. 'I'd been playing like that long before we'd ever heard of Duane Eddy,' he declares. 'I just used to play melodies down there at the bass of the guitar and play them strongly, so that sound just happened. It wasn't anything you could put your finger on, yet it turned out to be one of those things that went down in musical history.'

John had met Flick when he was playing in The Bob Court Skiffle Group alongside the Seven on a support bill for Paul Anka the previous year, and had been impressed by his playing. So when the original Seven line-up started to change, Flick was John's first choice.

Changes had become necessary gradually. Not only was there now a need to create a newer, harder, less brass-led sound, but some band members had begun to get fed up with being away from their families, and so it was time to recruit some new blood.

The new Seven line-up now included drummer Doug Wright, bassist Mike Peters, saxophonists Jimmy Stead and Dennis King and Flick's flatmate: keyboard-player Les Reed. The Seven had a new, tighter, slicker sound and it was to lead them and John to the top of the charts.

Initially, though, the band's next few singles only dented the charts' lower regions. But as time went on John began introducing more material of his own into the Seven's live shows and once they'd been tried out on a live audience, the numbers started appearing on the B-sides of their singles. By the following year, John's 'Pancho' was deemed good enough to be released as the A-side of their fourth single, but anyone looking for prototype Bond on this particular release should give up now. The record is a kind of tame rock and roll mambo, and the only remote hint of what lay ahead is in the fact that it sounds as if it should have come from a film – ideally an ersatz 1950s' party scene in Rio, with revellers bongoing the night away.

As the band began to spend more time in the studio down in London, it made sense for them to move to the capital full-time, instead of constantly commuting up and down the A1. For John the move was well overdue; he'd long been looking for an escape route out of York.

'If you go to York on a mid-October day when it's raining,' he says, 'you'd get the hell out of there as well. It's misery personified. All those people standing in queues waiting for buses in the rain. And then a bus comes and they get all excited: "Ooh look, the bus is coming!" I go back there and it hasn't changed a bit. They'll probably hate me for saying this up there, but it's true.'

Since he'd been a teenager, John had been coming down to London as much as he could, as well as visiting his aunt who lived in Liverpool. Like London, Liverpool was buzzing, and that was what John was thirsting for. He wanted to be somewhere where there was some life. He'd had three years out of York, but those had been in the strictly disciplined atmosphere of the Army and in the social backwaters of a small Mediterranean town. Now he was a budding pop star and London was where he needed to be.

So John and the band took rooms in Mrs Cotat's theatrical digs in Old Compton Street in the heart of Soho – at that time London's premier red-light area. John had discovered that 'strip-joints' made perfect rehearsal spaces and could be hired quite cheaply during the day, so now they had somewhere to live, somewhere to practise, and a lot less commuting to do. The rooms at Mrs Cotat's were pretty basic

1950s-style lodgings with one telephone on the landing for the whole
house, but the French Mrs Cotat did prepare a mean breakfast. 'She
used to cook us these magnificent fried breakfasts,' remembers Mike
Cox, 'which we never ate. She used to bring them into the room for
us, but we always woke up to find them congealed at the side of the
bed 'cause we couldn't wake up before midday. It was a terrible waste.'

Soho was still a small local community in those days, and though
John was regularly going back home to Yorkshire to see his girlfriend
Barbara Pickard at weekends, he often spent his evenings wandering
around the area getting to know his way around the jazz clubs and
coffee bars. In the 1950s and 1960s, Soho was still a world unto itself.
Bars and restaurants stayed open later, nightclubs were more risqué,
and the only people who actually hung out there were local residents
– apart from the select few in the know about jazz and rock and roll.
John quickly became a regular fixture on the social scene and London
soon seemed like home.

This was the beginning of John's new life in London. He wasn't a film
composer yet, but he was a lot closer than the young Barry Prendergast
who'd left the Army in 1956. His rock and roll plan had paid off, and
he'd unwittingly hit upon the instrumental twang sound that would
later be so crucial to the creation of James Bond. The John Barry Seven
were one of the best-known bands in the country, and that meant there
were plenty of people who knew exactly who John Barry was.

John Barry Prendergast had arrived and his musical career was definitely on its way.

5

FAITH IN FILM

As far as the film world was concerned in the 1950s, pop stars did not write film music. Film composing was a serious business, the domain of well-respected classical composers like William Walton and Vaughan Williams. But rock and roll changed all that, and so did John Barry. Suddenly youth had become a valuable commodity, and serious musicians who were young enough to understand the new culture were in short supply. John fitted the bill exactly, and Britain's first home-produced rock and roll film – *Beat Girl* – launched both him and the sound of pop into British cinema. With his title track for the film, John also created the blueprint for what would eventually become the most famous theme of them all – 'The James Bond Theme'.

If you look at John's career as a whole, Adam Faith is probably not the name that would stand out, and yet it was Faith who eventually became John's passport to the film world. Between 1959 and 1961, during what was essentially a rather fallow period in British pop, John scored more than ten hits for Faith as his arranger and virtual producer, and created some of the best records of the time. They reflected the optimism and exuberance of the newly affluent Britain, and they had a charm and lightness of touch that owed more than a little to John's use of strings.

[62]

During his collaboration with Faith, John learned invaluable lessons about strings and how to use them. Listen to those Faith records chronologically, and you'll hear the string sound developing from pizzicato pluck to the broader, lusher style which would later become such an integral element in the sound of John Barry.

But the start of that sound was no accident. In the same way that John had seen the rock and roll phenomenon and thought, How do I use this to get from A to B?, he looked at the task of arranging for Faith and brought to it the same analytical approach. John wanted to get inside the workings of pop. In his records for Faith and the Seven, he was constantly striving to find and create new sounds, and would take a hands-on approach in the studio, talking things over with the sound engineer in-depth before each session to work out exactly how they would tackle each track.

At the time John was virtually unique as an artist and arranger in this approach, and was recognised as such by the music business. In the pop scene he was one of a kind in another way as well. Since rock and roll had emerged, the industry had been split in two. On the one hand there was the old guard who had made their names with the Sinatra-style crooners, and really didn't understand what all the fuss was about. Most of them still thought it was a fad that would die out soon, or else as some alien beast that was all a bit bewildering. On the other side you had the new hustler-managers – mostly wide-boys out to make a fast deal – and the artists themselves, who were most often gauche, working-class kids with no musical training at all.

In the middle of all this came John – the perfect candidate to straddle the two sides. He was classically trained, could read music and on a personal level was both educated and sophisticated. At the same time he was young, hip and seemed to have rock and roll sussed. John understood what it was all about, and brought his own common-sense approach to it. 'Because John wasn't a regular three-chord rock and roller, he was always coming at it from a different angle,' says Adam Faith. 'Rock and roll is usually about emotion, but John had intellect and intelligence as well. He was very smart and thoughtful about his music and he wasn't a frightened insecure working-class lad like most rock and rollers at the time. He had an intellect that most of those other guys just didn't have.'

It was John's educated background, musical knowledge and sophistication that had impressed the old guard at EMI and at the BBC. The operators of these hefty institutions were quick to recognise that from their point of view, John was ideal. Here was someone who could happily discuss Prokofiev and Mahler, but who also understood the workings of this new 'rock and roll thing'. What was more, he was confident and ambitious, and left no one in any doubt about his potential. 'One knew he was a tremendous talent straight away, says Norman Newell, EMI A&R man at the time. 'When I first met John with the Seven, he was very, very ambitious, and you always knew he'd be a huge success. He had a great personality – he had that way of making you like him. He was also innovative and talented, and he was always talking about wanting to write for films right from the word go.'

John would eventually end up applying everything he'd learned during his years in pop with the Seven and Adam Faith to his film music. And it was his pop 'sensibility' that became one of the vital trademark elements that makes a John Barry score sound unlike anyone else's.

In February 1959 John landed what the press described as 'British pop music's plum job' – Musical Director on Jack Good's brand-new TV show *Oh Boy!* This was a major step up for John, and it wasn't bad for the Seven either, as it meant they were now on TV every week. But it wasn't just the sound of the Seven which had attracted Good's attention. Jack had met John on *6.5 Special*, and had been impressed by his self-assurance and musical capability as an arranger, and so immediately thought of him when he needed someone for his new show.

'John was clearly so different from all the other people who danced about – the Tommy Steeles and Terry Denes et cetera,' says Trevor Peacock. 'There were kids coming on *6.5 Special* who a month ago had been milkmen and the girls would all scream. They were as big as Michael Jackson for several weeks, and then most of them were never heard of again. And then, in the middle of all that was John. He was always the posh part of it, really. He always looked smart, he dressed

well, and he looked intelligent – kind of like a rather beautiful under-
graduate. And he had all those handsome men around him – the Vic
Flicks and all that. John might not have been the most consummate
instrumentalist, but he always *seemed* like somebody you would take
seriously as a musician, whereas nobody else on that scene was at all.'

The job on *Oh Boy!* was a real breakthrough for John and the Seven.
It meant regular exposure, good money, and it established them further
as major pop stars. John had also proved himself more than capable as
a Musical Director as well, and once the series ended, he was approached
by Stewart Morris, producer of BBC's rival show *Drumbeat* and asked
to do the same job again. Eager to match the success of *Oh Boy!*, which
had launched Cliff Richard's career, Morris turned to John for advice
in the search for new artists.

'We need an equivalent of Cliff Richard,' Morris told John.

'Yeah, they really grow on trees, you know,' John replied. However,
he recalled a photogenic young singer with James Dean cheekbones
who had been on *6.5 Special* and suggested they call him in for an
audition. His name was Adam Faith.

'I didn't know where the hell he was, but I remembered that his
real name was Terry Nelhams, so I looked him up in the phone book
and phoned his mum, and she said, "Ooh, he's out at Shepperton. He's
a runner." So I phoned him up there and said, "Are you still interested
in singing, or what are you doing?"

'He said, "Oh, I'm going to Turkey. I'm on this movie."

'I simply said: "I'm doing this new show for the BBC and I've told
them you'll be terrific, so if you want to come down and audition on
Saturday morning, keep your day job and we'll see how it goes." At
the audition Stewart Morris took my advice and said, "Yeah, John,
fine" – so they signed him for six weeks. He cancelled Turkey.'

Already grateful to John for having got him on the show, Faith was
to end up feeling indebted to him for a whole lot more. Over the next
two years John would become responsible for creating the sound that
would make Faith a star, but he also took him under his wing and
helped steer his career in the right direction. 'The way I saw my
relationship with John,' says Faith, 'was that he was captain of the boat

[65]

and he plotted the course and told us how to get there. If you were shipwrecked on a desert island, John's the sort of person you'd want to have around.

'He always came across as a kind of wise, elder statesman. He was very softly spoken, always very quiet and considered, and he had a middle-class confidence about things – the way he bought furniture, the way he moved flats. I think I was always slightly in admiring awe because he was always in command. He didn't question how things happened. He just knew and he was always in control of his own destiny.'

John liked Faith and saw straight away that he had potential, but it was obvious that he needed direction. So John recommended him to the woman who had by now become his own manager – the redoubtable Evelyn Taylor, later described by Faith as 'making Cruella de Vil look like Snow White'. Evie – as she was known – was in fact probably midway between Margaret Thatcher and Malcolm McLaren, and by all accounts that's being kind. 'She looked and sounded like Thora Hird and behaved like Attila the Hun,' says Faith. 'She was a cruel, destructive woman who liked to control the people around her through intimidation, and she abused her power at every opportunity.

'She didn't treat John like that though. John wouldn't be mucked about. Nobody could ever have owned him. He was always very strong, self-determined and incredibly mature. John was used to an existence that encouraged him to be his own man early on, and Evie's tactics just wouldn't have worked on him.' But although Taylor may have been a nightmare for Faith on a personal level, intimidating him and browbeating him at every opportunity, she also had great strokes of managerial flair.

First of all she got Faith signed to Rank where he recorded a few singles (including one produced by Tony Hatch), but to no avail. The records made zero chart impact. Evie then, to her credit, managed to get him signed to EMI on the back of another artist in her stable – the bekilted Scottish child star Jackie Dennis. If EMI wanted Jackie Dennis, she told them, they'd have to sign Faith as well.

John had meanwhile been pestering EMI, practically since the start of the Seven's contract, to let him have a go at arranging for other artists on the label. He was by now confident enough of his own abilities to know that he was more than up to the job; it was just a question of getting the chance to prove himself. Finding themselves with this new singer Adam Faith on their hands, whom nobody was very excited about, the A&R men at EMI felt perhaps now could be the time to give John Barry the chance he had been hankering after for so long.

John couldn't believe his luck. All he needed now was a decent song. But finding one was easier said than done. In the pre-Beatles era, when singers were singers and songwriters were songwriters, the two rarely crossed over. The music industry was still locked in the old Tin Pan Alley showbiz system, for it was only in the wake of rock and roll that record sales had begun to take off. Prior to that, the mainstay of the business had been in sales of sheet music – and these still accounted for a significant part of the overall revenue. Consequently the music publishers had great clout, and songwriters were at least as important as the pop stars, if not more so. The pop stars might bring in the teenagers, but without songs, they were nothing.

Even geographically the music business was still based in and around Tin Pan Alley, aka Denmark Street – the narrow cluster of music publishers, managers and musical instrument shops off London's Charing Cross Road. EMI's offices were of course larger, but at that time were situated nearby in Great Castle Street. The A&R men had the fourth floor to themselves, where they each had their own offices kitted out with an upright piano in the corner. Here George Martin, Norman Newell and Norrie Paramor would receive visiting pluggers who would come in, sit down at the piano and play the latest song their writers had come up with that week and say, 'I think this'd be great for Marty Wilde,' or, 'I've got just the thing for Tommy Steele.'

So when it came to finding a song for Adam Faith, John's first port of call would have been one of these professional songwriters. As it turned out, he didn't have to look that far. One of the regular bands on *Drumbeat* – The Raindrops – was fronted by a good-looking wannabe

[67]

songwriter called Johnny Worth who approached John one day at rehearsal. He'd written a song which he thought could be perfect for Faith, and so accompanied by his friend Les Reed on piano, he sang it to them. It was called 'What Do You Want'.

John immediately saw the song's potential, checked it out with EMI A&R man Norman Newell and started thinking about how to arrange it. He spent a long time working out what would be the most commercial way to do it, but in the end decided to forget about trying to please the public and record this one the way they themselves wanted it to sound.

They recorded 'What Do You Want' in Abbey Road's Studio Two – later to become legendary as the home of The Beatles – one evening in about three hours, with the Seven as backing band and four string-players. Norman Newell was due to produce the session, but having just got back from America where he had seen Elvis live, he realised that with this whole rock and roll phenomenon he was way out of his depth. Newell had made his name signing and producing old-style artists like The Beverley Sisters and Russ Conway, and was part of the old school. To his credit he recognised not only the importance of this 'new' music, but the fact that his generation really didn't quite understand it. This is something absolutely new, he thought. So he decided to send his young assistant John Burgess – who was the same age as John and Faith – to officially 'take' the session.

This usually meant doing what is now called producing, but in the late 1950s, producers as such still hadn't really been invented. The whole concept of having a separate person in charge of recording was unknown, mainly because the whole process was still so basic. All you were usually doing was little more than physically recording a live act which had already been recognised as sounding good the way it was. The role of the early A&R men/producers such as Newell and George Martin was merely to ensure the record sounded as close as possible to the live sound. The only exception to this was if there was an arranger involved, such as John, who had brought in his own musicians to play the song. If that happened, it was assumed that the arranger might well

[68]

have their own ideas about how things should go. And in John's case, although Burgess was the official 'producer' of the Faith records, he had the wisdom to recognise that John knew what he was doing and to let him get on with it.

'John Barry effectively produced those early records, with John Burgess more as associate producer keeping an eye,' says Adam Faith. 'John Burgess had a very good instinct for what was right, but John Barry was definitely the architect of that sound.'

Not only did John have a very clear idea of the way he wanted things to sound, but he was also constantly striving to find new techniques to do it. 'John was one of the few artists I worked with who was very particular about the sound side of things,' remembers John Burgess. 'He would listen to everything very closely, and I used to let him have free rein.'

One of John's key allies in this was sound engineer Malcolm Addey who, like Burgess, was also in his twenties and more adventurous about experimenting with new sounds. 'John was very, very much more involved with the engineering side than most arrangers were at that time,' he says. 'He would call me over sometimes and say, "Let's talk about this and see what we're going to do", rather than just take pot luck as to what happens in the studio, which was largely the attitude in those days. Usually some guy'd come in, write the arrangement, and we'd know what the instrumentation was, and maybe we'd have a chat with them on the phone if we were a little doubtful as to what was going to transpire, but John always made sure that we talked beforehand.'

It wasn't that John was interested in sound technology as such. Cables, wires and decibels were never really his thing. He was just fascinated to find different ways of creating new and better sounds. Later on, this approach became a key element in his film scores from *Zulu* to *The Ipcress File* and *Born Free*. It was like everything he did: if he was going to do it at all, it had to be done as well as conceivably possible.

Happily, the sound that John created for Faith was to become not only a fast-track to commercial success for both of them, but also John's trademark sound, both on his work with the Seven, and on his arrangements for other artists. John had worked out that as Faith didn't

[69]

have an enormously strong voice, a pizzicato string backing could be just the thing. The sound had first been heard on Buddy Holly's 'It Doesn't Matter Any More' where it had come about almost by accident. The record had been a last-minute affair, and as Holly's arranger Dick Jacobs didn't have time to write harmonies, he had scored simple pizzicato string arrangements.

How the device first came to be used on a British record is now the subject of much debate, with a seemingly never-ending stream of people claiming credit for the idea. Depending on who you talk to, this may have been Les Reed, Joe Meek (who engineered a record called 'Be Mine' which John had arranged for singer Lance Fortune at around the same time), Bob Kingston who was 'Be Mine's publisher, or John Barry. The debate aside, however, John's reasons for using it on Faith's record made perfect sense, and his way of doing it started an English trend of its own.

'The thing about Adam was that he sang quietly in a relaxed way,' says John, 'as opposed to the frantic shouting style which was the thing at the time. Gene Vincent and Eddie Cochran were like the heavy metal stars of the time and they had loads of loud guitars on their records, but that would have been much too powerful for Adam. So I took the light Buddy Holly strings from "It Doesn't Matter Any More" and miked them differently to get a hard sound. I'd get four violinists sat in a circle and put a load of echo on it so it had an almost electronic punch. That way the whole thing was relatively polite, the punch just coming from the way I did those strings.'

After the session, John took the acetates round to Norman Newell's office for his reaction. Instead of the expected approval though, what he got was utter dismay. 'This is horrendous!' snapped Newell. 'He can't enunciate his words! He says "biyabee" instead of "baby" and it sounds like nothing else that's out there.' If this was the best John could do, once left alone in a recording studio, he told him, it definitely wasn't up to much.

John was deeply disappointed. He thought he'd ruined his long-awaited chance and apart from anything else, he was frustrated because he personally liked the record and was convinced it worked. But he was up against an A&R man who was looking for something that sounded like everything else in the charts, meaning Gene Vincent *et al* and not Buddy Holly. Fortunately, Newell agreed to release the record as it was, in spite of his doubts. But the fact that EMI weren't behind it meant that it received virtually no promotion; only about three boxes were ever sent to the shops, so little was the demand anticipated.

Things began to look up though when Jack Good took the record on board. As well as producing *Oh Boy!* on TV, he also wrote a highly influential column in *Disc* magazine, which at that time was the closest thing to street-cred music writing there was. He gave the record a glowing review, and because of *Disc* magazine's power, that was enough to help significantly. Another key champion of the record was disc jockey Brian Matthew, who began playing it on his Saturday morning radio show *Saturday Club*. In those pre-*Top of the Pops* and pre-Radio One days, *Saturday Club* was one of the only programmes on air where you could actually hear pop music, and so the show consequently had the power to single-handedly create hits.

By Christmas that year – 1959 – the record was number one. And by the following year, the song had become so ingrained in national culture that director Karel Reisz included it in a pub scene in his landmark film *Saturday Night and Sunday Morning*. Suddenly Norman Newell had changed his tune. 'Hasn't it gone well!' he phoned John to say. 'Would you like to do the rest?' The answer was a most definite 'yes', and over the next few years John and Faith were to notch up eleven Top Ten hits, many of them also written by Johnny Worth, including 'Poor Me' and 'Someone Else's Baby'. Before long Adam Faith, alongside Cliff Richard and Billy Fury, had become one of the biggest stars of his day.

Although none of Faith's subsequent hits were quite as memorable as 'What Do You Want', compared to other records of the time they still have an innocence and exuberance to them which makes them stand out. There's also a peculiarly English charm about John's arrangements, which was set off perfectly by the fact that in spite of his ludicrously contrived pronunciation, somewhere along the line you could always tell Adam Faith came from Acton and not Mississippi.

Another important element in the records' success was that throughout his whole time at EMI, John was given a free hand in the studios
and access to whatever orchestration and backing he required. 'There
was never a budget in those days,' says John Burgess. 'If you wanted
to do something really expensive you had to get it okayed with your
superior, but generally that was never an issue.'

The only thing that was an issue was the amount of acetate used
up when the records were cut. In the backrooms of EMI's studios,
there was a silent army of technicians in white coats, who would start
complaining about the waste of valuable supplies if you used up too
much acetate. This was 1959 and recording technology was still stuck
in a Neanderthal Dark Age where cutting directly onto vinyl was a
thing of the future. Recordings were made using one track directly
onto acetate, so if you didn't get it all perfect on the first take, that was
it. You just had to record another take and risk the wrath of the men
in white coats.

The necessity to record everything in one take often meant sessions
could be quite major events. Everybody on the track was there playing
and singing live, and the studios were often jam-packed with people.
Sessions were always night-time events as Faith was apparently 'not too
good in the mornings'.

For the recording of Faith's single 'Who Am I?', the session was held
in the large Studio One at EMI's Parlophone studios in Maida Vale.
Crammed in under the bright white glare of the lights was a full string
section – as John's arrangement featured the lush sweeping orchestration
which was already becoming his trademark – backing singers The Vernons Girls – all eight of them – plus the Seven, Faith and John. The
Vernons Girls and Faith stood behind separate hardboard screens, with
only a glass panel at eye-level for them to see John conducting. Once
they were all there, John and Faith went into a huddle in a corner to
discuss cues and effects, and then, after a few run-throughs, the thick
steel soundproof door of the studio was wedged shut and the red light
on the wall switched on – indicating that recording had now begun.

John counted a brisk, 'One, two, three, four,' – and they were off:
Faith, the orchestra and The Vernons Girls, all held together by John,

elegantly holding the slim gold pencil with which he always used to conduct. Once finished, John and Adam were called up to the control room to listen to the playback on the speaker monitor.

The need to record on one track in mono meant that the balance of instruments and voice had to be absolutely right from the start. 'The voice always had to be number one,' says John Burgess, 'and the orchestra – including the rhythm section – number two, but it was difficult to get it exactly right. John always had a very clear idea of the way things ought to sound, but this didn't prevent the occasional difference of opinion between him and Faith, who was always keen to be louder, while John was often equally concerned about his orchestra, demanding, 'Where the fuck is my trombone? You can't hear it at all!'

Faith's hits had turned him into a major pop star, and his success duly reflected on John as his arranger, but in December 1960, something happened which was to have a lasting impact not only on Faith's career but on pop music in general. He was asked to appear on what was at the time the most intellectually prestigious show on TV. It was called *Face to Face*, and its previous list of interviewees included Martin Luther King, Bertrand Russell, Carl Jung and Henry Moore. No pop star had ever been invited on the show, mainly because most thinking adults still considered 'pop' to be a passing fad perpetuated by moronic rock and rollers who'd have trouble stringing two words together let alone a whole sentence. Adam Faith's interview was to change all that and more. By presenting himself as a thoughtful, articulate and intelligent young man, Faith altered people's perceptions of pop overnight. Suddenly pop was the word on everybody's lips and the sound on their turntables. It had become hip to like it.

Faith was soon on tour around the country with The John Barry Seven as support and accompaniment for him, and John was eager to enjoy the trappings of his new-found success. Far from slumming it in the communal rock and roll tour bus as the Seven had done earlier, John was now getting used to travelling in style. He had always naturally gravitated towards the better things in life, but thanks to his generous nature, he wanted those close to him to enjoy the same standards too.

'He was a cool dude, John. We were in Manchester one night,' remembers Adam Faith, 'and John came back to the hotel calmly announcing that he had just bought a new car. "I was wandering around earlier," he said in his gravelly Yorkshire accent, "and I saw a Chevy in this American car dealer's. So I bought it."

' "You're joking," I said.

' "I'm not joking, it's outside. See for yourself." And there in the street was this spaceship, this huge great mass of fins and chrome and aerials. I've got to have one of those, I thought.

' "They've got a Ford Galaxy down there," John told me. "A real beaut – yellow and white. Go and have a look."

'Twenty minutes later I'd traded in my two-tone Ford Zephyr and I was sitting outside in my new £2,800 American Ford Galaxy, beeping my horn for John to come and see.'

From then on, the A roads, B roads and C roads of Britain should have come with a certified government hazard warning. 'John and I used to race each other all the time,' Faith recalls. 'It was like being in a Grand Prix but without the track. We weren't drunk or anything, we were real straight. We'd just finish a gig in Manchester, race the two hundred miles back to London and arrive within seconds of each other. All you could smell by the time we got to London was burning rubber.'

More importantly for John, Faith had also been noticed by film producer George Willoughby, who was planning a film called *Beat Girl*. Centred around the coffee bars of Soho, and the so-called 'beatnik' culture, the film was to become Britain's first attempt at addressing the new breed of young people called 'teenagers'. In 1955 even the word 'teenager' was unheard of, and so although it was now 1960, the whole concept was still new. Just like everything else that was considered new and exciting – from home gadgets to supermarkets and advertising – the idea had arrived from America.

The image of the angry, rebellious teenager in jeans and a black leather jacket was personified first by Marlon Brando in *The Wild One* and then most famously by James Dean in *Rebel Without A Cause*. Over the next forty years, that look was to boost a thousand careers, from Adam Faith's to George Michael and Wham's, but in the 1950s, it was associated with America's beatnik movement. 'The Beat Generation' as exemplified by writers William Burroughs, Jack Kerouac and Allen Ginsberg had seized on a celebration of jazz and a rejection of traditional bourgeois values and both these ideas were now beginning to seep into mainstream culture.

By late 1959, everything that was 'cool' had to be 'beat' related: *Easy Beat* was on the radio, *Drumbeat* was on TV and now there was *Beat Girl*, the film. Faith was given a medium-sized role in the film, and it was to consolidate his success still further. But more significantly, it was to prove the opening John had been waiting for, to enter the world of film. Once again, when it came to managerial manoeuvrings, Eve Taylor came up trumps. As Geoge Willoughby wanted Adam, and the film was to be a musical one, surely they would be best off using the very man who arranged all Adam's music for the film too, she said – and so John was in. He'd been commissioned to write his first film score.

The idea of using a pop musician to compose for a film was revolutionary at the time. The British film world was a close-knit community of old-school professionals, who put a high value on craftsmanship, and as far as music went, they rarely strayed from the upper echelons of Britain's classical composers. But *Beat Girl* was an attempt to capture the 'youth' phenomenon and what George Willoughby needed was a young composer who could write 'young' music. And with John, that was what he got.

'It's strange the way things work out,' John says now. 'Who'd have thought starting off with Adam with that song, that he would then have a movie career which would put me in a movie situation? Who would ever have thought that would be the way in? I guess it's what they call the luck of the game.'

But amid the excitement of his first film commission, John also had to work out exactly how he was going to write the thing. He may have studied arranging with Bill Russo and by now certainly had extensive studio production experience, but nobody had ever sat down and said, 'This is how you score a film, John.' Although it was what he'd always wanted to do, it was also daunting. 'I was very excited, but there was nobody around to talk to and ask about technique, so I formulated my own. I worked out a whole graph of timings just based on logic – one bar per four seconds, metronome mark at sixty, or if it was uptempo – one bar per two seconds, metronome mark at a hundred and twenty. I just worked it all out with a metronome and a stopwatch, so then all I needed to do was get the score paper and write the times from bar to bar and then just compose it. It was as simple as that.'

It would have been that simple – if John had had peace and quiet to write. However, with only two weeks left before the score was due, he suddenly found himself booked onto a variety tour with the Seven. There was nothing he could do but work around the situation, and so he ended up writing most of *Beat Girl* in the Midland Hotel in Manchester and at digs in Glasgow, finishing off the rest in between rehearsals at ballrooms around England.

Having written it, going into the studio should have been no problem – in theory. When recording began, however, the facilities organisers at Elstree, where the film was being shot, had put the musicians in a small dubbing theatre, with the excuse that the main sound stage was already booked.

The dubbing theatre was, as John puts it disgustedly, 'the deadest-sounding place in the world'. He had gone out of his way to book the top jazz session-players of the day, as well as bringing in dry-ice machines to recreate the muffled fug of a nightclub, but in that space it was to no avail. 'So there I was,' he says, 'with this twenty-piece orchestra – like the Seven with a big band around it – and we went into the dubbing studio with an engineer who couldn't have cared less, and it was absolutely awful. We started off and after a while, I just said, "I'm not going to continue".'

In his straight-talking manner, John got on the phone to producer George Willoughby and said, 'George, take a listen to this. It's deadly. This is supposed to be a movie with a contemporary score, and with the big mikes they've got in that studio, it's making the whole thing sound archaic.' A few minutes later, Willoughby got on the phone and booked the main sound recording stage for two weeks later. After checking it out to make sure it would work, John said, 'This'll be fine, George. This is where we should have been to start with.'

[76]

Over the years, John developed a reputation for being 'difficult', but within the film world, as in most cases, it's usually more a question of people's annoyance at anyone sticking their neck out to get what they need. 'People sometimes say, "Were you always stroppy?" ' says John, 'and I say, "Well, actually on my first movie I refused to continue 'cause it was so bad. So yes, I always was." '

Meanwhile, the fortnight hiatus between recording proved no bad thing for John. 'In a way it all turned out to be a bit of a lucky break for me,' he admits frankly, 'because while we were still in that awful studio, we'd had one morning actually putting the music to film and I realised that I'd been writing too fast for the scenes. Nobody else commented on it, but I knew I was making a big mistake. My tempo choices hadn't been right, so I learned from that. I had two weeks before we were in the studio again and so although I didn't actually rewrite anything, I reorganised the whole thing.'

When the final recording eventually took place, everything went according to plan. But after the previous wrangles, John was understandably anxious. 'He was tight as a drum,' says Sid Margo, violinist on the session and later John's orchestra-booker, 'but he didn't show it. He would never give out any degree of his nervousness, and it never came into his work. But occasionally I could feel it.'

Beat Girl was the first film in Britain to have its soundtrack released on what was still called a 'long-playing record'. Today you could see *Beat Girl* as a groovy mix of smoky jazz, swinging jazz, moody atmospherics and tame rock and roll, but that would be to miss the point. John's unique combination of Stan Kenton-inspired big-band jazz styles with Vic Flick's edgy guitar twang was unprecedented at the time, and formed an early blueprint for not only 'The James Bond Theme' itself, but the entire musical genre which John was to create with subsequent Bond scores. Anyone looking for a precursor in style to 'The James Bond Theme' need look no further than the *Beat Girl* title theme, recorded in 1959 – three years before the first Bond film *Dr No*.

Beat Girl itself is cult B-movie material. Shot partly on location in the coffee bars and strip-clubs of Soho in moody black and white, it's based around the teenage Jennifer and her 'beatnik' friends. It covers similar ground to Julien Temple's unfortunate 1986 fiasco *Absolute Beginners*, but does it a whole lot better. *Beat Girl* manages to take in the themes of jazz, juvenile delinquency and prostitution along the way, and also features some classic moments of 1950s' dialogue: 'Love – that's the gimmick that makes sex respectable, isn't it?' Or: 'If you wanna fight, go join the Army – that's for squares.' And: 'He sends me – over and out.'

The star of *Beat Girl* was fifteen-year-old Gillian Hills. In theory she had all the right attributes for stardom at the time – long blonde hair, an oversized pout and voluptuous curves – but God had been less kind when dishing out the charisma, and the celluloid bears evidence to it. More interestingly, the film also featured Shirley Ann Field, singing the delightfully camp 'It's Legal', and an extremely young Oliver Reed.

In Britain the film was given an 'X' certificate – the equivalent of today's '18' – on the grounds that not only did it feature so-called 'juvenile delinquents' who were challenging authority and might therefore be a dangerous influence on the nation's youth, but that it also included several striptease sequences – one of which is in fact a superb moment of erotic cinema, albeit tame by today's standards. Abroad, concern that the central character Jennifer was rude to her parents was so strong that the film was actually banned in Italy, South Africa, Turkey and Singapore.

At home, the film's release was delayed, as the British censorship board could only allow a certain quota of X-rated films to be released at once, and there was a glut of them that month. In the meantime, word spread that Faith was actually not a bad actor and he was offered a part in another film, *Never Let Go* starring Peter Sellers and Richard Todd, and as the film was set against a background of jukebox-filled coffee bars, John was once again asked to write the music.

Never Let Go was conceived as a serious drama about a stolen-car racket, with Sellers as the main villain, and Faith as a beat generation car-thief. The contrasty film-noir-style lighting and John's jazz score combine to give it what we now think of as a classic 1950s' B-movie atmosphere, but at the time it was considered an important mainstream release with major stars. Its cast included young actress Carol White,

[78]

who later went on to star in the groundbreaking 1960s' dramas *Poor Cow* and *Cathy Come Home* and who, along with Shirley Ann Field, became one of John's growing legion of 'close friends'.

Thanks to the problems over *Beat Girl*'s release, *Never Let Go* ended up coming out first, and although it still stands up as a very good B-movie melodrama, the public were unconvinced. It may have been that Sellers was hugely popular already for his comic roles and so seeing him playing a heavy dramatic role as a villain was perhaps not what people wanted. *Beat Girl*, on the other hand, obviously was. The film was a successs and although the soundtrack wasn't an enormous hit, it did well enough to convince film companies that soundtrack LPs could have a future.

The album also yielded another, albeit more controversial minor hit for Adam Faith, before it was banned by the BBC. 'Made You' had been banned first in America, when it was covered by teen idol Fabian. Over there, if you said you'd 'made' someone, no one had any doubt what it meant, but the BBC took some time to pick up on the saltier side of life, and so in their clipped tones, happily carried on announcing the record to the astonishment of expat Americans nationwide.

By 1961, on the back of *Beat Girl* and *Never Let Go*, John had been offered work writing two more film scores: *Mix Me A Person* – another teen vehicle for Faith, and *The Amorous Prawn*. The latter was a light-hearted drawing-room comedy in the old-fashioned British theatrical style, and was definitely not cutting edge, but for John, if it moved on celluloid, he was up for writing it. And there were better films just around the corner.

By 1960, John's life was frenetically busy. He was still touring and doing TV and radio with the Seven, and following his success with Adam Faith, EMI had signed him up for a three-year contract as an arranger. Within no time he was working on songs for a vast array of artists: mostly minor pop stars who have since vanished into the mists of recording history, such as Peter Gordeno, Danny Williams and Dick Kallman. One or two would crop up later in John's career, like Johnny De Little – a Welshman who'd been discovered by Jack Prendergast singing in York and would later go on to sing the vocal theme on *The Knack* – and Nina and Frederick, the Danish husband and wife team who John worked with intermittently over the next few years.

Through his contacts in the music-publishing world, he had also gained work doing 'library music' for Chappells. Then as now, library records were usually instrumentals, issued by publishers to be used as backgrounds for speech on radio or to fill time, and for John they were perfect. It meant you got regular money, royalty potential if the music was used, as well as useful writing experience. It also provided him with a valuable source bank of his own material ready to be drawn on at any moment, which he frequently did, not least on *Beat Girl* which featured several numbers originally written as library tracks.

At the same time, John had also been approached by Brian Matthew who was looking for a resident band for his new Sunday morning radio show, *Easy Beat*. The programme was to be recorded in front of a live audience every week at the BBC's Playhouse Theatre Studios in London, and so Matthew needed a house band. It couldn't be just any old band, though. 'I needed a band with a leader who ideally was also a good and fast arranger,' says Matthew, 'because the band's duties included not only playing their own spot, but also accompanying any other guest artists. The Seven were an obvious choice.

'I never knew how John had the energy to be doing all the things he was, though,' says Matthew. 'He was permanently rushing from one recording session to another, and everything was always last-minute. Barbara would come tearing in frantically with copies of all the sheet music for the band, and she always seemed to be racing around town sorting out something or other for John.'

By this time, Barbara Pickard had become Mrs John Barry Prendergast and the couple had moved into a small flat in London in Redcliffe Gardens, near Earl's Court. The wedding itself had not been anything grand. 'It was strange how they got married,' remembers Seven drummer Doug Wright. 'We were at Chiswick Empire one night getting ready for a show and John just came in and said, "You can congratulate me, lads. Barbara and I got married today." We had a bottle of champagne and then we went onstage, but that was it. No fuss, no nothing.'

Barbara was by now playing a keen role in the Seven's career. She would sit down with the band and discuss what type of venues they should play, and she'd take care of the band's accounts, making sure they all got paid on a weekly basis. 'I think she must have led a terrible life,' says Matthew, "cause John was flying all over the place. He did so many recording sessions with the Seven as accompanists as well as his own stuff, there was always so much going on. He was getting all the radio he could, writing arrangements like mad, and he would leave "B" as he called her with his finished score and say, "Get that to the copiers, and when they're done, fetch the parts and bring them down to the Playhouse Theatre." He would then turn up at the theatre with only half the scores he needed, and he'd say calmly, "It's all right, Brian, don't worry. They'll be here." And then she would arrive with these things hot from the copiers. It was utterly nerve-wracking. I don't know how we survived!' Fortunately, Barbara always managed to keep her cool.

'She was a very responsible person,' says Vic Flick, 'and she had her head screwed on her shoulders. She knew what was happening and I think she played a big part in John's early success, keeping on top of everything he was doing.'

Amid all the tours, radio shows and arranging, John hadn't forgotten the Seven's own recording career, and after his hits with Faith, he was eager to repeat the success with his own band. Two months after the release of 'What Do You Want' the Seven went into the studio to record their next single, 'Hit and Miss'. Using the same pizzicato-style string arrangement as in 'What Do You Want', but this time pushing Vic Flick's twang guitar to the fore in place of a vocal, John used the same format – the Seven plus four violinists.

From the beginning John was always liked and respected by the musicians who worked for him. They appreciated his quiet, laid-back manner and his understanding towards them. But he could also be a hard taskmaster. He was a perfectionist, and if it took two hundred takes to get something sounding exactly the way he wanted it, then that's what they'd do. 'Plucking away pizzicato at that E-string got incredibly tense and sharp on your fingers,' says Sid Margo, violinist on the session. 'After thirty-two takes on "Hit and Miss" getting it absolutely the way John wanted it, our fingers weren't just sore, there was blood gushing from them.'

'It sounds even better when you get down to the bone,' John would tease, but meanwhile he got straight down to finding a practical solution to the problem. Rather than give up on getting the sound he wanted, he would hire eight violinists instead of four and have one group as a reserve. That way, he'd use the reserves for the run-throughs and the first group for the actual take. Failing that, when one group's fingers started bleeding, the other could take over.

'Hit and Miss' went straight to number ten in the NME's national chart, and it established John and the Seven beyond any question as one of the biggest pop acts of the day. The record was also featured on the star TV show *Juke Box Jury* – a kind of celebrity panel review in which star guests were played a selection of the week's new releases and had to vote on them being a 'hit' or a 'miss'. The Seven's new single was voted most definitely a hit, and what was more, presenter David Jacobs decided that it was a whole lot better than the programme's current theme tune; from then on they'd use 'Hit and Miss' instead.

With 'Hit and Miss', John's trademark marriage of twang guitar and pizzicato strings – 'stringbeat' – reached its creative peak. The combination worked better on this one record than it would on any other future Seven single. 'Hit and Miss', like all the best pop records, was utterly of its time, and yet seems somehow timeless.

More singles followed, and although none matched the success of 'Hit and Miss', some of them deserve a mention. Following the *Beat Girl* LP, *Beat for Beatniks* was released and although not a big chart success, it was enough to impress the critics. In the still jazz-dominated *Melody Maker*, Maurice Burman wrote: 'I put on the record without a lot of interest, but after the first four bars, I nearly fell through the floor! The record is like nothing Barry has done before – it is modern jazz with a fresh approach tinged with Kentonism. It stamps Barry as a first-class modern arranger and composer with a daring mind.'

Along with the craze for all things 'beat', the other recent import from America which had captured everyone's imagination was the Western. The Western wasn't of course new, but the arrival of John Sturges' *The Magnificent Seven* in the cinemas in 1960 sparked off a renewed passion for all things of that ilk, with *Rawhide* and *Gunsmoke* following fast on its tail on TV. John loved Elmer Bernstein's score for the film, and the Seven recorded a twangy but tame version of the classic title theme. Even with Vic Flick's guitar, there was no way that a single string guitar line, albeit augmented by tremelo and reverb, could ever really compete with the punch and drive of Bernstein's original.

'I'd been watching all these cowboy movies,' says John, 'hence "Rodeo" and the rest of those cowboyish titles. But the things that I wrote weren't successful because you can't write a piece like that when it's really based on the Yorkshire Moors.' Later on, of course, John would capture the vastness and expansiveness of the American landscape on *Dances with Wolves* and *The Beyondness of Things*, but at this stage of the game, The John Barry Seven's twang style didn't quite measure up to the task.

In the studio, John was still eagerly trying to work out new ways to record, but was becoming increasingly frustrated with the limitations of even the best-equipped London studios. He could hear how much better American recordings sounded, but couldn't work out how they did it. There was a simple solution, he decided. He'd go to America and find out for himself, even if that meant paying for his own trip. At that time, going to America was not something that most people just got up and did. Your average Englishman in 1960 had probably never been abroad, and if they had it would only have been in the Army. But being John and being EMI's Golden Boy arranger by that time, he organised it.

He would go to Los Angeles and Las Vegas, and while he was there he'd also go to New York, see the musical sights and do some career networking. So in his inimitable style he flew to America and was soon ensconced in the Plaza Hotel, New York. Over the next two weeks he went to legendary jazz club Birdland and saw Joe Williams with the Harry Edison Quartet, Leonard Bernstein at Carnegie Hall and Quincy Jones at Basin Street East.

EMI had arranged for him to be taken round the recording studios

[83]

in Los Angeles, and after settling into the best hotel in Beverly Hills, John was immediately whisked through town to the home of the hits – EMI's Capitol Tower. 'I met a lot of people and I saw a lot of things that really opened my eyes,' he says now. 'I got to meet Phil Spector, for instance. He was one weird guy. He'd get on a plane and when it was going to take off he'd run up the aisle shouting: "This plane's going to explode – I've got to get off!" I met him in a management office once and I needed to go to the bathroom. Someone told me that I had to get a key and Phil said, "Why? Has someone been stealing shit?"'

John also got to sit in on sessions with Lee Hazlewood – then Duane Eddy's producer – and learned the studio secrets which were to transform the sound of the Seven and everything else John was to do in future. Brian Matthew remembers his excitement on his return. 'I've cracked it, Brian!' he said. 'I've found out how they do it. Do you know how many mikes they use on the drumkit over there? Seven, that's how many!'

'"That's all the mikes we've got," I said, but we did what we could. John was always very interested in technical developments and was very meticulous about the way things sounded. That was pretty unusual for a musician at that time. Most people just got out there, played and didn't really care. But John always cared passionately.'

John had been so excited about his new discoveries that he'd phoned John Burgess in London from America and told him to hold the next John Barry Seven single back so he could re-record it using the new studio techniques he'd observed. Not only did the Americans use more mikes on a drumkit, it was where they put them that made the difference. Instead of having just one microphone hanging above the kit, they placed a different microphone under each part, and it was this that gave those American records their punchy sound.

Once home, John lost no time in applying his new skills to the Seven's first and only album – *Stringbeat* – still considered by some to be a minor classic in its own right. In a way *Stringbeat* was one of the first ever concept albums. Contrary to the way things work today, where singles are released to promote albums, many pop artists in the early 1960s never got round to releasing an album at all. LPs in those days were still regarded as a collection of singles which you might get

[84]

the opportunity to put out if you'd had enough hit singles, and although other instrumental bands like The Ventures were recording themed albums, *Stringbeat* was the only one of its kind to use its own trademark sound of twang guitar and pizzicato strings as the linking element. Over fifteen tracks John tackled a mixture of his own compositions, Flick's, Reed's and standards such as Lionel Bart's 'Handful of Songs' and Lieber and Spector's 'Spanish Harlem' with his characteristic musical ingenuity.

Throughout the LP he experimented with unusual combinations of instruments – glockenspiel, acoustic guitar, violins and castanets. He also introduced the clavioline, a kind of early prototype synthesiser which he got jazz pianist Ted Taylor to play. The rubbery electronic squeal of the clavioline would later figure largely in the success of one of John's contemporaries, producer Joe Meek, who used it to great effect on his hit for The Tornadoes – 'Telstar'. Although John's records had the sound, they lacked the energy of Meek's later ones; Meek's were recorded in his bathroom and perhaps it was the crudity of his recording techniques which brought more life to his records than the superbly clean sound of EMI's studios.

The precision of John's records with the Seven reflected the perfectionism of the man, but although today *Stringbeat* would definitely be called 'easy listening', like all John's later music, even here there are darker, much more complex, dramatic elements which belie the description.

Stringbeat was not a big hit, but it became a steady seller nevertheless. The album was John's first and only LP with the Seven, but it had given him fantastic opportunities to experiment in the studio with different sounds.

During his time with both the Seven and Adam Faith, John had acquired an in-depth knowledge of strings – how they worked and what they could do. He'd also mastered the art of the three-minute pop song. These were important skills which would form a vital part of his film sensibility. Adam Faith and pop had – indirectly – got him into film, but it was his own intellectual fascination with the mechanics of pop both technically and structurally that had created the John Barry sound. Up to now that sound had been pop . . . but it was about to become something quite different.

[85]

6

BOND AND THE KITCHEN SINK

At the end of the 1950s, British cinema was in a sorry state. There had been a massive slump in box-office takings and Pinewood – England's largest studio – had laid off huge numbers of staff. Television had a growing audience and people found the programmes on the box at home a lot more entertaining than anything the big screen had to offer.

Two things changed all that – and John was part of them both. One was the eruption onto screen of Secret Agent 007 with *Dr No*, and the other was the arrival of a new generation of young British directors with a new style of realism – the so-called 'kitchen-sink' school of films. Both breathed life into what had become a stagnant and rapidly dwindling film industry.

Dr No was unlike any kind of action film cinemagoers had seen before: its hero was a new breed of person, leading a lifestyle that was light years away from most British people's daily experience. In 1962, the austerity of the war years was still not that far behind, most town centres were still desperately awaiting a lick of paint, and although a new kind of life was beaming its way into people's homes via TV advertising, for most it was still far from reality. Here, though, was a spy who was modern, dashing, daring, sophisticated and immaculately groomed: he wore Savile Row suits, he knew the best wines and got all the best-looking women. He even had a sense of humour. It was the ultimate fantasy.

The Prendergast family. *Left to right, back row:* Jack Prendergast, John's elder brother Patrick, Doris Prendergast. *Front row:* June and John

Doris Prendergast

Jack Prendergast

Doris and Jack (*2nd and 3rd from left*) with Louis Armstrong
at the Casino Theatre, York

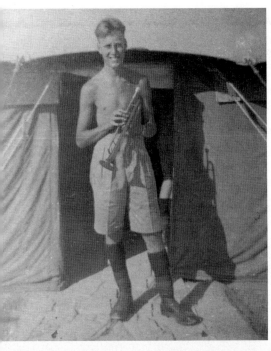

Jazz in the desert. John
outside his army tent in
Egypt

The Green Howards at
Liverpool Station. John,
3rd from left, back row

The John Barry Seven backstage with their NME prize.
Left to right: Les Reed, Vic Flick, John, Mike Peters, Jimmy Stead, Dennis King, Doug Wright (kneeling)

ohn Barry, popstar. Blackpool Sands, 1960

John with Adam Faith at
Abbey Road Studios

At home in Cadogan Square

John and Shirley Bassey with gold discs for 'Goldfinger'

The Bond men: Saltzman, Fleming and Broccoli

Conducting a Bond session in the studio at CTS

Dr No was important cinematically as well, not just because of what the film represented, but how. Editor Peter Hunt had worked on numerous films before and knew that a film's editing style had the power to transform the whole feel of it. He had been watching the latest American films and realised there was a new way of doing things that was different from the high drama style that Hollywood had established and Britain had followed. The old style was beautifully lit, beautifully shot and moved at a slow, dignified pace. The new style was quicker, snappier and punchier and it whizzed the whole thing along faster than an Aston Martin. It also took the film far away from any attempt at realism, and that was what Hunt wanted.

'What I tried to put into the editing style,' says Hunt, 'came out of my thinking about the whole way we should tackle it. I thought that the people who were reading those Fleming novels were essentially bored commuters, coming up to London from the suburbs. They were probably people who worked in an office or some dreary job they didn't care for, and so what they'd be looking for in those stories was fantasy and escape, and that's what I tried to give them.'

And so the Bond phenomenon was born. The success of *Dr No* was John's 'in' to big-time film-making, and became his springboard to international and lasting success. But it was the other school of British films that would consolidate his reputation as a serious composer. The kitchen-sink films were the flipside of the coin to Bond. They were independent, socially realistic films that were about life in Britain as it really was. But just as *Dr No* broke the established rules of film-making, so did the new British films. They just did it in a different way. Instead of the technicolour of Bond, they were black and white and gritty. They had close-up shots of puddles, 'Ban The Bomb' posters and brought the truth of life all the way home. They were the opposite end of the spectrum to Bond's escapism, but in their own way they were equally daring, and they sparked off a decade of dynamic, indigenous film-making. This period was to be a turning point both for British cinema and for John's career.

★   ★   ★

In 1962 James Bond was definitely not a household name. Spy novels on the whole were pretty much a non-starter in sales terms. They had a small cult following, which supposedly included President Kennedy, but generally they were far from mainstream.

Ian Fleming, an ex-British naval intelligence officer and journalist, had written his series of Bond novels in the 1950s in the hope that they would bring him fame and fortune as an author. But having found neither he was about to kill his hero off. In film and television, where new source material was at a constant premium, the stories had been noticed by one or two producers, but nothing had materialised. Sir Alexander Korda had requested the manuscript of *Live and Let Die* but rejected it, while CBS in America had made an instantly forgettable – and consequently long-forgotten – one-hour TV version of *Casino Royale*. For Fleming so far, his only real moment of financial luck had come when film producer Gregory Ratoff had bought the film rights to *Casino Royale*, but he took so long bringing them to celluloid that Fleming never lived to see the results.

Two other film producers meanwhile had separately noticed the Bond books as possible film material – Harry Saltzman and Albert 'Cubby' Broccoli. The latter was a gregarious Italian-American who had been in London for years. With his partner Irving Allen he had set up Warwick Films and produced several successful films including *The Trials of Oscar Wilde* in 1960, but recently he had begun to feel he was not getting as much credit for his input as he would have liked. He decided to go it alone, and so his next move was to find a new project to embark on. He had always dreamed of making films of the Bond thrillers, and thanks to the encouragement of scriptwriter and theatrical impresario Wolf Mankowitz, Broccoli decided to contact Fleming's agent and find out if the rights were available.

As it turned out, they weren't. They had already been optioned by one Harry Saltzman, a large, brusque Canadian who had worked in advertising and vaudeville and been involved in various entrepreneurial ventures before coming to England. Basically he was a hustler, a man who was perhaps short on social skills, but who knew how to make a deal and knew how to get on with it. In England, his reputation for

[88]

financial nous had led him to become the monetary arm of Woodfall Films, the production company set up by theatre director Tony Richardson and playwright John Osborne. With Saltzman as producer they had made the groundbreaking *Look Back in Anger* with Richard Burton, and the equally important *Saturday Night and Sunday Morning* with the then unknown Albert Finney.

On discovering that Saltzman had optioned the Bond books, Broccoli immediately offered to buy them, but the answer was a definite 'no'. Saltzman initially tried to put him off by telling him: 'I've tried to set the Bond books up with every studio in the business, and they're just not interested.' Then, on second thoughts, he said that if Broccoli was still interested, perhaps they could go into partnership and see if they could get further by working together. Reluctantly Broccoli accepted the deal. He wasn't keen to enter into another partnership, but he wanted James Bond. And so the pair started their own production company – Eon – for 'Everything Or Nothing', and set about looking for finance.

It was to be a long, hard search. In 1960 the spy film as a genre was less than buoyant. There had only been one successful spy film that year – Carol Reed's *Our Man In Havana* with Alec Guinness – but that had been a comedy and hardly a box-office smash. Broccoli himself had approached Columbia with Bond a few years earlier but their enthusiasm had been decidedly lukewarm. 'This Fleming seems to write travel books,' they said, after their research department, in a marvel of efficiency, had confused Ian with his travel-writer brother Peter.

Everywhere Saltzman and Broccoli went, the whole idea was swiftly dismissed. 'Spy films are a thing of the past,' they kept being told by one distributor after another. Finally Broccoli remembered there was yet one avenue they hadn't explored. He had met a lawyer called Arthur Krim on a Warwick film, and Krim was now President of United Artists – one of the key American distributors and backers. So Broccoli and Saltzman flew to New York in a last attempt to try and sell their Bond vision. The meeting with Krim dragged on interminably, but finally, after heavy consultation with his colleagues and staff, Krim agreed to back Bond, on the condition that the film could be made cheaply. He was offering one million dollars, but no more. This was not big bucks by 1960s' standards, but it wasn't that bad either. 'Harry,' said Broccoli, 'we are now in the Bond business.'

Once Saltzman and Broccoli had the contract in their hands, they were on the first plane straight back to London. Now they had the money, all they needed was a script, a director and an actor to play Bond. *Thunderball* was to be the first film, but perhaps fortunately all round, a rethink became necessary as there was a dispute over legal copywright ownership of that particular novel.

Instead they decided to go for *Dr No*, which had the added attraction of topicality. America's air base Cape Canaveral had been getting an extremely bad press at that time, as its missiles had repeatedly misfired or gone astray. This had obviously caused more than a little embarrassment for the US Defence Department, and so with *Dr No*, Fleming's villain provided a perfect 'culprit' for the public's imagination to seize upon. The book's plot mirrored the situation perfectly, while assigning all blame to the ruthless villain and his quest for world domination.

A director was found in the form of the young, debonair, and not entirely un-Bond-like Terence Young – a 'gentleman' of the old school who had directed several films both for United Artists and Broccoli's Warwick Films. None of them had been great commercial successes, but Young had shown himself to be very competent, imaginative and good at storytelling – just the qualities they required.

The other key factor was the question of who would play Bond himself. Ian Fleming had originally wanted David Niven – who was later to play him in *Casino Royale*, while other names bandied around included James Mason, Richard Burton and James Stewart. But Broccoli and Saltzman had been convinced from the word go that they wanted an unknown actor to play the role. They had had a vision all along of making the films into a series with an identity of its own, and they knew that an established actor would never have been able to commit himself to more than one film. An unknown, however, would be made a star by the role and would also become identified with the character. And that was exactly what they needed.

Patrick McGoohan was the producers' first choice, but he turned it down on the grounds that Bond was too immoral. Others considered included Roger Moore – rejected because he was too 'baby-faced' – Richard Johnson, Terence Cooper and a little-known Scottish actor called Sean Connery. With Connery, Saltzman and Broccoli thought they saw potential. 'What impressed me,' said Saltzman at the time, 'was that a man of his size and frame could move in such a supple way.' Broccoli put it more bluntly: 'He looked like he had balls.' And he did. Connery had been a boxing champion in the Navy, as well as a Shakespearian actor and a Carnaby Street model, and he had exactly the right combination of sophistication, sex appeal and virility. Importantly he also had an accent that was British – as opposed to American – but at the same time was neither working class nor upper class. The fact that he had a slight Scottish burr was the perfect evasion of this potentially audience-dividing issue, and so Connery was the perfect choice all round.

This kind of detail was crucial to the success of the films with audiences on both sides of the Atlantic – as was the film's location. In the same way that Connery's classless accent avoided an issue, the choice of location did the same. Again, a perfect compromise was found by setting the film in Jamaica – technically British soil, and therefore simple for union and crew logistics, but also much more glamorous and exotic than grey old England, or at least it was when the sun shone. For most of the shoot it rained torrentially, but after spending weeks waiting for the sun, and going way over budget, Young, Saltzman and Broccoli decided to bring everyone back to England and make the best of what they'd got in the editing.

The sound of James Bond is undoubtedly the sound of John Barry. And yet it almost wasn't. John's crucial role in creating the Bond phenomenon was one of those accidents of Fate that very nearly didn't happen. While casting the film, Saltzman and Broccoli had had to think about who they would get to do the music, and in doing so, unknowingly embarked on what would end up as a complex web of commissions, de-commissions and gentleman's handshakes which in years to come would make Watergate look simple.

Saltzman knew a songwriter called Monty Norman who had worked on various stage musicals. Like John, Norman had originally come from a jazz background and had been the singer for Geraldo, leader of one of the big bands of the time. So when Saltzman offered him the music for *Dr No*, he jumped at the chance. Saltzman wanted him to write incidental music and a title theme which would work for the whole series, and so he suggested Norman came out to Jamaica to get the feel of the film and record some local music. This he did, drawing on traditional Jamaican calypso for the recurring 'Underneath the Mango Tree' song and compiling other hi-life and calypso melodies for the rest.

Peter Hunt, editor on *Dr No* as well as the next four Bond films, remembers: 'He came back with hours and hours of this Jamaican steel-drum stuff, and some of it ended up as background music in the film. When he first got back, though, he sat down with Terence Young and I, and we told him where we needed the music to go, and then he went off and did the writing. Then the first time we really heard anything was at the recording session, because in those days that was the way things still worked: a director wouldn't really hear how the music would sound until you were on the session with an orchestra.

'Well, we arrived at Denham, where they were rehearsing, and it was not at all the sort of music we'd expected to have on the film.

'So I said, "I think the most sensible thing to do would be to pull up stakes now, and let's go and talk to our producers."

We knew we had to rethink the whole thing and we set up a meeting with the producers that afternoon.

'I went back to the cutting room in between, and on the way there I was talking to my assistant and I said, "Terence has got all these grand ideas about composers, but they'll never be able to do that. Who could we get to arrange it instead?" And my assistant said, "I've just worked on a TV show that featured The John Barry Seven."

' "Ooh," I said. "I like them. Could that John Barry guy do music for a film, do you think?"

' "Well, I don't know," he said. "But he's very good. And he's a new fellow and he's young."

[92]

'So I went to this meeting and during the conversation Terence was trying to talk them into William Walton or someone and Harry and Cubby were saying, "We don't have the money for those sort of people. We've got to find someone who's efficient and practical and who'll do it and not be extravagant." So I piped up and I said, "What about John Barry?"'

In the hours leading up to the meeting, Saltzman had also got on to Noel Rogers, the head of United Artists' music division and explained the situation. According to John, Rogers then called his friend Teddy Holmes who was head of Chappell Music Publishing to find out who might be good at rearranging instrumental music that needed to be lively, contemporary and most importantly, hip.

Working on these criteria, Holmes considered the two top instrumental groups in Britain at the time – The Shadows and The John Barry Seven. In The Shadows there was no one who could arrange. In the Seven, John was known as being the man behind Adam Faith's hits and a skilled instrumental arranger. He'd also already scored two films. Holmes reckoned he'd found the man for the job and told Rogers, who told Saltzman.

Saltzman was someone who always needed at least two people's back-up on every decision, and so by the time Peter Hunt came to mention John's name at the meeting, he picked up the phone to his secretary and said, 'Get me John Barry on the phone. *Now*.'

'I was called in for a Saturday-morning meeting with Monty Norman and Noel Rogers,' says John, 'and asked to arrange this theme. I never saw the movie though. I was just given a timing and told that it was about this Secret Service guy. And at that time, even though I'd heard of Ian Fleming's Bond books, I'd never actually read one.'

Even though John hadn't seen the film, and no one at this point had any idea what a cinematic sensation Bond would become, this was still a big-time film for him. Broccoli and Saltzman were both well-established, respected producers, United Artists was a major distributor, and even though the budget hadn't been massive, compared to *Beat Girl* and *Never Let Go*, it was huge. This film was in colour, and it was definitely in another league.

'He was quite nervous to start with,' says Peter Hunt. 'Even in those days, before Bond took off, those two producers were pretty big names in the film business and they were pretty overbearing. Harry was a big bully and Broccoli was always trying to be nice, but never quite succeeding, I don't think. They were tough guys – and it was a tough business. They were never really kind or sympathetic unless it suited them, so they would have been daunting for John.

'But I said to him, "You don't need to worry. I'll hold your hand, and we'll get it all sorted out," and as he knew I'd been editor on a number of films and knew about music, he trusted me. So I advised him whenever I could, and then he came up with this marvellous sound, which was exactly what was needed, and which was really part of the creation of the whole new era of James Bond, secret agent. Without the music, we just wouldn't have had the same sort of film.'

Monty Norman has himself been reported saying that his first attempts at the 'Theme' were not quite right. He had proposed 'Underneath the Mango Tree' as a possible, but this was turned down as not being strong enough to carry an entire series of films. He had also put forward what would appear on the soundtrack album as 'Dr No's Fantasy' – a piece of moody jazz twang. Having then gone back to the drawing board once more, he had hit upon the idea of re-using a melody he had written for an aborted stage musical called 'The House of Mr Biswas'. As no soundtrack for this was ever recorded, we have only Monty Norman's vocal rendition to go by, and from that we hear the basic melody of 'The James Bond Theme' guitar riff as we know it, albeit at a much slower pace.

It is interesting to note the presence of John's arrangement of the 'Theme's' opening four-note motif in the backing vocal to The John Barry Seven single 'Black Stockings' released in 1960. Also worth a listen are the first few bars of Adam Faith's 1960 hit 'Poor Me' which was written by Johnny Worth under the name Les Vandyke, but arranged by John. And to go back even earlier, the same motif can actually be traced back to a significantly earlier jazz source – jazz clarinettist Artie Shaw's 1938 recording of 'Nightmare', a popular big-band number.

Most importantly of all, what made the arrangement of 'The Bond

Theme' as we know it the groundbreaking start of an entire genre was John's unique combination of the dominant guitar twang – the sound of the Seven – with the brass-heavy jazz style of Stan Kenton. The blueprint for this orchestration can easily be heard on John's theme for *Beat Girl* recorded two years earlier in 1960, and to a lesser extent in the Seven's signature tune – the Barry composition, 'Bees Knees' – but John hadn't invented this mix overnight. It was a natural progression of everything he'd been doing.

'What I did for Bond, that whole sound – that mix of two styles – was completely new at the time,' says John. 'But what that style was, was me. I never sat down to concoct a "Bond sound" as such. It was just a mixture of the rock guitar twang stuff I'd been doing with the Seven, plus that brass thing I'd got from studying with Stan Kenton's arranger Bill Russo. Those were the two main areas I was coming from, so it just came out of me that way.'

Putting those two elements together in the arrangement was John's masterstroke, but the whole idea of changing style in the middle of a record was at the time considered just as groundbreaking in itself. ' "The Bond Theme" breaking into a swing middle was absolutely unheard of at the time musically, but it worked. I remember Paul Anka, who was also on EMI at the same time, doing a song which changed key in the middle – and that caused a big fuss. In those days you didn't even change key, let alone style.' With the Bond arrangement, John had broken all the rules.

When it came to recording 'The Bond Theme' though, John had learned from the lessons of *Beat Girl* and had a very clear idea in his mind of the way he wanted things to sound. 'We didn't have a lot of money,' says Peter Hunt, 'and so John couldn't have a massive great orchestra. He had to be clever with what he had in order to make it sound right.' And John was determined that it would sound right, in spite of the limitations.

As a teenager studying with Dr Francis Jackson at York, John had gone into the Minster one day to find a whole orchestra playing in there. The almost religious experience of hearing this extraordinary sound reverberating around the heights of the building had had a lasting effect on him and so when it came to Bond, he knew what he was looking for.

John Burgess remembers him paying special attention in the studio to the way the brass section was recorded in order to get the big sound he wanted, using the echo chamber on the trumpets and trombones to give them all extra breadth. It was what he wanted himself, but he also had Broccoli and Saltzman in mind. 'Film people are always very impressed with big sounds,' John told Burgess. 'If you can't win them over with melody, win them over with sound.'

Dr No was the birth into popular culture of Agent 007. It was also the birth of what was to become one of the most influential musical genres of the century – spy music as created for James Bond. *Dr No* was an entirely new kind of action film, and the 'Theme' was an entirely new kind of sound.

The idea of moody jazz heavy on the minor chords for *films noirs*, spy or detective films was in itself nothing new. Henry Mancini's theme for *Peter Gunn* had been a hit first in its own right in 1958, and more influentially for Duane Eddy with his guitar twang in 1959. Elmer Bernstein had also created the mix of big-band jazz with an orchestra for *The Man With the Golden Arm* and all these can be seen to have influenced John's arrangement for Bond.

But whereas the earlier themes of Mancini, Bernstein *et al* were about lowlife, sleaze and mystery – the seamy underbelly of urban living – 'The James Bond Theme' had all that and then some. It had the darkness and intrigue, but it also had a sense of sophistication and anticipation that was more than a little to do with sex. From the driving rhythm of Vic Flick's guitar lead to that swing break which just oozed excitement, the 'Theme' enthralled from beginning to end and it suited Bond's schoolboy fantasy antics perfectly.

When John finished work on the 'Theme' and delivered it to United Artists, he had no idea what would become of the film, nor did anyone else. Cubby Broccoli showed it to a friend of his who ran a chain of cinemas in America, hoping to test the water. 'This film is not showable,' he declared to Broccoli at the end of it. Broccoli was devastated;

the best thing seemed to be to try the film out on the public and see if it did any better there.

Dr No was previewed at Slough and when the audiences roared with laughter, director Terence Young felt decidedly put out. As far as he was concerned, the film was not supposed to be a comedy, but a serious spy thriller. Saltzman and Broccoli, however, were wiser. They recognised that although they hadn't intended it that way, the audience had picked up on Bond's humour in a way they could never have imagined, and they had the sense to realise that this might not be a bad thing.

As United Artists were still uncertain whether anyone would bother to go and see it, they opened the film at B-list cinemas across the country. But in no time Bond's licence to kill quickly became a licence to print money as the public flocked to see it. It seemed that the Cold War had thawed enough by this time to allow for Bond's playful approach to the world of international intrigue and espionage and the potential dangers of global war, and the film had captured the new confidence and optimism of the time. Bond was a spy but there was nothing drab, depressing or even faintly realistic about his existence. He moved in a world where the villains always got their come-uppance and a ready supply of glamorous women were constantly available to him. Who could resist so seductive a notion? Especially when it came wrapped in an enticing package of fast-paced American-style editing, futuristic set designs and gripping music.

John himself had to wait alongside the general public before he could see the finished film. 'I stood in line outside the Pavilion Cinema in Piccadilly one Sunday afternoon after it had opened on the Friday, paid my money and went in,' he remembers. 'I thought the whole thing was very fresh, having a new lead actor and all that. But I'd also thought I was only doing the title sequence and there I am, sitting there watching this movie, and this thing just kept coming in every five minutes. I thought, They've got their £250 worth here – 'cause that's all I was paid.' By that time, John had parted company with Eve Taylor, and was temporarily negotiating his own deals.

John had indeed only been commissioned to arrange Norman's title

'Theme', but Peter Hunt had liked the finished article so much that he'd decided to use it throughout the film. 'It was so good as a theme,' says Hunt, 'that I used it deliberately all through, so that any time Bond was going to do something – there it was, as a kind of signature. I used it to underline the humour of the whole thing, because Bond did everything with such style and with never a bead of sweat, and so the music helped the humour of the film. That's why it was there each time.'

This was all very flattering to John, but it was certainly not what had been agreed. 'On Monday morning I called Noel Rogers at United Artists and I said, "What's going on?" says John. He said, "Oh my God, I knew this call was going to come." So I said, "Well, what are you going to do about it?" He said he would speak to Harry Saltzman and get back to me.'

Saltzman and Broccoli were immovable on the terms of John's *Dr No* deal. There was no more money, and he couldn't have a writing credit but, they said, if *Dr No* did well, there might well be another Bond film sometime very soon, and if there was, they'd definitely be in touch. As it turned out, *Dr No* did plenty well enough. The public lapped it up. It wasn't an instant smash but a word-of-mouth thing. Little by little, more and more people were talking about the film, and *Dr No* was soon making money, and lots of it.

'The James Bond Theme', as recorded by The John Barry Seven and Orchestra was released as a single on Columbia in September 1962 to coincide with the release of the film. It entered the Top Forty straight away, and spent nearly three months in the charts. As much as the public loved the film, they loved the 'Theme' too. And this was not only good news for John and the Seven, it was also to have a lasting effect on the film industry. Suddenly film music was news. As John Burgess recalls: 'Up to that time, film companies didn't see music as very important. They weren't used to spending time or money on it. So the success of "The James Bond Theme" really helped to change all that.' And as film music became more important over the next few years, so would the composers.

But although *Dr No* was an enormous success, in 1962 nobody could

[98]

have foretold just how famous Bond films and 'The James Bond Theme' itself would become. Nor could anyone have guessed that nearly forty years after the first Bond film was made, the origins of the 'Theme' would be under discussion in London's High Court of Justice. In March 2001, Monty Norman successfully sued Times Newspapers Ltd over an article published in the *Sunday Times* in October 1997 under the heading: 'Theme tune wrangle has 007 shaken and stirred'. The piece had inferred that John, rather than Norman, was the author of the 'Theme'.

Norman refuted this claim, stating that he was indeed entitled to credit for composing the 'Theme'. He also claimed that it was he himself – not Noel Rogers – who had originally brought John in to arrange the 'Theme'. After a two-week hearing, in which both John and Norman gave evidence, the jury deliberated for four hours before reaching their unanimous verdict in Norman's favour. It was a complex case in which music experts had been consulted, and based on their final agreement the judge noted that Norman had made 'a very substantial contribution towards the composition'. On the basis of the evidence presented, the case had been resolved and Norman was awarded £30,000 in libel damages.

In 1962, while *Dr No* was the glamorous, shiny new side of British film, another more serious black and white version had also emerged. During the first half of the 1960s, it would run parallel to Bond as the alternative, but equally important face of British cinema. While John had been busy forging a musical career for himself with the Seven, there had been dramatic developments in the film world. Just as rock and roll had been a revolution in music, a new generation of young British film directors had transformed British cinema.

Things had started to change in 1956 with the emergence of the Free Cinema Movement. Calling it a movement suggests it was on a scale much larger than it actually was, for Free Cinema was essentially the work of three young directors: Tony Richardson, Karel Reisz and Lindsay Anderson. They had started making low-budget documentaries which focused on the two areas of life that were fascinating the left-wing intelligentsia of the time – jazz culture and youth culture.

Films such as Reisz's *We Are the Leather Boys* and Richardson and Reisz's *Momma Don't Allow* never reached a wide audience, and outside the film-history books are generally long forgotten, but their importance lay in their unconventional subject-matter and the way they were shot. These semi-documentary films were a universe away from the terribly proper drawing-room dramas and stiff upper-lip war epics that were still the mainstay of British cinema. Instead of the meticulously lit, theatrical style that had been copied from Hollywood, the directors used natural light, odd camera angles and showed their subjects in an altogether freer, more spontaneous way.

In commercial terms, Free Cinema was just a blip in film history, but what was important was that it gave birth to the now famous 'kitchen-sink' school of socially realistic films which, in the hands of directors Reisz, Richardson and John Schlesinger, would re-energise the British film industry.

The turning point for them had been John Osborne's landmark play *Look Back in Anger* which Richardson had directed at the Royal Court Theatre in 1956, and which he had subsequently filmed for Woodfall – the company he'd set up with Osborne and Harry Saltzman.

Look Back in Anger's central character Jimmy Porter was the archetype of the new breed of Englishman that the media had seized upon – 'The Angry Young Man'. His generation were the first products of the post-war Education Act, which had made a grammar-school education available to working-class children. Now there was a newly articulate working class, and they still had reason to be angry. As John had seen at his first BBC audition, the old values of Britain's Empire days were still very much in place, and Britain was still an essentially conservative, socially deferential place where how you spoke mattered more than how bright you were.

Jimmy Porter was the figurehead of a generation's frustration. He was the 'rebel without a cause' of British intellectual society. The 'kitchen-sink' directors picked up where *Look Back in Anger* had left off and started filming books and plays by Northern, working-class writers, featuring Northern, working-class actors. With films like Karel Reisz's *Saturday Night and Sunday Morning*, John Schlesinger's *A Kind of Loving* and Tony Richardson's *A Taste of Honey*, they started showing a more real side of British life. These films overtly tackled the previously unhallowed issues of life in Northern towns, the class divide, sex, abortion, homosexuality and race. But the difference between these films and the earlier Free Cinema was that they were commercial, made to be seen by regular cinema-going audiences and although they were essentially the 'art' films of their day, they did have an effect on the industry.

By 1962, writer/director Bryan Forbes had seen what was going on and started work on *The L-Shaped Room*. Although it was set in London's Notting Hill, instead of the North, its story of a single girl's pregnancy in a low-rent boarding-house carried on the 'kitchen-sink' themes and also featured several scenes in a jazz club. And this was where John came in. The jazz sequences represented the height of what was spontaneous, new, vital and young, and Forbes needed music that would express that.

The world of film composing at the time was still very small, so it was hardly surprising that within a week of *Dr No* opening, Forbes contacted John and asked if he could write a jazz sequence for the film.

'I needed a little nightclub sequence,' says Forbes, 'and John's fixer – as we called musical bookers in those days – brought this thin, spindly creature onto my set. I'd never met him before and he was like a beanstalk in those days – "If you stood him sideways you couldn't see him," Michael Caine once said – and so his fixer brought this young man on the set. I remember I was very busy that day, but he came along and said, "I understand you want a bit of music." I said, "Yeah, I want three or four minutes of nightclub music with a trumpet maybe – a solo," and he said, "Fine." I didn't know much about him but I said to the fixer, "If you believe this young man is good, I'll take your word," 'cause I knew him and trusted him. Then, within what seemed like seconds almost, this young man had returned with some material. He'd obviously gone home and written it immediately, 'cause the following day I had the music and it was very good. So we put it in the film and it worked beautifully.'

John's jazz sequence may only have formed a very small part of the film, but it was a significant one. Only a few years earlier, screenings of *The Blackboard Jungle* had caused riots simply because the film featured Bill Haley's 'Rock Around the Clock' over the opening titles. And *The L-Shaped Room* wasn't a 'youth' film like *Beat Girl* either. This was a serious drama by a well-respected member of the film industry. But the whole notion of anything that could genuinely be called 'popular' music in a respectable motion picture was still daring. As Eric Tomlinson, engineer at CTS Studios where John recorded 'L-Shaped Room' and many of his future film music recalls: 'We'd been getting all these British films with people like Muir Matheson and symphony orchestras for years, and this was a new sound and a very modern sound, so that was important.'

The film itself enjoyed a moderate success, in spite of being labelled by critics as 'a ragbag of kitchen-sink clichés'. Seen from today's viewpoint, it's still very watchable and apart from anything else, is awash with classic early 1960s' social references, from the parking meters – which had only just been introduced – to lines like: 'Between her and the bomb, we don't stand a chance' and, 'What's the verdict – hit or miss?'

During the 1960s, John would end up working on a broad range of films, but there were two important collaborations which would span the decade. One was with Saltzman and Broccoli on the Bond films, the other was with Forbes.

John's musical contribution to *The L-Shaped Room* may have been small, but it marked the beginning of his working partnership with Forbes, one that would eventually give him the opportunity to prove himself as a serious and versatile composer. Forbes and his black and white dramas provided John with a chance to show the world that there was more to him than big thrills action music. Here was his opportunity to be subtle, innovative and experimental – and that was what he needed.

His work on 'The James Bond Theme' had been a milestone in John's career. Almost forty years on, that one track has lost none of its punch. Even familiarity hasn't managed to blunt its edge, and in spite of the infinite changes in musical styles and recording technology, it still sounds fresh.

It was the beginning of what would become John's most famous series of work and maybe it's his own sense of thrill and excitement that you can still hear on that brass. It also marked the bridge between his career as twang maestro and arranger with the Seven, and the start of his role as a fully-fledged film composer.

7

FOOL BRITANNIA

Someone once said that life is like an aeroplane flight. Most of us are the passengers who just sit there and wait for the pilot to take charge of the route, while some are in the cockpit from the start. They decide where they're going and how, and never stray from their path once it's marked out.

John Barry was always one of the pilots and he had always known where he was going. He was going to make it as a film composer, and with *Dr No*, he was well on the way. But he needed to do the full score for the next Bond film to really set him on the path. In the meantime, he still needed to earn a living.

For all he knew, the film-music bubble might burst at any minute, so it was important to consolidate his reputation in the music business. People already knew him as the man behind Adam Faith as well as the Seven, but John still wanted more recognition as a producer, arranger and musical director. He needed to be known for doing those things and for doing them well.

His chance came when Jeffrey Kruger, owner of the small, independent record label Ember, offered him carte blanche to come in and be its Musical Director. With Ember, he would no longer be just another EMI employee, supplying them with hit arrangements for little reward and less recognition. This time he was the boss. At least artistically.

On the film front he also needed to prove himself as more than just a pop musician who'd had a few lucky film breaks. He needed to show he was capable of working with a full orchestra, of using it to its full advantage, and of being innovative with it. He had shown what he could do with the Seven's pop recordings and his work for *Beat Girl*, *Never Let Go* and *The L-Shaped Room*, but he needed to apply all that he'd learned to a major film score.

In 1963 John won the chance to do so, with two very different films. One was the follow-up to *Dr No* – *From Russia With Love* – and the other was *Zulu*. And both would make a significant difference to his professional standing.

'Until the Bond films got going, or at least until *Zulu*,' says Michael Caine, 'there was definitely a bit of snobbery around the film circles. John was perceived as a bit of an upstart, 'cause he was a rock and roll musician. Not by me, but by the film people. According to them he had this group that weren't that famous, and here he was writing for movies. People didn't realise that he had this musical education, 'cause most of the pop guys you met – they could do four chords on a guitar and were making a million quid a week. But John was in actual fact a real musician, but 'cause he had this pop group, no one thought of him in those terms.'

1963 was an important year for John in more ways than one. It was a year of dramatic social change at every level of society and in all aspects of British culture, but it was also a year of scandal, both on a national level and for John on a personal one. By the end of the year, both his professional and personal situation would have altered considerably.

Dr No had been a great success at the end of 1962, but while John had been working on *The L-Shaped Room* for Bryan Forbes, he was still anxiously waiting for Saltzman and Broccoli's call. He was dying to know if they were really going to keep their word and offer him the next Bond picture, and in 1963 the call finally came. They'd begun work on *From Russia With Love* and although they'd already commissioned the title song from Lionel Bart, they wanted him to score the rest of the film.

[105]

John was ecstatic. 'He was thrilled to pieces,' smiles Sid Margo, who had by now become John's regular 'fixer' or booker. 'He called me up straight away and said, "I've got the Bond film, Sid! I can't believe it!"'

But the decision once again had only been made after lengthy discussion, even though with the rest of the crew, Saltzman and Broccoli had opted for continuity and employed the same people as they had on *Dr No*. Terence Young was directing once again, Peter Hunt was editor and Ken Adam was set designer. The key cast members were all the same, but the producers had still had doubts about the music. 'I don't know why,' remembered Terence Young in conversation with John Williams, 'but Saltzman and Broccoli were awfully wary of John. They thought he was too young and inexperienced in film music and I had a little bit to do with his finally doing *From Russia With Love*. Somebody wanted Lionel Bart to write all the music, but I said that if John Barry was inexperienced then so was Lionel, and I thought we owed it to John to give him a chance. I told them I liked Lionel very much, but I could not see why they were doing down John because he was inexperienced. If they had been suggesting someone like Williams who was one of the classical composers instead, it would have made more sense. But Cubby Broccoli was on my side, and in the end it was two to one. I think Cubby was the decider that we should go with John. In the meantime I think Harry had committed to Lionel Bart, and that's why Lionel wrote the title song, which was charming. But John wrote a hell of a good score.'

John did indeed end up writing a good score, and this time he got the full composer treatment from the word go. Now he was a fully fledged member of the Bond 'family', it was off to Istanbul for two weeks to soak up the atmosphere on location. And the atmosphere was far from dull. 'Istanbul was absolutely hilarious,' says John. 'If ever I walked into a page of Kafka, this was definitely it. One night me and Noel Rogers went into this bar – this gorgeous place with a really long bar and a fifty-foot brass rail holding it all together. There was no one else in there, but we sat down and ordered a couple of drinks. The next thing we knew we'd leaned on this rail and the whole thing just collapsed on top of us, every nut and bolt. We'd been told this was the place to be, you know? I guess you had to be there, but it was a very strange evening. Istanbul's like that. You get in a cab, go half a mile and then three old ladies get in holding chickens!'

Having recovered from the ardours of Turkey, it was back to London and reality. Writing the score was rather less eventful than the trip to Istanbul, although no less exciting for John. On the back of *Dr No*'s success, *From Russia With Love* was allowed a bigger budget, and so although Bond was still not quite the cultural phenomenon it became later, compared to the low-budget British films that were still the norm, this one was in an altogether different league. It had glamour, prestige and most importantly for its commerciality, American money behind it. Getting the Bond score was a coup for John, and getting it right was definitely a priority.

But even though he had by now worked on several films, he continued to have other commitments, not least with his band. At the same time as he was due to write *From Russia With Love*, he was also due on tour with the Seven, and as the dates had been booked months earlier, there was no way of pulling out now. The only thing for it was to get into the ballrooms early, before rehearsals, and sit down at grand pianos around England and write.

John realised straight away that to maintain continuity in the films it was important for 'The Bond Theme' to feature again in the next score. It had been such a big hit in its own right, that it made sense to capitalise on that too. And so having seen the way Peter Hunt had used it so effectively in *Dr No*, he carried on the tactic himself, weaving it into his own music.

But he also established two other elements which were to become regular features of his Bond soundtracks. One was the technique of writing orchestral variations on the title theme. Now that he had full musical control and a budget to work with, he had opted for a full orchestra and intended to use every bit of it. The other key element was the addition of his own signature '007 Theme' – an alternative to the main 'Theme', which he would likewise use intermittently throughout the film to reintroduce Bond. In order for it to work, though, it had to be recognisably different from the original, whilst at the same time conveying some of the same characteristics.

His solution was to use a combination of hard, military-style percussion and brass for the main thrust of it, while transferring the melody to honeymoon strings in the middle. And in doing so, John created a theme which told you everything you needed to know. You sensed completely that whoever Bond was, he was a man on a mission, and that you'd get danger, drama and adventure, but that somewhere in there you'd get romance as well.

John had put no less effort into his arrangement of Bart's title song, and when it came to recording, he was determined to get things sounding exactly the way he wanted them.

'Recording the *From Russia With Love* song took up most of the session,' remembers Margo, 'much longer than usual. Normally we'd get several tracks done in a session, but that song took all afternoon. John was very particular to get the strings sounding exactly right. The poor string players had to play so high up the top of the violin, they were practically picking their noses.' But after umpteen takes, John had finally got the sound he wanted.

When the film came out, it was an even bigger success than *Dr No*. John rerecorded the title song as an instrumental, with the Seven plus orchestra, and issued it as a single, backed with his own '007 Theme'. The record just scraped into the Top Forty, making it to thirty-nine, and would probably have done better, had there not been three vocal versions out at the same time – not least Matt Monro's, which became a major hit.

The success of *From Russia With Love* in the autumn of 1963 established the Bond films as a world cult. *From Russia With Love* was also an important step for John. By proving to Saltzman and Broccoli that he could successfully write a whole score, he now had the confidence to hold out for even more scope on the next one. With *Goldfinger* he would demand to write the whole thing including the title song – but in the meantime he still had a career in the record business to deal with.

★   ★   ★

While John was scoring *From Russia With Love*, EMI had acknowledged his arranging talents and promoted him to A&R Director. This was a major step up from his pre-Adam Faith days, but although John now had a title, he still wasn't getting as much recognition as he wanted. Until then he had been getting £50 per arrangement – which wasn't bad money at the time – but what he really wanted was a named credit for his role as producer on the records, as well as more money and a share of the royalties. After all, as arranger and producer, he was at the very least partly responsible for the records' success, and he had been bringing in the hits on a regular basis. As his contract was now due for renewal, it seemed that this could be the perfect time to renegotiate.

EMI, however, were not forthcoming with an improved offer. Although by today's standards what John was asking for would seem no more than reasonable for any successful producer, in those days the music business was still heavily stacked in favour of the record companies – at the expense of both the producers and the artists. Feeling confident that one of the other major record labels would snap him up, John allowed his EMI contract to expire and got on with working with the Seven while he waited for another offer. To his surprise none came, until one day he received a call from a Jeffrey Kruger, who said he wanted to talk to him about his independent record label, Ember.

Kruger was known in the London music business as a rather shady character who managed the Soho jazz and blues club The Flamingo. Ember had mainly been releasing blues and R&B artists, but over drinks at the Carlton Tower Hotel in Knightsbridge, Kruger told John: 'What I want you to do is come and take over the label. I own it, but basically you'll be running the show.' What he was offering John was complete artistic freedom to release whatever records he wanted, and he was making it very attractive financially. Until then John had been earning £20 a week from his publishing deal with Campbell Connelly, plus anything else he was doing on top of that. This wasn't too bad by the standards of the time, but the Ember offer was in a different league. Kruger was offering him £400 a week, plus expenses, as well as a producer royalty and even more importantly for John, a producer credit. On a personal level, Kruger may not have been John's cup of tea, but he was not one to let personal preferences get in the way of sound economics. And so, in the absence of any other offers, John signed on the dotted line.

Running Ember was a new challenge for John and he was determined to make the label very much his own. His first move in his new role as Creative Director, therefore, was to apply the marketing skills he'd learned at his father's cinemas and get the company logo redesigned to look cool and contemporary. The result was just that. Drawing on the London Underground logo for inspiration, animator Richard Williams – who later went on to do the Pink Panther and Roger Rabbit – came up with the distinctive red, black and white circular design. It was a marked contrast to EMI's uninspiring black labels, and with a combination of its new, swinging logo and the then revolutionary policy of releasing all records in picture sleeves, Ember was on its way.

Having revamped the label's image, John's next task was to sign some acts and find something to release. He had by now started up his own artists' management agency – Topline Artists – with fellow musical arranger Geoff Love and theatrical impresario Edward Horan. They had all seen how often performers were mismanaged, and had been on the receiving end of it themselves, so they thought, Why not start our own company? That way, things'll get done properly and we might make some money too. It also gave John and Love a steady supply of artists to arrange for, which didn't hurt either.

The man they got to run the agency on a day-to-day basis was Tony Lewis, an obsessive music fan who knew everything and everyone in the business. Aware that John was on the lookout for new talent, Lewis called him up one day and said, 'John, there's a guy I think you should hear,' and took him down to Tina's, a wine bar in Albemarle Street where a young duo called Chad and Jeremy were playing folk songs at lunchtimes. John immediately saw hit potential, signed them to Ember and within weeks had produced and released 'Yesterday's Gone'. It was the label's first release under John's supervision and it was a hit.

At around the same time John was also approached by hit songwriting team Leslie Bricusse and Anthony Newley. They'd just scored a big success with their musical *Stop the World, I Want To Get Off* and Newley was a pop star in his own right. Now they'd recorded a live comedy LP in New York with Newley's then-wife Joan Collins, and Peter Sellers. It was called *Fool Britannia* and it was hilarious. The only problem was that no record company in London would go near it because of its content, and that's why they were coming to John.

Fool Britannia was a merciless send-up of the major political scandal that gripped the nation that year. For most of 1963 you hardly needed James Bond in the cinema when you could open the *Daily Mail* and read about Russian spies, glamorous girls and sex – all in one story. And this story was actually true. The married Minister of Defence John Profumo had been discovered having an affair with a glamorous young 'model' named Christine Keeler. This in itself would not have been that scandalous. The problem was that whilst entertaining Mr Profumo, Keeler had also been involved with one Eugene Ivanov, of the Russian Embassy.

Throughout the summer the country talked of nothing else. But whereas in the previous decade something of this magnitude might have been considered an outrage, the Profumo case came at a time when there was such a spirit of freedom, irreverence and optimism in the air, that sending it up was almost par for the course.

Since the start of the decade the staunchly reactionary old-style values had begun to crumble. In 1960 National Service had been abolished, and the earlier Suez Crisis had badly damaged Britain's vision of itself as guardian of an Empire. The obscenity trial for D. H. Lawrence's *Lady Chatterley's Lover* and its subsequent publication had vanquished the old guard of prudes, and the arrival of the Pill the following year was to mean freedom with a capital F. That freedom also extended to the media, and with the arrival of *Private Eye* in print, *Beyond the Fringe* on stage, and *That Was The Week That Was* on TV – political satire as we know it was launched.

It was against this background that Leslie Bricusse and Anthony Newley went to see John. On hearing *Fool Britannia*, John was on the floor, laughing helplessly. 'I love it,' he told them, 'but if we're going to release it, let's make it look classy and let's get it out soon.' He reckoned if they were going to put out a potentially scandalous album

– fine, but he wasn't going to have any record on his label going through the shops in some brown paper bag-style sleeve. It was going to look good – and with its glossy black cover, simple graphics and geometric photos, it did.

In spite of the atmosphere of new-found freedom, doing something like this was still subversive, but John's gamble paid off. Within days, the reaction from record-shop dealers was ecstatic, and the distributors loved it as well. Once he had them on board, success was almost a sure thing. 'There I was all of a sudden at Ember with a number one selling album and I also had this hit single with Chad and Jeremy. It was great and all the majors were so pissed off,' says John.

Less successful commercially, but much admired was John's third release for the label – an album by bebop jazz singer Annie Ross – *A Handful of Songs*. Although John produced the album, he brought in Johnny Spence to arrange it and conduct it, as by now he had other projects to work on, and was also busy running the label.

To celebrate Ember's relaunch, John organised a huge party at the Mayfair Hotel, and personally supervised everything, from the décor to the catering. The Ember launch was a classic 1960s' party – the must-be-seen-at event of the week. On the walls there were huge black and white blow-ups of the Ember artists, there was good food, good wine and a chic-looking glossy white press pack. The stars of the day turned out in force and John seemed to have the golden touch.

John's success with Ember was an important achievement for him. In the early 1960s, the record industry was still dominated by the major labels: HMV, Columbia, EMI, Decca, Pye, Philips and Top Rank – and there were generally very few independent attempts to challenge them. Joe Meek had tried it a few years earlier with his Triumph label and failed, but now John was doing it and proving that it could work. 'It was a big change,' says John. 'The majors were the masters, and then all of a sudden there was this small company with freedom that was getting through and it was like I was one of the first real independent English producers. The only other one really was Joe Meek, but we were the only two.'

★   ★   ★

By now, John was living what to many seemed a charmed existence. He and Barbara were more than comfortably off, they had a new baby daughter Susie, and although his frantic schedule of writing, arranging and filmwork meant that he was rarely at home, family life had become fairly settled.

'He and Barbara always seemed so wonderful,' says Trevor Peacock. 'Whenever you went there Barbara, or "B" as John called her, was always smiling, and I remember thinking, how nice. They live in this lovely flat in Redcliffe Gardens, and they seem so happy together. But then again, one did wonder about the au pair situation. Whenever I went to Redcliffe Gardens there was *always* a rather attractive au pair girl . . . and so, although I knew Barbara, and things seemed so perfect, I do remember wondering about that.'

The au pair was a young Swedish girl called Ulla who had already been with the family for a few months when she went back home for the summer holidays. As the weeks passed, John began to notice her absence more and more, and remarked to close friends, 'You know what? I think I really miss Ulla.' By the time she got back in the autumn, John had reached a decision about his feelings and told her. The affection turned out to be mutual and an intense, passionate affair began.

An affair in itself wouldn't have been that shocking to conventional society, even in the early 1960s, and John was well-known among friends and colleagues as being 'a bit of a ladies' man', but for him this was more than an affair. Within a few weeks he announced he was leaving Barbara and setting up home with Ulla.

'One wasn't surprised in a way, though,' says Peacock, 'because he was a very sexy person. He had this very slim figure and was very good-looking, but he also had this sort of academic look to him and a sort of vulnerability which musicians or poets might have, and so women did tend to fall at his feet a bit.'

A few months later Ulla was pregnant, and that year John's second daughter Sian was born. Marriage was discussed, but having just left one marriage John wasn't in that much of a hurry to enter into another one. As he says, 'It was the Sixties,' and a new feeling was definitely in the air.

In the air it may have been, but in the minds of the conservative older generation it certainly wasn't, and John quickly found himself ostracised by a lot of the people who had until now been his friends. 'I guess I was one of the original sinners,' says John ruefully. 'Left his wife, lived with a woman, had a child. That was not done at the time, and with a lot of the friends that I'd had – especially business associates at EMI – I was out. I was like a big social outcast, it was a real social scourge. Suddenly people just blanked me.'

Sometimes the situation led to some more entertaining episodes though. One evening an Italian couple who were neighbours came round to the flat. 'What a lovely baby you have!' they said. 'How long have you been married?'

'I haven't, actually,' replied John innocently, beginning to try and explain. 'I *was* married and I have another daughter called Susie – she's three years old, but now I'm living with this Swedish girl and we've just had a child.'

'You should have seen the look on their faces,' says John. 'And this friend of theirs was with them and was saying to me, "What are you thinking of? These people are Italian Catholics!"' But caring what 'people' might think had never been in John's nature. So as far as he was concerned, life carried on as normal.

John's neighbour turned out to be film producer Philip D'Antoni who later went on to produce *The French Connection*. At the time he was working on an hour-long TV special for ABC called *Elizabeth Taylor in London,* in which Ms Taylor took the audience on a historical journey through the capital, and he offered John the music.

A few days later John drove down to Shepperton where the show was being filmed. He wasn't usually one to be star-struck or impressed by fame, but meeting the legendary Elizabeth Taylor was an event, even for John. 'She was staggeringly beautiful,' he says, 'and had these extraordinary blue eyes. What was really sweet though, was that she said, "I love all your music".'

John subsequently wrote and produced a string-soaked score in the high-Hollywood romantic style. It was slow, languid and lush. There were harps, flutes and more strings than a puppet-masters' convention, but it wasn't saccharine. There were gorgeous, 'Greensleeves'-ish melodies in it and a lightness of touch on the jazz variations that lifted the whole thing beyond the standard run-of-the-mill sentimentality of so many scores of that style. *Elizabeth Taylor in London* was nominated for an Emmy Award in America and John was soon approached to do the producer's next project – *Sophia Loren in Rome*, a TV show in the same style.

Loren had specifically requested 'that Englishman who worked on Elizabeth's show', and so John set off to Rome for the recording. Rome had been where the chic set went since the 1950s and the Dolce Vita had practically been invented there. Rome's film studio Cinecittá was a swarm of stars and glamorous wannabes, and if there was style, glamour and sex happening in one place at the same time, John would never be too far away. Since he had started earning proper money, he had got into the habit of flitting over to Rome for the weekend, so when it came to actually doing some work over there, John knew the place inside out.

All went smoothly on the session, except for the fact that the whole thing took three times as long as it would have done in London. 'It was impossible,' John recollects. 'I could never get more than two minutes of music recorded at a time. Each time we'd get started, one of the musicians would pipe up, "Mr Barry, please Mr Barry. I have to go put money in the parking meter." Then, five minutes later, another one would start, "Please Mr Barry, would you excuse me. I also have to put money in the meter." I'd never seen anything like it. That session should have taken an afternoon, and in the end it took about two days.'

In spite of all this, John managed to complete a score which although as sweeping as *Elizabeth Taylor in London* was this time less lush and more fittingly Mediterranean and melancholic. It also featured a vocal track by Sophia Loren – a gentle, pensive ballad called 'The Secrets of Rome'. Loren obviously had a yen at the time to become a singing star and it wasn't long before she stepped further into pop's cloudy waters with Peter Sellers to record the deliciously outrageous 'Goodness Gracious Me'. But John had by then moved on.

Around the same time, John was also commissioned to re-orchestrate the theme for the British TV series *The Human Jungle*. Starring Herbert Lom as a psychiatrist, the show was a weekly noir-ish thriller with strong echoes of the American private detective films of the 1940s. The theme had been written by a TV writer called Bernard Ebbinghouse, but John was asked to do it again as the Seven were still known as a top instrumental act, and the producers thought it might help promote the series.

'We went up to this crappy studio where they made it,' says John, 'and they showed me some bits of this and bits of that to just give me the flavour and character of the piece. I never saw the whole thing, but you're better off not knowing too much about things like that. It can stagnate the imagination.'

John's masterstroke was to use the clavioline he'd employed on *String-beat* and it gave the theme a new, gloriously psychotic dimension. 'I just wanted a weird sound,' he says. 'I've always been attracted to actual sounds that have a very specific thing that grab your ear, like I did afterwards with *The Ipcress File*. This was the same deal.' The final result ended up like a battle of wills between the stealthy menace of Vic Flick's guitar, the theremin-like squeal of the clavioline and wailing strings on one side, with John's favourite alto sax grasping the melody on the other, begging for mercy. All in all it was a triumph of alone-in-the-city, late-night paranoia production, and although it wasn't written by John Barry, it sounded like it should have been.

John's scores for *Elizabeth Taylor in London* and *Sophia Loren in Rome* were firmly rooted in the Hollywood tradition, as of course their sub-jects demanded, while *The Human Jungle* was somewhere out on its own. What John wanted now was a more challenging subject, to allow him to explore a broader musical canvas; fortunately, he didn't have to wait too long. His next and final recording for Ember was the soundtrack album to his second big film – *Zulu*.

Zulu was a major British war epic, recounting a small nineteenth-century British battalion's defiant stand against the Zulu army. At the time, grand-scale epics were big news and Hollywood had recently churned out *Spartacus*, *El Cid* and *The Fall of the Roman Empire*. *Zulu* was therefore an attempt at creating the same kind of thing in Britain.

Actor Stanley Baker was the star and co-producer, and he had asked his close friend Lionel Bart to do the music. Bart had agreed initially, but according to John, had read the script and realised that in an epic war film set in Africa, there wasn't really a lot of room for a song, as such, and so declined. Rather than leaving his friend completely stranded, though, he was keen to offer an alternative. He had been impressed with John's work on *From Russia With Love* and so thought of him now. 'Why don't you get John Barry to write it?' he suggested. 'He's good at doing scores, he'll be perfect.'

Zulu was an important step in John's film-writing career, and it also proved a breakthrough in the career of an as yet unknown actor called Michael Caine. Caine had turned up to audition for a small part as one of the Cockney soldiers in the film, and after doing his bit was just about to leave, when the director Cy Endfield said to him: 'Hold on a moment. You don't look like a Cockney.'

'What does a Cockney look like?' replied Caine.

'Not like you,' he said. 'You look like one of those faggy officer types.'

'But I'm not a fag,' said Caine.

'I know you're not,' said Endfield. 'But you look like one – and that's what I need. We're after a foppish sort of weak officer type to combat Stanley Baker's tough working-class officer lead. Can you do an upper-class accent?'

'Absolutely,' Caine nodded. 'I've been in rep, you know. I've been doing one for years.'

And so Caine got the part. Previously it would have been unheard of for a working-class actor to be cast in an upper-class role, but the changing social climate and the arrival of actors like Albert Finney and Tom Courtenay was ushering in a new era. Endfield was also part of the new influx of more cosmopolitan directors who had begun arriving in Britain as a result of the McCarthy committee's witch hunts in Hollywood, and he brought with him a broader approach. He was also broad-minded when it came to music. While filming in Africa, Endfield had enthusiastically recorded hours of local Zulu music, and once he got back to London, he gave the tapes to John to work from.

John liked the music Endfield had brought back, but he knew all along that it would be a question of finding melodic themes and orchestrating them in his own way. 'When Cy Endfield gave me those rough tapes, there was one – a wedding song – which I really liked. I liked its repetitive motif, so I took that for the main *Zulu* theme and developed it into this heroic thing. I just took the original African music and Westernised it. But those original themes were so good, so very basic, so wonderful and simple. Just two chord changes and yet so *good*.'

The idea of using original ethnic folk melodies and Westernising them was not new in classical music. As John explains: 'I guess my role model for that was Prokofiev when he did *Alexander Nevsky*. He took very basic Russian folk tunes and set them in a large dramatic scale. There's a whole history of that with Stravinsky and Bartók and I was thinking along those lines.' In pop music, however, the whole concept definitely was new, and with *Zulu*, John was pioneering exactly the kind of mix of styles for which Paul Simon was to get so much acclaim, twenty years later, with *Graceland*. Pop was still in its infancy in the early 1960s, though, and the whole notion of analysing and deconstructing something as 'trivial' as a pop record had not yet surfaced.

Once it came to the orchestration, John knew instinctively that for it to really work, he had to create an authentically African sound with the instrumentation. 'John used every conceivable type of percussion on that,' recalls Sid Margo. 'He went down to a repository in Archer Street where they kept unusual musical instruments and said, "I want African, African, African. African everything." So in the end he had drums, bongos, bell belts and boobams. Boobams were like mini-tablas all laid out in a row, like a piano keyboard in half tones, but you played them with drumsticks. In the end, that studio was so packed with gear, there was hardly room for the orchestra with all that stuff in there. Also, normally you had three percussionists. On *Zulu*, John had six as well as a wacking great orchestra. But John always had large orchestras; he never stinted. He always said: "Either I get the orchestra or I don't do it." And it made sense, because if you start skimping on the orchestra, you can't get the colour you want.'

John's musical version of Africana would have major repercussions on his career, for *Zulu* represented the start of a long musical relationship between John and Africa. It wasn't that he'd been particularly struck by its musical tradition – things just worked out that way. Later on, he would win Oscars for his other two Africa-based films: *Born Free* and *Out of Africa*, but with these scores his interpretation of the continent would draw solely on Western musical traditions.

The original *Zulu* soundtrack, when it was released on Ember, featured the music from the film on Side One, while Side Two featured a selection of wonderfully hilarious pop twang reworkings of the main themes. The idea, which was pretty revolutionary at the time, was the Sixties' equivalent of a dance remix and had been Stanley Baker's. Even though he was by now in his late thirties, and a well-established film actor, he, unlike most people his age, had discovered pop and liked it.

'Stanley Baker was into pop music,' says John, 'and between him and Cy Endfield, the idea was hatched that it might not be an uncommercial move to release a "pop" version of my music.' And so the "Zulu Stamp" was born, complete with its own dance steps created by Lionel Blair. As Cy Endfield so memorably put it in his original sleeve notes: 'A number of these great traditional dance and song themes have been studied by the brilliant composer and arranger John Barry . . . and converted . . . so that all of us who listen to this record can do a little dancing of our own. If you learn to Zulu Stamp you will be doing the exciting, groovy dance movements that the Zulus themselves use.'

Zulu did well and so did the soundtrack album, and that was good not only for John but also for Ember. But in spite of his success there, John was becoming increasingly impatient with the label. It was an ongoing struggle, battling it out against the major record labels, who had far greater resources at their disposal for distribution and promotion, and Kruger was also beginning to want a hand in things. He was convinced that American Country singers would be the next big thing, but that wasn't quite what John had had in mind, and so eventually, John decided to leave.

He had plenty of other ventures to occupy him. As well as Topline Artists, the Seven were still a viable concern commercially. For John, the Seven plus Four format was useful when it came to tackling TV projects like *The Human Jungle* or his Dave Brubeck pastiche 'Cutty Sark' – the *Dateline* theme.

What mattered most to John was writing music for moving images. If he was in between film-score commissions, the next best thing was TV, and the next best thing after that was advertising. The whole concept of television and commercials was still relatively new, and someone had pointed out to John that writing music for ads could be rather lucrative. Musically for John, it was a cinch. Thirty seconds of music here, two minutes of music there, and from his Topline offices in Great Newport Street, John set up his own company called Jinglewise.

Advertising was still a small industry and John found it easy to get work. 'You'd just ring up people from the agency and you'd get work,' he shrugs. 'And doing ads was very profitable.' Over the next few years he ended up creating signatures for Ingersoll's Trendsetter watches – for 'go-ahead people', Eastern Airlines and later on, the most legendary one of them all, Silvikrin's 'The Girl with the Sun in Her Hair'. TV ads also brought John together with some of the big-name directors of the day, working on Black Magic with Richard Lester and the glamorous Izal Toilet Paper with Karel Reisz.

With all these different ventures going on, John by now needed a full-time secretary to run his office; his father's former assistant Miss Ackers was the perfect candidate. The redoubtable 'Ackers' as she was known, was soon the linchpin of John's working existence – a kind of twinset and tweeded Mother Superior who ran the office with an iron rod.

'She was a tower of strength,' says John's old friend and Army colleague Pete Varley. 'She was the paymaster, the brains and the clerical side of it all. But she was very bossy and stern, and definitely no glamour-girl.' Later on, friends would remember her motherly efforts to moralise with John about his social life, and vain attempts to 'keep him on the straight and narrow', but she was less successful there than on the business side. On the work front, however, she was exactly what John needed.

TV themes and advertising gave John the opportunity to tackle different musical styles, while the success of Ember had consolidated his reputation as an important player in the music industry and given him the satisfaction of getting the recognition he wanted.

With *Zulu* and *From Russia With Love* he was able to experiment with a large orchestra and different types of instrumentation, and everything he had learned on both those films would serve him well over the next few years. He was by now coming to the end of his life as John Barry, pop musician, or even pop mogul. He had already said goodbye to his old married life, and over the next year he would begin to concentrate more and more on film and another type of life altogether.

8

LONDON GOES GOLD

As much as John Barry's music is part of the iconic 1960s' legacy, so too is the life he led. There's a common image of the composer as a grave professorial recluse, but John Barry was about as far as you could go in the other direction. John – as Trevor Peacock pointed out – 'looked like a film star'. And he lived like a pop star. In 1964, London had started to 'swing'. It was hailed throughout the world press as 'the most exciting place on earth' and John was at the heart of it both professionally and socially. It was an enormously fertile period for him: one of personal rebellion, of breaking free of the constraints he'd had imposed on him until then; a time of intense creative outpouring in which he produced some of his best work.

It was the period that would come to be characterised by The Beatles, the Kings Road, Carnaby Street, mini-skirts and 'dolly birds'. There was an entirely new mood on the streets: the social deference to 'one's elders' had given way to a new, more relaxed irreverence; politically the old 'do it for one's country' ideals of Empire had crumbled and been replaced by a new, more self-interested, inward-looking thrust for affluence; class barriers and regional prejudices were disintegrating by the minute and morally the whole notion of what 'nice' young people did and didn't do before marriage had become obsolete. The 'angry young man' had been replaced by the 'man about town'.

By this time, perhaps conveniently, John's relationship with Ulla was over. She had left and gone back to Sweden, taking their baby Sian with her. 'We fell in love, we had a child, then she departed and went back to Sweden. That was all there was to it,' says John, matter-of-factly. 'It was the Sixties,' he adds, offering this as his all-encompassing explanation for a multitude of events. Although John and Sian would pick up their relationship years later, for the meantime, she had gone back to Sweden with her mother, and he had a life in London.

It was an extraordinary time to be young, attractive, successful and single, and John enjoyed it to the full. He had the ultimate designer flat in Chelsea, an E-type Jaguar and a social life to die for. There were nights on the town with Michael Caine, Peter Sellers and David Bailey, and John's little black book of girlfriends and dinner dates included Shirley Bassey, Britt Ekland and Charlotte Rampling.

It was John and his friends who made the Sixties what they were, but it's often forgotten that they themselves were not from the new post-National Service generation – the war babies who'd been let off the rigours of Army life. They had grown up with the old life, they had lived through World War Two, they revered Churchill as the nation's saviour, and they had experienced the rigidity of the Army. As opposed to the younger influx, John *et al* knew exactly how much of a turnaround had taken place. They had lived the other life, and when a different one arrived, they grabbed it with both hands.

'The life I was living was fifty times more fun than anything that was in *The Knack*,' John says now. 'I had been brought up with a very strict Irish-Catholic father. My first education was by nuns in the Bar Convent, then there was St Peter's and more discipline. After that I worked for my father for three years, before going into the British Army. So by the time I came out, I started thinking: I want my own life. The discipline that I had lived under till then was extraordinary. So when I started becoming successful, and had money and my own apartment, I just let go. I was making up for lost time.' And somehow, in between making up for all that lost time, John and the others still managed to get some work done.

1964 turned out to be a pivotal year in John's career; by the end of it, his reputation as a film composer was established. His days in the pop world were over and he had written what would become one of the biggest-selling Bond records of all time – 'Goldfinger'. His score for the film would also turn out to be the quintessential Bond soundtrack, just as the film itself became the blueprint for all future Bond movies.

During 1963, while still running Ember, Topline Artists, Jinglewise and writing Bond scores, John had also carried on doing tours and working as Musical Director for other artists. Capitalising on the success of the Bond records, he went on the road with Shirley Bassey and Matt Monro. With his own orchestra, he played the first half of the bill, closing it with 'The Bond Theme', and then they accompanied Bassey and Monro for the headlining second half. It was all very well making the most of Bond, but having to spend time away from London was becoming more and more of a bind, although John did find time while on tour to develop a brief 'liaison' with Ms Bassey.

By the end of 1963 the musical world in which John had established himself was also beginning to change irredeemably. At Christmas the *Evening Standard* published a special supplement headlined simply: *1963 . . . The Year of The Beatles*. The Beatles had erupted onto the music scene. Their second single 'Please Please Me' entered the charts at number four; 'She Loves You' went in at number one and sold over a million copies, and their debut album stayed in the charts for thirty weeks. Their success was to be revolutionary, both musically and socially.

The arrival of the 'Mersey Beat Boom' effectively spelled the beginning of the end for the old hierarchical record-business system of which John had by now become a part. Throughout the 1960s A&R men would continue to wield power over artists, but gradually the latter began to assert their own creative identity – and the fact that The Beatles wrote their own songs inspired others to do the same. Suddenly, having lost control of many artists' material, the influence of the A&R men became drastically diminished.

The 'Mersey Sound' had also become 'the Liverpool Phenomenon', and thereby a subject of national debate, way beyond the norms of the relatively small world of pop. The *Sunday Times*, hitherto unknown to write about 'pop', in an eerie precursor to the way dance music would be defined by the Criminal Justice Bill some thirty years later, described the Mersey sound as: 'vigorous, aggressive, uncompromising . . . exaggeratedly rhythmic, high-pitched, thunderously amplified and full of wild, insidious harmonies'. Conversely, by the end of the year, *The Times'* music critic William Mann was hailing Lennon and McCartney as 'the outstanding English composers of 1963'.

Whichever way you looked at it, the sound of The Beatles and the groups who emerged in their wake was nothing like the sound of The John Barry Seven. And before too long John was sending the Seven out on the road on their own, fronted by Vic Flick, and no one seemed to notice or mind.

The Seven carried on touring in various guises over the next couple of years, serving as a useful promotional tool for the 'Seven plus Orchestra' format which John was still using to record his film themes. Flick and his colleagues soon left to take up session work in London, and their replacement line-up released one single of their own – the R&B style 'Seven Faces' – before finally disbanding in 1966.

The birth of The Beatles was the dawn of a new musical era – and the death of the old one. The Beatles sensation had saturated the media and it seemed like nothing could overtake it. But at the end of 1963, one event did. It was of global and personal significance to millions throughout the world, including John.

Whilst working at Ember, Danish aristocratic husband and wife folk stars Nina and Frederick contacted him. He had often worked as their arranger in his earlier days at EMI, and now that they were booked to do a run at the Savoy just before Christmas, they wanted him to be their Musical Director. 'John,' they said, 'it's midnight for half an hour – every night for two weeks – but we'd absolutely love you to do it.' John was hugely busy with other commitments, but as they got on well, and 'they were such charming people', he said: 'All right. I'll do it.'

The memory of that fortnight would remain with him for the rest of his life. 'I had this great little group,' says John, 'a harpist, a jazz organist and a flautist, and it was the last week of November, first week of December. I used to go down there to the Savoy every night at midnight. And I remember it was a Friday night and I hadn't heard the radio or seen the TV and it was torrential rain when I was driving down to the Embankment. As I crossed the road I saw this *Evening Standard* placard which said *Kennedy . . . something*. Because of the rain, the newsprint had bled and all I could see was what I thought looked like *Kennedy Sensation*. And so I went into the Savoy lobby, and someone ran out to me and said, "You know what's happened, don't you?"

'And I said, "No, what?"

' "Kennedy's been assassinated," he said.

'I just couldn't believe it, and I said, "There's no way we can go on tonight."

'And he said, "John, I've just talked to the manager and he's said, "Just as you didn't know what's happened, most of the people here have been sat there since seven o'clock and they don't know either. So you have to go on."

'It was awful. There we were, all devastated and nobody out there knew. Some of those Nina and Frederick songs still kill me – they just take me back to that night.' Years later John would bring his memories of that night to 'The Day the Earth Fell Silent' on his 1998 *Beyondness of Things* album, and it's still something that haunts him. 'It was tragic,' he says, 'the lost potential of what he could have done.'

The young President John F. Kennedy had captured the dreams of half the world. He was the embodiment of youth, efficiency, excitement and nonconformity – qualities that had grown in popularity since the mid-1950s. And he also played a large part in furthering Britain's – and John's – fascination with all things American. He had swept away the cobwebs of the old era. He himself had declared that, 'the Presidency needs someone creative and dynamic'. And so his assassination on 22 November 1963 was an event that had a global emotional impact not witnessed again until Princess Diana's death thirty-four years later. For four days after John Kennedy's death, Britain and the rest of the world were stunned, and media coverage went into overdrive.

The assassination had marked John's shows with Nina and Frederick indelibly in his mind, but another event occurred during the run that was to do so still further. 'A week after Kennedy's death,' says John, 'I was late for the show and I was running down a corridor in the Savoy. As I came round the corner I ran straight into two big guys pushing this old man in a wheelchair. I hit my leg on his chair and my shin was bleeding like mad. While I was standing there swearing, with my hand covered in blood, this old man was looking at me, saying, "Are you all right?" And then I looked at him, and it was Winston Churchill, because the Savoy was where he used to go. I was just kind of speechless, but blurted out: "Yes, I'm all right, sir." And he kept saying, "Are you *sure* you're all right?" and I just about managed a "Yes, sir". I was just so stunned.

'When I got to the dressing room, Nina and Frederick were frantic, going, "We're late, we're late, where have you been?" and I was in this daze, saying, "I just fell over Winston Churchill." I took down my sock and I kept rubbing my gash, saying, "I'm not gonna let this heal. I want this mark on my leg for the rest of my life." And so I didn't even change. I went out there with blood all over my sock and we did the show. So there we were for two weeks. Kennedy got assassinated in the first and I fell over Winston Churchill in the second. Two of my heroes – it was such an emotional thing.'

John had long been enthralled by politics. He had grown up through World War Two and seen Churchill as the hero of the nation. Then, later, with the arrival of Kennedy, he had identified with this young, handsome, driven man who was tough enough to reach the top of the political arena, but also charismatic enough to charm the world. John was also intrigued by the mechanics of politics, and even though it was a far cry from film and music, it was something for which he felt a natural affinity.

'The whole political thing fascinated me, and Churchill in particular,' says John. 'People often say to me, "If you couldn't be a composer, what would you rather be?" And I say, "The next best thing would be to be a politician in the tradition of a Churchill or a Kennedy." I think if politics are exercised on a level of excellence, it's such a calling.'

★   ★   ★

Once the media hysteria over Kennedy's death had died down, it was back to The Beatles as the national obsession. The group had by now become more than just a musical phenomenon. They had become a social one. Whereas two years earlier John had played a BBC audition with the Seven and been practically blacklisted for speaking with a Yorkshire accent, The Beatles' success stuck two fingers up at the stultifying fossils of the Establishment. Here was a group who had more than cleaned up: they had taken the nation by absolute storm and they had done it with 'long hair' and more importantly, they had done it with Liverpool accents.

These weren't Oxbridge graduates who had come up through the 'system', nor were they working-class puppets, content to have their careers controlled by svengali managers and record company A&R men. The Beatles not only wrote their own songs, but they thought for themselves as well. Yes, they had a manager, but in their off-the-cuff, irreverent interviews they showed that they also had minds and personalities of their own. This was what was different. And it affected everything.

But it wasn't just The Beatles who were changing society. Change was happening at every level, and London was where it was happening first. Society had been moving towards these changes since the mid-1950s, and The Beatles were just a symptom of the general shift. In 1960 Princess Margaret had married a commoner, Anthony Armstrong-Jones – something which would previously have been unimaginable for the sister of the Queen. Likewise the grammar-school educated Edward Heath had been elected leader of the Conservative Party – something else which before, would have been considered equally horrific. Meanwhile Britain had practically full employment and so without the prospect of joblessness, people could worry about how to enjoy themselves instead.

These were all-important contributory factors to the changing mood of society. The other most vital one was the arrival of the Pill, which had become readily available in 1961. While its effects had begun to be noticed throughout 1963, its impact really took hold during the following year.

Suddenly John and his peers couldn't believe their luck. They had spent their youths in the sexual Dark Ages where 'nice girls' didn't go 'all the way' without an engagement ring, and if you did, you ran the risk of pregnancy and social disgrace. The arrival of the Pill changed all that. If you were young and single, it was as if you'd spent your whole life outside a cake shop never getting more than a crumb here and there, and now, all at once, someone had said, 'OK – in you go. You can have as much as you like, whenever you like.'

John was by now at the heart of a social scene that included David Bailey, Jean Shrimpton, Peter Sellers and Michael Caine. There were weekend parties at country houses, nights out and afternoons in. And they were nearly always eventful. There were key points on the social circuit where at certain times or days of the week, you knew you'd find practically everyone else. Places like the bustling Italian restaurant Alvaro's on the Kings Road, the Lotus House – a huge, dimly lit Chinese restaurant on the Edgware Road – the Trattoria Terrazza in Soho, and the Ad Lib Club.

These places had become havens for the 'in-crowd', partly because they were the only places that were still open once theatres or shows finished. They also had a generally more relaxed attitude to the whole idea of eating out than traditional British restaurants.

'In those days there were no restaurants that were open late till the Italians came,' says Michael Caine. 'All the restaurants were a pain in the arse 'cause you had to wear a tie and stuff and they had these waiters who started looking at their watch at nine o'clock 'cause they wanted to go home. So people never used to go to those. What happened was that the other places became social centres for people in showbusiness because ordinary people never went out. The Tube had always stopped at eleven until the Sixties when everyone just said, "Sod this – we're gonna go out."

'But for us lot it was a regular circuit. The Terrazza, the Lotus House and then the Ad Lib Club. That was the disco and to my mind it was the best disco ever. It was on top of where the Prince Charles Theatre is in Leicester Square, in the penthouse. Johnny Gold and Oscar Lerman ran it and it was the only time I've ever seen all four Beatles and four Rolling Stones all dancing on the floor.'

The other main place on the circuit was the Pickwick Club in Great Newport Street. The Pickwick was a 'members only' club which had been opened by Leslie Bricusse, Wolf Mankowitz and Sammy Davis Junior, and it immediately became the exclusive hang-out of anyone who was 'happening' in showbusiness at the time. It was where The Beatles went, David Bailey, Terence Stamp and Mary Quant, as well as any visiting stars who happened to be in town, from Frank Sinatra to Nat 'King' Cole. It was small, dark, intimate and served great food. And because it was strictly membership only and no press photographers were ever allowed in, the club became a haven for stars eager to escape the unwanted attentions of autograph hunters and paparazzi.

'It was a place where stars could go and nobody could get at them,' says Leslie Bricusse, 'cause it was all closed doors. The most amazing people used to come in there. It was at a time when all the Sammy Davises and Sinatras were coming regularly to London, so they all used to come down to the Pickwick. It was rather like Alma Cogan's home. She was a friend of everyone's and a big star at the time, and every Saturday night the stars of all the shows would end up at Alma's flat in Kensington High Street – Stafford Court. You'd meet fantastic people there – everybody from Nat 'King' Cole to Danny Kaye at midnight on a Saturday night. It was just an open house every week, and the Pickwick ended up being the same sort of thing.

'It was probably the only unofficial place where The Beatles ever performed. They just improvised one night. Peter Asher who was Jane Asher's brother was there all the time, and he and Gordon Waller – Peter and Gordon – used to play downstairs. That was when Paul McCartney wrote "World Without Love" for them and they had their big hit.'

When the Pickwick opened in July 1963, John was an obvious candidate for membership. Both his own offices and Ember's were just over the road, opposite the club. It was almost inevitable that he would become not just a member, but virtually semi-resident.

It was over lunch in the Pickwick one day that John met the actor who was to become one of his closest friends during the next few years. 'We used to have a Friday lunch club,' says Bricusse, 'consisting of John, Tony Newley, me, Terry Stamp and an unknown actor who was flat-sharing with Terry called Michael Caine. There was no particular game plan, it was just that we'd had a lunch one Friday and we had such a good time that we said, "Let's do it again next Friday." And so it became a regular thing. Michael Caine does it to this day at Langan's.'

John vaguely knew the 'unknown actor' as he'd seen him on screen in *Zulu*. 'When I first saw him in the film, he was doing this English Officer thing,' says John, 'and then when we met, it was like "'Ello, John, mate," and I thought, That was obviously a good acting job. So we struck up a friendship and then he ended up staying in my apartment.'

John by now had the luxury flat at Cadogan Square to himself, and it was kitted out as the ultimate bachelor pad. He had furnished it with a mixture of antiques, Charles Eames chairs – which in 1964 were the furniture 'must-haves' of the year – and walls and walls of records, as well as a collection of the latest hi-fi gadgetry. 'The Barry living-room scheme is essentially modern with strong Renaissance overtones,' wrote the *Daily Mail*. 'Walls are white, the carpeting avocado green and the dramatic curtains are in a cerise linen weave. John Barry is fascinated by early antiques, and although his armchairs and luxurious four-seater settee are modern . . . they are upholstered in antique gold suede. [There is also] a 16th-century oak chest, packed with LPs, and a 17th-century English oak refectory table.' What the flat also had was a spare room, and so when Michael Caine got thrown out of the flat he'd been sharing with Terence Stamp, it was to John's that he immediately came.

It was a Sunday night and John was at the Lotus House with his girlfriend of the moment, when Caine came into the restaurant and walked straight up to his table. 'I knew I'd find you here,' said Caine. 'Terry and I have been thrown out for rent arrears. If I can't find a place to go, can I stay at yours for a few nights?'

'If you've got no place to go, fine,' said John.

Much later that night, John was in bed with his girlfriend when the doorbell rang. It was two o'clock in the morning. 'Who is that?' she asked. Then on the intercom they heard, 'Hello, it's Michael. I haven't got anywhere to sleep.'

'All right, Mike,' said John wearily. 'There's a spare bedroom down the corridor, first room on the left. But I'm busy right now, so just let yourself in, OK?'

What started off as a few nights soon turned into a few weeks and soon a few months. And London, or at least Cadogan Square, probably never quite recovered. The flat had already been the scene of John's bachelor existence, but with the two of them there, the hallway must have looked like Piccadilly Circus.

'It was the Sixties and the nights were incredible,' says Caine. 'We'd be out at restaurants and discothèques every night, and we were both heavy drinkers. That period was all drink, it wasn't drugs. There didn't seem to be any around. There was a lot of alcohol around and everybody wanted to go out and go to restaurants, and drugs were illegal so you had to stay in for that. But you could go out and get bombed on alcohol as much as you liked. There was also the constant search for young ladies, so naturally you went out for that.'

And so they did. Every night. 'I would say we were extremely active on that particular front,' laughs Caine. 'We had more than our share actually. He was a big ladies' man, John. I mean, the Sixties was an incredible time to be young, have money and some kind of fame, so none of it was difficult. I was also very good at manipulating social life 'cause I'd already shared a flat with Terence Stamp for two years and he was always bringing girls back. So really, as long as you had two doors you could get one out through the back while the other one came in the front. It was like being a flight attendant dealing with a crash landing – trying to get everyone out the right door.'

And activity wasn't confined to night-time, either. The atmosphere at lunchtime in the restaurants of the Kings Road or Soho was equally highly charged. 'The whole place was buzzing,' says John. 'Because the Pill had just come in, it was a very crazy, exciting time. The whole creative energy of all these young writers, young actors, young directors and playwrights . . . And then all the young women – all the young ladies that were coming out, the Jean Shrimptons. And there were so

[132]

many! You'd walk into a restaurant and there would be seven or eight beautiful girls, there would be seven or eight handsome or not so handsome gentlemen all around having lunch and going table-hopping. That wasn't just once, it was every weekday; it was lunch, it was dinner.'

And the table-hopping was less for passing the time of day than for passing phone numbers. 'Every lunchtime,' says John, 'you'd be calling the head waiter, saying, "Would you give this note to that lady over there." Then a little note would come over with her phone number, or nothing or bad news. But a *lot* of the time it wasn't bad news. "Noonies" they were called. Sexual episodes after two o'clock in the afternoon.'

'There was this tremendous feeling of excitement,' says Caine, 'and among our friends it was a tight circle. Everybody you knew who was unknown suddenly became famous. You couldn't wait to pick up the papers or see them in a restaurant and suddenly they'd be somebody. Something would happen, there'd be a review of a film or a record'd come out – it happened to John with the Bonds and *Zulu* and everything – and it was just happening all the time. Everybody was a success and you didn't know anybody who wasn't. And it wasn't because you were a snob and you only went out with famous people. You just went out with the people you'd always been out with, except that now they were rich and famous. And John and I were part of that.'

One of the great mysteries of the 1960s seems to be the way that during this unbelievably hedonistic period, enormous amounts of work were still produced by all the key figures, whether they were composers, film directors, photographers, actors or playwrights. And yet at the same time, by all accounts, everyone seems to have been out – all night and every night.

John himself combined work and pleasure in his own idiosyncratic schedule. 'The thing about John was that he used to write music at night,' remembers Caine. 'I would get up in the morning, and he'd be there banging away at the piano, having been there all night. Then he would go to bed in the afternoon, and we'd have dinner together in the evenings. Then I would go to bed, and he'd keep working.'

There was one particular piece that John was 'banging away' at during most of Caine's stay with him, and that was 'Goldfinger'. Having written a successful score for *From Russia With Love*, when it came to the next one, John told Saltzman and Broccoli he was going to do the song as well. 'I was breaking my butt to do the whole thing,' says John. 'I wanted to have the song that one could integrate throughout the whole picture.' This time he was adamant, but by now he had shown that he could write, and the producers had also been swayed by his self-assurance and professionalism. He believed in himself and he had the ability to make others do the same.

'John obviously impressed Cubby Broccoli and the others,' says Trevor Peacock, 'because he always had this air of quiet authority, of knowing what he wanted, and you somehow always knew he would deliver the goods. He had this natural air of, "This can be done – and I'll do it." If he'd turned round and said, "I've been made the conductor of the London Symphony Orchestra," I'd have said, "Oh good," and you somehow wouldn't have been surprised.'

But having successfully persuaded Saltzman and Broccoli to let him do the song, now John had to deliver. Caine remembers John working on it for what seemed like forever, but as John says, 'When you're trying to get to sleep, it probably does seem like weeks. It didn't take me weeks – but it didn't take one night either. It was my first title song and it was a strange one. With *From Russia With Love*, you could be romantic and lyrical, but with *Goldfinger* it was something else. This was a song about a villain and that took a lot of figuring out. How do you make a song about a man who paints women gold sound good?'

After hours, days and more than a few nights spent at the piano, John had finally got what he wanted. But the lyrics were to prove as elusive as the music initially had. John had worked with Trevor Peacock on songs for Adam Faith, and he was his first port of call.

'What *is* Goldfinger?' Peacock enquired. 'What does it mean? Is it a new brand or something?'

'No,' said John. 'It's the name of a villain.'

'Oh, I see.' said Peacock, trying to sound confident.

Peacock was to have more than a few headaches trying to get the lyrics right. 'I sat there,' he recalls now, 'trying to work out rhymes, thinking, "Goldfinger, mustn't linger . . . plays right-winger . . . singer – ooh no, that's a Lancashire accent and people won't get that," and I just kept on like that. And so I struggled and struggled, and in the end I said, "John, I'm having a bit of trouble here. I can't seem to work this one out. It's very difficult, you know." Fortunately, he said, "It's alright. You don't have to worry about it any more. Leslie Bricusse is going to do it." It was a great pity, but at the time, it was actually a kind of relief.'

Leslie Bricusse and Anthony Newley were by this time well established as one of London's wittiest song-writing teams. As John had got to know them on *Fool Britannia* they seemed ideal for the task.

So the pair came to Cadogan Square and John sat down at the piano and played them what he'd written. He'd just got past the 'Goldfinger' vocal line's opening three notes when Bricusse and Newley both sang out in unison – 'wider than a mile'. It was 'Moon River' all over again, they thought.

'No no,' said John. 'That's only one bar and then it goes off in a completely different direction.' He demonstrated – and they were off.

As it turned out, of course, Bricusse and Newley's lyrics not only worked with John's music, they also worked with the whole Bond style. The gloriously camp lyrics with their outrageous rhyme of Gold-finger with 'cold finger' picked up on the Bond humour and really brought it home.

With the exception of 'The James Bond Theme', 'Goldfinger' is certainly the most famous song to emerge from the whole Bond canon. Thirty years since its release it has lost none of its potency, and yet what's interesting is that unlike many successful songs of the 1960s, 'Goldfinger' was unique even when it was first released. Look at the charts from 1965 and you'll find Petula Clark's 'Downtown', The Beatles' 'I Feel Fine' and Sandie Shaw singing 'Girl Don't Come'. Nothing even comes close in style, feeling or structure, but this was no accident. Neither John, Bricusse nor Newley belonged to the new breed of self-taught songwriters who'd learned their craft by tinkling away at a piano, or strumming away at guitar chords in the back of a van. They had honed their songwriting skills emulating the Broadway musicals of the 1920s and 1930s, and came from a school where there was a recognised craft and structure involved. The lyrics weren't casual or colloquial, nor were the melodies. As John explains: 'That structure – two eights, a middle eight or bridge, and a last eight – that's classic song structure from the Twenties. It's probably the most successful songwriting structure that anyone's ever come up with, but it's so weird that it still doesn't sound that pat. "We Have All the Time in the World" and "You Only Live Twice" are the same.'

With the song complete, Shirley Bassey was chosen to sing the title theme. 'Choosing the singer was like casting a movie; it had to be the right choice. Shirley was great casting for "Goldfinger". Nobody could have sung it like her. She had that great dramatic sense. When it came to the studio, she didn't know what the hell the song was about, but she sang it with such total conviction that she convinced the rest of the world.'

John's next task was to make sure the song worked with the images for the title sequence. Right from the start, one of the Bond films' most famous features had been their openings. When *Dr No* had first hit the screen, the whole notion of having a virtually self-contained section of the film with images of its own was still revolutionary, and reflected the influence of TV advertising. It was a great way of drawing people's attention the moment the film started. 'You grab the audience in the beginning,' says Peter Hunt, 'and you won't lose them. That was the secret of those title sequences. It has to be a crashing bore to lose them.'

Robert Brownjohn had designed the wonderfully lurid fantasy for the opening of *From Russia With Love*, and now that he was preparing *Goldfinger* he was desperate to hear John's music. At that stage though, he only had a rough-cut with some early images and so the idea was to have a session with the orchestra and Bassey to see how the whole thing could work together. 'I want to hear the music,' he told John, 'so I can start putting all this stuff together so it works.'

And it was seeing Brownjohn's images that suddenly made it clear that the musical arrangement still needed a little something extra. 'All I had at the beginning were those Wagnerian chords – the F to the D flat,' says John, 'and when I saw Brownjohn's images, I realised it needed something else. It was just too down, so at the break everyone went off and I went back to the piano. I came up with that line' (the sleazy *wah wah wah wah* brass line) – 'and it was like a common scream, but it worked like a bitch. So when they all trooped back in, I told the trumpeters: "I need *wah wah* mutes on this new line that we're adding in," and when they did it everybody went, "Wow! That's great!"'

And it was great. It was the addition of the Vaudeville brassy sleaze to John's heady mix of brooding, Wagnerian drama and Sixties' sexuality that made 'Goldfinger' so special. Plus, of course, that impaling Bassey interpretation. Shirley Bassey had been selected because she was a well-established star, and Saltzman and Broccoli had by now decided that each Bond song should be sung by the biggest star of the time. With Bassey's star status, however, came the star behaviour. 'She was certainly quite an outspoken lady,' remembers Eric Tomlinson, the engineer on the session, 'and she used to throw quite a few tantrums, especially if you made her do several takes.'

John had by now developed a reputation with musicians for being a perfectionist, albeit in his own quiet way. He was never one to go with the first, second or even third take, if there was still time to try another ten, and this didn't exactly please the star. 'Shirley Bassey used to get a bit uptight when she was doing take after take,' says Tomlinson. 'But I suppose it was just a clash of personalities, really: the quiet one and the loud one.' Eventually the song was recorded and John did indeed get the perfect take. Now he had to work out the rest of the score. And this time he didn't have nearly as long to do it.

The whole project had been behind schedule virtually from the start because Sean Connery had been working on *Marnie* with Alfred Hitchcock and so filming had started late. But Saltzman and Broccoli refused to put back the film's opening date, and decreed that *Goldfinger* would open on 26 September 1964 at the Odeon Leicester Square, London, come what may.

'I had to start the first week without Sean,' remembers director Guy Hamilton, 'just doing car chases, so we were already tight at that end. Then a lot of the aerial stuff of Fort Knox had been done by a second unit and didn't work out too well, so I had to go back and redo that. So by the time the picture was done, the editor Peter Hunt and I were frantically putting it together imagining that the producers in their wisdom would delay the opening date, but not a bit of it.'

There were now only three weeks before the film was due to open and John was scoring scenes fresh from the cutting-room. But he had worked out his Bond masterplan and knew exactly how he was going to tackle it. John may have let Bricusse and Newley reflect Bond's tongue-in-cheek humour and ham up the lyrics for the song, but when it came to his music, he was going to take Bond very seriously indeed. John saw early on that just as the Bond films themselves were bold in every way, likewise the music had to follow suit – even if that meant disobeying all his usual film-scoring rules. Normally he would always try to avoid what he called the 'Mickey Mouse' school of film-composing . . .

'When the the action and the music happen at the same time, that's what I call Mickey Mouse music,' says John, 'and that's obviously what I try to avoid like the plague when I'm scoring movies normally. But that style was right for Bond. The movies were big, especially by the time they got to *Goldfinger*, and so the music had to be big to match. I took the whole thing for real. I didn't treat it fliply or tongue-in-cheek. We all knew the format because it was always the same: at the end of it, James would get the girl and the villain would be out of it. But musically you couldn't play it that way. There was always just under an hour's music in all those movies – it just worked out that way – so when he was in danger, I played it in the most serious way. I was always thinking of a twelve-year-old kid and what he wanted to go through. He wanted to be on the edge of his seat, excited, like, "James, look out! There's somebody behind you!" and so I played on that the whole time, from the saxes when the sultry girl walks into the room to everything else all the way through. I just played it to the hilt for all it was worth.'

As John explained to *Showtime Magazine* in 1965: 'Consider the scene in *Goldfinger* where Bond is captured. He's taken off to Goldfinger's headquarters and it would appear that he's had it. But the audience is not convinced it's really the end of Bond. They know there's a button.

So what do you do when writing the music for this scene? Do you relax the music? No – you keep an edge on it. If you suddenly gave it a negative mood – which would suggest it was *really* the end for Bond, it would be foreign to what the audience was feeling, so you keep the tension in the music all the time. Then, when Bond presses the button and all hell breaks loose on the screen, you increase the tension and let every man in a sixty-piece orchestra give his everything to produce a vast tumult of sound.'

But although John had gone for boldness with his score, that didn't mean for one moment that it was simplistic. On the contrary, the whole score stands up way beyond its basic premise of drama via theme and variations, and the 'Mickey Mouse music' label really belies the complexity and refinement of what John actually created.

Right from the start, having got the audience's rapt attention with Bassey's opening title, John wasn't going to let them go in a hurry, and the title theme practically segues into the 'Into Miami' music of the film's first scene. It's only a short cue, but with its enticing saxophone and its cocktail hour swish, it sets the whole film up perfectly. Throughout the score the permutations of both the 'Goldfinger Theme' and the original 'Bond Theme' are more than diverse. Listen to 'Teasing The Korean' and you'll find the maddest, headiest version of 'Goldfinger' you're ever going to hear. It starts off all classic Sixties-party-scene beat-group-twang, but as it edges up to its anarchic climax, you get pounding, moaning, cat-on-heat strings over rumbling surf guitar. And it's all driven along to its thrashy end in four-four with frightening, literally military precision.

These sounds had started off in John's head; once conceived, he had to find the recording techniques to bring them to life. By now he had started using CTS studios in Bayswater quite regularly. They were in what had previously been an old Wesleyan Chapel, and the building had strange acoustics. 'That studio contributed so much to the distinctive Bond sound,' John reveals. 'The brass sound on that was a lot to do with the echo in the studio. Because it was an old chapel, you couldn't control the sound the way you can now. It wasn't a phoney echo on that score, it was real.'

[139]

Going into the studio could often be a fraught affair. John would be trying to convey his own musical vision to an orchestra full of musicians and a sound engineer, but he'd also have the film's director in the studio, looking over his shoulder, making sure everything was working with the images.

This time the director was another old-school, English director, Guy Hamilton, who had started out assisting John Huston and Carol Reed, and had since directed numerous films. 'At all the sessions you would have a screen running the picture,' explains Hamilton, 'with the conductor facing it, and the orchestra with their backs to it. The film is sometimes marked up to suit the conductor because, if it's a piece that runs for, say, three and a half minutes – which is a fairly average section – he's probably got half a dozen sync points in it where he's got to be there, just as the person jumps out of the areoplane. And so if the orchestra's playing for two minutes they're likely to get slightly ahead or behind, and so the conductor's got to drive that orchestra, pick them up, slow them down to hit all these sync points. That's the way it works. And you, as the director, are watching as a spectator to see that the sync points are hit. Also, as it's the first time you've heard it with the orchestra, you probably put on some cans to check that the music isn't drowning out the dialogue or the timpani aren't being over-enthusiastic.'

Attending the session also gave the director the opportunity to see if the music worked with the action. And to do something about it, if he felt it didn't. 'I remember on that session there was one bit of music which was for the part when Goldfinger's troops are turning up at Fort Knox, and for some reason it didn't work. It was over-orchestrated or there was something wrong, and I went to John who was on the podium conducting and I said, "Look, it's not right for this thing." And I was convinced that John was going to have to work all night because we'd got another music session the next day. So I was quite anxious about it. But he just listened, took the point and then suddenly turned and said to the orchestra – "Right, the violins are tacit, the brass will repeat the next six bars from G, the drums will do so and so," and off we went again. And it was a totally different piece. He'd re-orchestrated it there and then and it worked magnificently.'

This flexibility and professionalism was enormously appreciated by directors. Both Bryan Forbes and Anthony Harvey – director of *The Lion in Winter* – later commented on how much easier these qualities made their lives. Here was a composer who not only delivered the goods but was willing to make any appropriate changes, adeptly, quickly and with no fuss. Being a successful composer in this instance was just as much about the ability to be adaptable and to make amendments without prima-donna tantrums, as about writing music.

On *Goldfinger* John had done well to keep his cool, bearing in mind that not only was it the first Bond score he'd done from start to finish, but that he'd been given less time than usual to get it done. Now, having completed the recording on time, he anxiously awaited his bosses' reaction. He felt that this score was what he had been working up to practically since the start of his career, and having put so much energy and so much of himself into it, he now needed some praise. He was pleased with what he'd done, but he also needed to know that after hassling Saltzman and Broccoli for so long to let him prove himself, they were going to be glad they had.

'Harry Saltzman hated "Goldfinger",' says John. 'He just kept swearing, saying: "John, I need to get kids in the cinemas, and I can't do it with a song like this." He wanted to get rid of it and was adamant about it, but in the end he capitulated, saying: "The only reason this song is staying in the movie is because we don't have any goddamn time to redo it. The print's wet and it's got to be in the theatres by next week." Cubby liked it though and the director Guy Hamilton loved it,' says John. 'He said, "I don't know whether it's a pop song at all, but it works brilliantly with the beginning of the picture. It just sets the whole thing up."' This was better, thought John, but Saltzman's scathing wrath was like a wet blanket in his face, and the thrill of his first entirely self-scored Bond film opening was not the joyful event it might have been.

When the film finally opened at London's Odeon Leicester Square, it was practically a national event. Since the tentative opening of *Dr No*, two years earlier, Bond's popularity had been growing as fast as the film's budgets. 'The sheer weight of hundreds of fans broke through a police cordon and shattered a twelve-foot-high glass door,' reported the *Daily Express*. 'The cinema door fell in with a crash. Girls screamed, but no one was hurt,' it continued. Connery appeared, looking suitably suave, while Honor Blackman – the film's unforgettable 'Pussy Galore' – turned up in a shimmering gold dress, complete with solid gold finger attachment.

It was the *Star Wars* and *Jurassic Park* of its day, and *Goldfinger* launched Bond as the cinematic cult of the decade, on a global scale. In America it gained a place in the *Guinness Book of Records* as the fastest grossing film of all time, and *Playboy* magazine hailed Connery as the man of the decade, while in France he was, appropriately, the 'Don Juan of the year'. There, Bondmania had reached epidemic proportions. Within a fortnight of the film opening, it had broken all cinema attendance records. 'Some houses report one hundred and five per cent capacity turnout,' stated the *Daily Telegraph*, 'which means people are sitting in the aisles.' Chic Paris department store Galeries Lafayette quickly opened its own 'Bond Boutique' selling Bond suits, trenchcoats and cuff links, as well as 007 negligées. And it wasn't just Paris that had gone Bond-mad. At London's Hilton Hotel you could drink 007 vodka in the Bond Bar, before going home to your Bond pyjamas and waking up to toast made from Bond Bread.

Bond was a success across all levels of society as well. The Queen Mother sidled up to Connery at a Royal function to tell him that *Goldfinger* was the best film she'd ever seen; the Duchess of Windsor told a French newspaper that Bond was her 'idol' and when Paul McCartney saw the film, he went straight out and bought himself an Aston Martin DB5. Even respected authors like Kingsley Amis and eminent sociologists were beginning to write essays and theses on the Bond phenomenon. Bond was more than a hit. It was hugely successful. Now John just needed to see that his music was a success too.

In Britain the Shirley Bassey 'Goldfinger' single only made it to number twenty-one, although it stayed in the charts for nine weeks. In America, however, it was a diffferent story. 'The album went in at about ninety or something,' remembers John, 'and then the second week I got the charts and I looked in the nineties and when it wasn't there I thought, Oh, it's gone out. Then I looked in the eighties and it wasn't there either, and I thought, Oh, have I blown it now! I wasn't in touch with anybody else, and I remember in the evening I was thinking, God, this is such bad news. Then I picked up the magazine again and looked at the top, and there it was: *Goldfinger* – number one, and The Beatles' album *Hard Day's Night*, which had been up there at number one, was now number two. I went crazy. I just couldn't believe it! And that's how it went, from this despair in the morning – thinking I'd failed miserably and maybe Saltzman was right. I was beginning to think, OK, it's lousy, inappropriate – all those recriminations were going through my head. And then to this joy in the evening.

'Harry Saltzman hardly said a word about it, though. I was sat in the Pickwick Club with Mike Caine one night and he came in and walked over and said, "Thanks, it works." But it was such an off-handed compliment that it didn't really make up for anything at all. Saltzman never understood the accuracy of the drama of that song, which I'm always very proud of. I still like it dramatically, and that was my main concern. And he was thinking "pop music" in some other way, and it didn't seem obvious to him that it was going to be a popular song.'

Whatever Harry Saltzman may have thought, 'Goldfinger' turned out to be an extremely popular song. Within weeks of its release there were three other recordings of it in the charts, including Billy Preston's masterful Hammond version. John's album meanwhile stayed at number one in America for three weeks and remained high in the charts for nearly two years. It sold over two million copies and was nominated for a Grammy Award, while the title song sold a million. James Bond had become an international cult and it had made John Barry a star.

Following the triumph of *Goldfinger*, even more than before, John was now Mr Success. He was at the heart of the British film world, and the heart of the London scene. And he was still only just past thirty. But that was the joy of it all. The mood on the streets and in the clubs was about optimism and it was about being young.

'This was so up,' says John. 'There was such joy in it. We were all young, we were all getting the breaks, and the Establishment had been told to go fuck itself. We were the young money that went to Turnbull and Asser; it wasn't the old farts. It was the David Baileys, the Michael Caines, the Terry Stamps. The money that was being spent in the Sixties was being spent by all these young guys and young women. They were the people with the new money, you know. It was a big, big change.'

'This is a young people's town,' said Ad Lib club manager Brian Morris at the time. 'In the old days, the middle-aged dominated the nightclubs. Now the young run the place.' And it wasn't just the clubs. It was everything. And it was exactly that spirit of youth and optimism that would be the subject of John's next film.

9

THE KNACK . . . AND HOW
TO GET IT

By 1965 John was no longer simply John Barry. Or at least not in the
eyes of the tabloids. He was John 'Bondman' Barry, and it was a moniker
that stuck. The success of Bond had made John virtually a household
name, and yet it was the smaller, non-Bond films John worked on over
the next few years that would get him noticed at another, more serious
level.

During the course of the 1960s, John wrote for no less than six
films with director Bryan Forbes, and although they weren't the most
commercially successful of projects they gave him the most scope for
experimentation and innovation. John had already shown he could do
action music: these films gave him the chance to prove he was more
than a one-trick composer. 'It's very easy in this business to get typecast,'
says John, 'and so I was always very grateful for those Bryan Forbes
films because they stopped that happening to me. Throughout the time
I was working on the Bonds in the Sixties, I was also doing those films
for Bryan, and it was a nice list. It was also terrific working for Bryan,
'cause he's such a gentleman.'

But even with the prospect of more Bond films pretty much assured,
and a steady flow of work from Forbes, John was not content to rest
on his Cadogan Square laurels. He may have given up tearing around
England with a pop group, but he was never one to turn down interest-

ing work if it was offered, whether it was films, TV or even musicals.

Somehow during the course of 1964 and 1965 John would end up scoring, on average, about five films a year, and not one of them was a bad job. On the contrary, during this time he was to produce some of his most memorable scores. And it was one of these – *The Knack* – another small independent British film, that would get him noticed by Hollywood.

In the days before Bond, Britain had been seen by America as a small, parochial backwater where the odd successful film might occasionally get made – but if it did, it was most likely a fluke, rather than part of any particular trend. All that was about to change, for with the social climate having altered so drastically not just in Britain, but across Europe and America, it was only a matter of time before films started to reflect this.

The Bond films had been the first to feature a sexually liberated leading man, surrounded by readily available women, but Bond was a world unto himself. It was another British film that captured the feeling on the street, and its impact caused deafening reverberations in the British film industry as a whole.

Tom Jones, Tony Richardson's film of Henry Fielding's bawdy eighteenth-century novel, was *The Full Monty* of its day. It had been made relatively cheaply and earned vast amounts of money in America, as well as winning four Oscars including 'Best Film'. This was the first time a British film had won the coveted top Oscar prize since 1948, and the impact was profound.

The film had broken new ground in its combination of very contemporary, naturalistic camera work with period drama, but its success was important to the British film industry for a different reason. *Tom Jones* was made by Woodfall – the company originally set up at the end of the 1950s by director Tony Richardson and playwright John Osborne with Harry Saltzman as producer. Saltzman had since been replaced by West End theatrical impresario Oscar Lewenstein, who had got financial backing from United Artists in a deal not unlike that of Saltzman and Broccoli's Bond agreement.

By February 1964 *Tom Jones* had made over one and a half million dollars in the US, and on the back of its success, United Artists gave Woodfall carte blanche to make three more films. This in itself was not that surprising. What was important were the terms of the deal. United Artists were agreeing to finance three films with one hundred per cent financial backing and zero artistic interference. The deal was every director's dream. Now Woodfall had the money, the only question was what film to make with it.

Although *Tom Jones* was set in the past, its spirit of sexual freedom was an easy metaphor for the prevailing mood. The Bond films had likewise picked up on the new atmosphere in their sense of glamour and sexual bravado, but until now, no one film-maker had really attempted to portray Britain and more importantly London itself exactly as it was. Only one film had come close – Richard Lester's *A Hard Day's Night*.

A Hard Day's Night was the precursor of the 'Swinging London' films that were to come later with *Darling*, *Georgy Girl* and *Alfie*. It captured the widening generation gap and The Beatles' irreverence for the old guard. But the 'London' film as such had yet to be made, and it was only a matter of time.

Oscar Lewenstein's theatrical background sent him back to the Royal Court for inspiration and there he found it. Two years earlier the London company had put on a play about the newly 'permissive' atmosphere in the capital. It was called 'The Knack . . . and How to Get It', and it revolved around three main characters: Tolen, a sexual Lothario par excellence, offset by Colin – the sexually gauche and therefore frustrated inept – and Nancy – the young ingénue, newly arrived in London from the country and eager for 'experiences'.

Lewenstein decided this could be just what he was looking for; the play might transfer very well to the cinema screen. He also decided that if they were going to make a Swinging London film, they'd better get a 'Swinging London' director. Who better than the man of the moment himself, Richard Lester? So Lewenstein got on the phone. 'I have this film I'd like you to do,' he told Lester. 'I've only got £100,000 to make it, but I think you'll be perfect for it.'

[147]

Starring Michael Crawford, Ray Brooks and Rita Tushingham, *The Knack* captured everything that we now associate with that era. It had the look, it had the style and, eventually it had the sound too. Shot in black and white, half of *The Knack* was a David Bailey fashion shoot come to life, with its all-white room, sharp-suited guys and mini-skirted girls and stark, contrasty lighting. The other half was an exuberant jaunt around the capital: a stream of breezy motorbike rides, frolics in parks and an extended sequence journeying through the streets of West London aboard an antique iron bedstead.

The Knack was a feature-length snapshot of life in London as it was. As critic Alexander Walker wrote in his book *Hollywood, England*: '*The Knack* contains the al fresco experience of the capital in 1964, at which time all who lived there shared a great sense of unleashing – that young people had taken it over, or were about to stage a *"coup de jeunesse"*.' It brought home the generation divide and celebrated youth. Everyone young in the film is living life – or at least attempting to live it – to the full, while the fusty elders are the stolid face of conformity, conservatism and inertia. 'If you ask me, they're a new breed of person altogether,' says an old dear in vox-pop disdain at the new youth. 'It will end in tears,' dooms another. 'I know what she wants and it's not the YWCA!' 'I blame it on the National Health.'

Lester's film had the look. All it needed now was the right sound. So John, hot from the success of *Goldfinger*, was brought in. The two had already met when they'd worked together on TV ads, but the question now was: how to approach *The Knack*?

Lester had been heavily influenced by the French 'New Wave' directors – Godard, Truffaut and Resnais – who had emerged at the start of the decade, and so when it came to music, his first thoughts took him across the Channel. He had loved Michel Legrand's score for Jacques Demy's *Umbrellas of Cherbourg* and so laid it under *The Knack* as a guide or 'temp track' to show the producer and composer what he was looking for.

But John, as ever, had his own ideas. 'What it needed was protest, youth answering back,' he told the *Daily Mail* later that year. 'I could have used guitars, but that would have been a bit corny. So instead I used girls' voices humming a melody against the dialogue, and it was very effective.'

But *The Knack* wasn't just about protest. There was joy in it too, and that was John's real challenge. 'I can't stand cute, funny music,' he insists, 'and so the thing on *The Knack* was how to put some kind of heart in it, yet make it whimsical. And that's what I think I got right.' John did get it right, and on the way he called in Hammond organ jazz supremo Alan Haven to give the score the coolest, swingiest organ licks this side of Jimmy Smith.

He had discovered Haven one night down at the Cool Elephant jazz club and had already used him on the score for a low-key comedy called *A Jolly Bad Fellow*. Since then the electric organ had become the sound of the summer, not least on The Animals' 'House of the Rising Sun', but it was John's blend of Haven's improvisational style with his own soaring strings that created the gorgeous mix of mischievous flirtation and wistful romance that is so perfect for *The Knack*. It was also, arguably, more effective than Legrand's *Umbrellas of Cherbourg*, which may have featured one all-time-classic song, 'Ne Me Quitte Pas', but in terms of the score as a whole, didn't even come close. And if ever there was a score that conjured up lazy, carefree, sexy afternoons and wayward nights it was John's for *The Knack*.

Richard Lester, however, was ambivalent in his praise. 'You've done everything I wouldn't have done,' he said. 'But it works.' That kind of backhanded compliment wasn't exactly what John had been hoping for, but Lewenstein was full of praise, and so that softened the blow. United Artists were unequivocally thrilled, and having seen the success of the *Goldfinger* LP, were keen to try and repeat it with *The Knack*. They therefore commissioned John to record a vocal version of his title theme, so they could maximise the film's soundtrack potential.

Given free rein to use who he wanted, but at the same time not having much of a budget, John brought in his old EMI protégé, singer Johnny De Little – a Welshman his father JX had discovered at the Rialto. Once again Leslie Bricusse supplied the lyrics, and once more they were classics of their kind:

You can say you love her, when planning your attack,
But don't let her catch you — that's the knack.
When you play the lover, and scratch her pretty back,
Don't let her scratch you, boy, that's the knack.
A man chases lots of girls — and maybe catches one or two,
But if you have the knack, the girls chase you.

'It was the story of John's life!' says Bricusse. Somehow it seemed only natural that John, who was leading the ultimate Swinging London life, should score the ultimate Swinging London film. Bricusse, Lester and John were all at the centre of the new, hip London, and understood what it was about. *The Knack* brought it all to life, and via the combination of John's pop sensibility and Lester's fast-paced, stylised direction it made the film the ultimate pop promo for London and its youth.

The Knack ended up winning the top prize at Cannes the next year — the Palme d'Or — and its London première was the celebrity event of the month, with The Beatles in the row behind John. The furore it caused was intense. To everyone's surprise. 'When we were doing it,' says John, 'we didn't have any idea that it was going to cause any kind of sensation.' But maybe that was because for John and his friends, *The Knack*'s kind of life had become their everyday reality. Whereas, at least for some of the older generation, it hadn't.

Until now, no British film had dared to show the nation's youth behaving with such unashamed sexual abandon in a contemporary setting, and the fact that *The Knack* was made at all was a reflection of the changing mood in society. Two or three years earlier, the Establishment had been shocked by the 'kitchen-sink' films' acknowledgement that sex even existed. 'Compared to Rome, England was then like a monastery,' recalled film producer Joseph Janni in the early 1960s. 'In those days England denied that her people even had a sex-life: sex was regarded as an exclusively Continental pursuit.' Things had changed significantly since then and culture was beginning to reflect that change.

Both *The Knack* and *Goldfinger* had propelled John's career forward substantially, but he was still eager for the chance to work in Hollywood itself. And that opportunity was about to arrive, thanks to his old chum, director Bryan Forbes.

By 1963 Forbes had made a name for himself as one of the new 'realist' directors with *The Angry Silence*, *Whistle Down the Wind* and *The L-Shaped Room*. These were arthouse films, shot in black and white, on relatively small budgets, and although they received critical acclaim, on the whole a large proportion of the public never got to see them. What was important, though, was that Forbes, like Lester and Tony Richardson, had a new-found freedom in how he made his films. Until the Sixties, the British film industry, like Hollywood, had been dominated by the studio system, whereas now suddenly there was a host of new young producers and directors, all freed from the constraints of a strict dictum from above as to what they could and couldn't do, and who they could or couldn't use.

Forbes himself was slightly older than the new young generation that Lester and John represented; he had already been working for over ten years as an actor and scriptwriter with the big names in postwar British films, from John Mills and Kenneth More to Richard Attenborough. This meant that he knew what made actors tick and how to keep a crew happy, and he was keen to build up a steady team of regulars for his films.

Forbes had been impressed with the jazz sequence John had written for *The L-Shaped Room*, and so when it came to his next venture, *Seance on a Wet Afternoon*, he remembered the bright young chap who had delivered so swiftly before. 'I'll let you do the whole score this time,' he told John. 'I just believed in him from the word go,' says Forbes, 'and we struck it off as friends as well. On a set you've got to have people you trust and at that time, it was only my third film as Director and so I was still feeling my way.'

Seance was an eerily intense, 'Tales of the Unexpected'-style story of a childless, bickering middle-aged couple who kidnap a small girl. The woman is supposedly a medium who proceeds to have 'visions' of the child, to the growing disturbance of her henpecked husband, played by Richard Attenborough, who was also co-producer.

For John, scoring *Seance on a Wet Afternoon* was an entirely different challenge from the ones he had faced with the Bond scores. This time it was a question of 'less is more'. The entire budget for *Seance* was only £139,000 and music-wise, John was on a tight leash. But Forbes' independence from the studio system meant that John also had freedom.

In the old studio set-up, things had been different. 'In those days every Hollywood studio had its own orchestra of fifty or sixty pieces,' says John, 'so naturally all those guys over there used them. If they didn't, the producers would say to them, "What's the point of us paying all these musicians all the time if you don't use them?" But in Britain no studio had that, so I used to be able to match each orchestra to the mood of the film. On *Seance*, Bryan Forbes said to me: "I want a really strange orchestral sound." So I had four alto flutes, four cellos, and vibraphones. It was a small orchestra, but very effective.'

John's score was also small, but eloquent, and Forbes loved it. 'The kidnapping sequence is amazing 'cause he uses the violin as a screen for the action. It just worked so well.'

While John was working on *Seance*, he had a visit from a young aspiring film director, who was just beginning to work in advertising. 'I was in Los Angeles, years later,' says John, 'and this guy said to me: "You know, I came to see you when you were doing *Seance on a Wet Afternoon*." I said, "No, I don't remember." He said, "Yeah, you made me wait an hour, but you were my hero and I was young, so I did." I think he'd just wanted advice and to see how I worked back then, but years later he wanted me to work on a film *he* was doing.' The man's name was Ridley Scott.

When the film premièred on 4 June 1964 it was critically well received, but in true arthouse tradition it never achieved widespread release in Britain, and consequently dwindled into the flotsam of low-budget, rarely seen British B-films. It was important though for John's career, since it cemented his collaboration with Forbes and during the course of filming, the pair were able to devise their own particular working method.

Because *Seance on a Wet Afternoon* and most of Forbes' future films were not big money extravaganzas on the scale of the Bonds, Forbes was always keenly aware of the need to keep within budget. This was relatively easy as far as most of his crew was concerned, but when it came to the music, that was the one area over which – usually at least – the director had little control. Forbes found a solution and John was flexible enough to make it work.

'I always felt that composers get a very raw deal as far as film's concerned,' says Forbes. 'With actors, I can make them do a shot twenty times if necessary to get it perfect, but composers get just three weeks to do the whole thing – and then if it's not right, it's a big problem. You bring the composer in at the editing stage and you give him the lengths of time and say, "I want music from there to there," and he goes away and he's usually got three weeks in which to do it. You then turn up having never heard a note, you've got eighteen musicians costing you a fortune and on top of that, the recording studio itself, and if you don't like the music, you're dead. You've either got to scrap it and do it again – which is a costly business and few people can afford it – or you're stuck with music you don't like.

'So what John and I devised – right from *Seance on a Wet Afternoon* – was to involve him from day one. Every two or three weeks he would come down to the studio where we were filming, and I would run cut sequences. Then I would give him a small sum of money – not his entire fee – and say, "Go away and give us some themes. I don't care what they are – piano, guitar, Jew's harp, anything you like." Then he'd bring it in and I'd lay it into the film, and we'd look at it and say, "God, that works" or "That doesn't work." And so by the time I come to the recording session, I know what I'm getting and John knows what I want. And John has plenty of time. Instead of three weeks he's got twelve to sixteen weeks in which to finesse his work, which seems to me only fair, and it's always worked very well with us. Mind you, I've tried it with other composers since and they just won't wear it. It's usually the big name composers who say, "Oh no" – it's beneath them to do that.'

It was Forbes' next film – *King Rat* – which would finally get John across the ocean to Hollywood. This was the one big ambition he still hadn't fulfilled. And it hadn't been for lack of trying. Back in 1961, when he had gone to America as Musical Director for EMI, he had already been planting seeds, and had had meetings with Doris Day's manager about writing for her films. But nothing had really materialised. He'd been asked to write and record the music for a TV show pilot called *Area Code 212* with Robert Wagner, but the show was never commissioned. *King Rat* was to be his first real film recording in America.

King Rat was a World War Two drama, set in Singapore's notorious Changi prisoner-of-war camp. It starred George Segal, Tom Courtenay, James Fox and John Mills, and like the Bond films, it was financed by American money. In this case – Columbia. By this time, the old Holly-wood studios were beginning to run into financial problems as more and more films were shot either abroad or on location. They were still running studios and employing full-time orchestras which were costing them a fortune each day they didn't get used. Consequently Forbes was under pressure to make use of Columbia's music facilities, even though it would probably have been cheaper to record the whole thing in England.

Columbia were also less than thrilled at the idea of using a British composer. 'We've got all these composers of our own out here,' they told Forbes. 'Why do we need to bring someone new in, all the way over from England?' But Forbes stood up for John, and said, 'No. I want John Barry.' He and John would go over to record the music in Hollywood, with the studio's orchestra, he said. John had made it to Hollywood.

He now needed to prove himself. Not only to Forbes as someone who'd been worth fighting for, but to the studio too. And it wasn't going to be straightforward. Forbes wanted something that sounded like nothing else. 'I wanted the music for *King Rat* to be something quite different from the ordinary run-of-the-mill wartime epics,' says Forbes. 'I asked John to give me a quite different *sound*. It was a hard, rough subject, so we couldn't have five hundred violins, you know. He couldn't have given me a sort of *Dr Zhivago*-type score, because it would have worked against the picture. It would have romanticised an unromantic subject.

' "I want music which is ragged and awful," I said, "because that's what the film is about." So John got thinking, digging out obscure, little-used instruments and came back saying, "Why don't I use a cimbalom?" '

'I said, "What on earth's that?"

' "Don't worry," he said. "It'll be perfect. It's like a steel harp and it needs to be played with a stick, 'cause otherwise it'll rip your fingers apart, but it can make that jagged sound you want and I think it'll work." Then once he'd written it, he was so enthusiastic about it, he played me the theme down the phone.'

John had discovered the cimbalom via John Leach, an expert in foreign instruments. 'John Leach had this house which was crawling with instruments,' remembers John. 'You opened the front door and you had to climb over them. Every year he used to take time off and go around the world, picking up these weird instruments and learning how to play them. So he played this big cimbalom and I knew it was right for what I needed.'

The cimbalom was to prove a major discovery for John for his future work, but right now he had to make sure it was played right. John Leach was in London, and John was going to be using Hollywood musicians. He was by now more than used to the London studio set-up, but Hollywood was something new. And as soon as he arrived, he realised he was no longer on the visitor's tour. This was the real thing.

'The orchestral booker there was this guy called Jonie Tapps,' says John, 'and he had this calendar in his office with all these girls posing, and he said, "You know, John, most guys that come in here, they really love this calendar." The thing was, it wasn't a sales calendar. It was a roster of girls available to people who worked for Columbia and I was supposed to say: "Yeah, I'd like July, this afternoon, please. Four o'clock at the Beverly Hills Hotel." I just stood there speechless for about five minutes.'

When it came to the actual recording session, John was in for another surprise. Jonie Tapps had said to him, 'You need someone to play the cimbalom? I have just the guy. He's amazing.' And John believed him.

Perhaps that was at least one problem solved. But it didn't make the task ahead of him any less daunting. Feeling nervous as hell, John turned up for his first recording session in Hollywood, conducting a whole orchestra of veteran film-music players. These guys had all been doing it for years. They'd played for every great Hollywood composer going, and now they were sitting there waiting for John to come up with the goods.

That proved harder than John had anticipated. 'We did not get one piece of music recorded the whole morning,' he says. 'Can you imagine? My first Hollywood movie and not to record one bit all morning. Jonie Tapps had booked me this cimbalom player who couldn't play a note, and 'cause the whole piece is based around that instrument, it made the whole thing sound horrendous. The guys in the orchestra were all looking at me like, "Who's this limey that's come over here and brought us this godawful stuff?" I was *dying*.

'Bryan was terrific, though. Some directors would have said, "This is going nowhere," and that would have been it. But Bryan was so cool and unflappable and just said, "Well, we did do it in England, and it sounded superb. We're not stupid. We've come here and we've got problems. Let's try and sort it out."

'Fortunately I'd taken the tape of the demo we'd done in London, and so then when I played it back to the orchestra they saw how wonderful it was with this guy who could really play, and how tight it was. So that changed their attitude, thank God. I'd done this demo with just the cimbalom, four cellos and a bass – very sparse – and it sounded ten times better than this whole goddamn orchestra.

'So finally in the afternoon we hired a guitarist who had a few gizmos which made his guitar sound a bit like a cimbalom. In the end, the whole thing was a mixture of sections with the real cimbalom and sections with the guitar. From that moment on, I never believed anybody again. So now whenever anybody says to me, "Oh, I've got this great cello-player," I say, "Terrific, can I meet him?" I always check everybody out.'

John's score, although not one of his most memorable, fitted the film and proved how effective a cimbalom could be. *King Rat* had given him his long-awaited first taste of Hollywood and had also cemented his working partnership with Forbes.

In 1964, there was still major crossover between the theatre and film worlds, and actors, directors and producers frequently worked in both. Before getting involved with Woodfall Films, Oscar Lewenstein had run the Royal Court Theatre, Tony Richardson had been and still was a theatre director, and the new young stars of British cinema – Albert Finney, Tom Courtenay *et al* – had all started off on the stage. It was therefore not unusual when theatre producer and playwright Wolf Mankowitz approached John with a new project.

John knew Mankowitz socially from the Pickwick, which apart from anything else had become, according to Michael Caine, 'an unofficial Labour Exchange for people in showbusiness'. If you worked in film or the theatre, it was where you'd see producers, directors, actors – basically everyone who could tell you what was going on. It was the ultimate networking centre, before the term was invented.

'I've got this offer to do a musical called *Passion Flower Hotel*,' Mankowitz told John. 'It's about a girls' school, so it's right up your street, and Stanley Kubrick's been after the film rights 'cause it's kind of like a multiple *Lolita*.' Mankowitz was writing it, and he wanted John to do the music.

John had never done a musical before, and hadn't really ever thought about doing one, but as far as he was concerned, it was work, and it was something new. John had adored the Hollywood musicals of the 1940s, and still looked up to the great writers of that time – Richard Rodgers, Lerner and Lowe et cetera – as heroes. So now that the chance for him to write a musical of his own had come along, it was an opportunity. 'At that time I wanted to do everything,' he says. 'It wasn't part of a hugely well-thought-out plan. I read it and liked it, and that was it. I was just open to anything that came my way.'

Passion Flower Hotel was based on a successful book by Rosalind Erskine. Erskine was actually a man, and like *The Knack*, the premise of *Passion Flower Hotel* was pure male fantasy. A group of adolescent public-schoolgirls get bored, and decide to set up an unofficial bordello to sexually enlighten the pupils at the neighbouring boys' school – and themselves. The idea in itself had potential and so John set about writing songs. They needed a lyricist though, and John immediately thought of his old writing partner Trevor Peacock.

'I think Trevor would be great,' John told Mankowitz. 'He's not done a show before, but he's very bright, and I think he's a very funny writer.' So the two sat down for a series of meetings at Cadogan Square, and discussed how things should work. 'In films you always see the composer sitting at a piano,' says Peacock, 'and the lyricist standing behind coming up with lyrics on the spot, but we never actually did that. Sometimes he would write a bit of the tune, but usually I'd set off the structure of the line and the rhyming scheme, and he would set the music to that. John knew what he wanted, and he had a manner which was authoritative. I always remember him being very pro-fessional, but without any great fuss. He was always fairly laid-back, and he would never steam-roller your ideas.'

But morning sessions at Cadogan Square weren't just matter-of-fact discussions about song structure either. They would do that too, but everything about John carried a note of glamour with it, from his luxurious flat and immaculate dress sense to his passion for music. 'I was always hugely impressed because the rooms at Cadogan Square were rather large,' remembers Peacock, 'and the entire walls were shelves of LPs – you couldn't see any wallpaper at all. And I thought what an *enormous* collection. I remember him sitting at the piano saying, "Listen to this, Trevor," and playing me these chord jumps – majors to minors and trying things out. He'd talk about what makes an exciting jump, and then he used to shoot off to this vast wall of LPs and go, "Where is it? Where is it? It's Mahler, I think." And he'd bring out a piece of Mahler and it was all terribly impressive.'

The resulting songs were not quite so impressive, but were still reasonably standard Broadway musical fare. John had written some strong melodies and Peacock's lyrics were suitably 'jolly hockey sticks' gauche. Barbra Streisand later covered one of the songs 'How Much of the Dream Comes True'.

Now Mankowitz had songs and lyrics. So far, so good. The problem lay more with the choice of cast. The producers had brought in the most drop-dead gorgeous young starlets of the day and these included the extremely young Francesca Annis and Pauline Collins, as well as a then-unknown seventeen-year-old called Jane Birkin. The criteria for the casting had presumably been primarily visual – and it showed in the performance. As John put it: 'Nobody could sing and nobody could dance, but they all looked great.'

One number – 'The Syndicate' – ended up sounding like 'Big Spender' from *Sweet Charity*, sung by the choir of St Trinian's. And somewhere along the line, that was probably the idea, but nonetheless it made for a hilariously bad end result. In spite of all this, the show opened to star reviews in Manchester and the show's writers took the lion's share of the praise. 'Trevor and I were suddenly considered the Cole Porters of the new English theatre,' says John, 'and I remember thinking, Jesus, it can't be this easy, 'cause we were packed out every night.'

After six months in Manchester, the show transferred to the Prince of Wales Theatre in London's West End, but here the critics were less enthusiastic. 'Mr John Barry's music is lenient to performers whose singing voices are not their greatest strength,' said *The Times*, while *Queen* magazine was even less enamoured: '[This show] . . . simply ignores everything we've learnt about what makes a successful musical, from *West Side Story* on,' they wrote.

The show they saw though was quite different from the one that had wowed the Northern audiences. And the lack of structure commented on by *Queen* was the result of severe cuts to the original script. The producers had decided that the three-hour running time was too long for a London audience and so Wolf Mankowitz had sat down with the director William Chappell and started chopping. The cuts were not perhaps as sensitive as they might have been, and the result was disastrous. 'It was hacked down in the crudest way,' says John, 'and they hacked the life out of it. The dramatic thrust and humour of it was lost, so when it came to London it just wasn't enjoyable any more.'

Other critics, however, were obviously less bothered about the show's dramatic credibility and one journalist at least was more interested in the show's other attractions. 'Top marks to Jane Birkin,' gushed the *Financial Times*, 'who has precisely the type of looks that knock 'em dead in the Kings Road: glistening shoulder-length hair, immense Shrimpton eyes, pouting lips and legs that look marvellous in calf-length socks. And she moves beautifully.'

John had first met Jane Birkin briefly on *The Knack*, when she had made a 'blink and you'll miss it' appearance at the beginning of the film. But they first met properly on *Passion Flower Hotel*. 'I remember coming back from doing *King Rat* in LA on the Red Eye,' says John, 'and I got this call as soon as I got into London, saying the auditions for *Passion Flower* were down at Green Park. It was a nice sunny spring day and that's where I first really set eyes on Jane.

'I'd met her briefly before that in a lift in the Ad Lib club. She was this nervous, twitchy young girl. I remember it was a Sunday night party and David Bailey was there feeling miserable because Jean Shrimpton had gone off to America and was hanging around with Terence Stamp. We all felt sorry for him, but then a few weeks later he turned up with Catherine Deneuve, and nobody felt sorry for him after that.'

At that point Jane Birkin was not yet the Sixties icon she would later become. Several years before she would gain notoriety with her breathy delivery of 'Je T'Aime, Moi Non Plus' with Serge Gainsbourg, she was an unknown, albeit striking young girl who had only appeared in a couple of very minor acting parts. John at that stage was already the James Bond man, the star-about-town, and Birkin was soon smitten by the charms of the older, more experienced man.

Within weeks their romance was the talk of the cast. Jeremy Clyde – previously of Chad and Jeremy, and now in *Passion Flower Hotel* – remembers teasing Jane about it. 'Everyone knew about their affair,' he says, 'and we used to tease Jane 'cause she was in such a state of excitement about it. My thing was that I could do this rather good impression of John's deep Yorkshire baritone voice, and I used to sneak up behind her in the wings and say, "Hi Jane, do you fancy a quickie?" and she'd get all flustered. It was ever so sweet. We all loved her though, and it wasn't really a surprise at all, them being together. The thing about John at that time was, he had this habit of marrying women, and then suddenly not being married to them. But that was just him.'

Within six months of their meeting, John had proposed to Jane. By this time his divorce from Barbara had come through and in spite of the gap in age and experience between them, it seemed this was genuine true love for both of them. 'I used to take her home in this white E-type Jag I had and she used to climb out of the car and crawl on the bonnet looking at me through the window saying, "I love you John, I love you." So there I was with this beautiful little seventeen-year-old thing, sprawling on the bonnet of my E-type. It was all terribly romantic.'

And Jane was equally smitten. 'I couldn't believe I was the one he chose,' says Birkin. 'Not Pauline Collins, or Francesca Annis or any of the other beautiful girls that were in that show. I could hardly believe it when he fell in love with *me* and asked *me* to marry him. My mother had said that I couldn't possibly go out with anyone or live with them unless they asked me to marry them. So thank goodness, as he was carrying me into the bedroom, he asked me to marry him. And I remember thinking, Oof, phew, thank goodness for that. Now I'll be able to live with this divine man.'

The only problem with Jane's age, as far as John was concerned, was that it meant he had to get permission from Jane's parents to marry her. Luckily for John, Jane came from a showbusiness family and that meant they were at least likely to be marginally more liberal when it came to the prospect of their teenage daughter marrying a man who was sixteen years older than her, and had two children by two different women. Not to mention a reputation that would have put Casanova to shame. But even they, perhaps understandably, had their doubts. 'They weren't boring people who said, "Oh, who is this man from showbusiness?"' says Birkin. 'Not at all. They just thought, Maybe a bit dangerous for sweet Jane who's never met anyone and who's seventeen to go off with this dashing, remarkable, brilliant composer, whose friends are Michael Caine and Terence Stamp and all those people.

'But in the end they came round. John negotiated my marriage with my father in the garden. My father wanted me to wait a tiny bit before

[161]

marrying John because I was so young. He wanted me to be a ward of court. But John was in such a hurry, John persuaded him. John persuaded everyone.'

'James Bond Theme Man Marries' wrote the *Evening Standard*, after they were married at Chelsea Register Office on 10 October 1965. *Newsweek* also famously commented: 'the groom drove off in his E-type jag with his E-type wife.' But the ceremony hadn't been all glamour. Since John had long ceased using his real surname – Prendergast – there seemed no reason to start again now. Legally he could get married in the name of John Barry and that's what he did. But not without a few objections first.

'The thing I remember most about the wedding,' says John, 'was that my parents were there and Jane's mum and dad were there, and Carol Reed who was her godfather, and we got to the part of the ceremony where the guy said, "Do you John Barry . . ." and suddenly my father booms out, "What the bloody hell is wrong with Prendergast?" I just ignored it, but there we were, in the most romantic moment of our lives and he just comes out with that!'

A traditional honeymoon wasn't on the cards either. As Jane was performing six nights a week in *Passion Flower Hotel*, going away properly was out of the question. So John in true cavalier style suggested that if they couldn't go the whole hog for a real honeymoon, there might be something they could do instead. 'Let's go to Rome for the weekend,' he said. 'We'll fly out there Saturday night after the show, we'll be there by early Sunday morning and I promise to get you back to London in time for Monday night's show.' And he did.

It was fabulously romantic, and it was a change for John. Up until then, in spite of his success both professionally and personally, he wasn't necessarily always happy. For several years he'd played Mahler's less than uplifting Ninth Symphony every day, and his friends often noticed his sullenness. 'I remember going to a party with Stanley Baker at Cy Endfield's house,' says John, 'and I was stood there so miserable – I was never very good at parties. Stanley came up to me and said, "John, why have you got to be so fucking miserable?" And I said, "Well, what's there to be happy about?" And he fell on the floor, and he thought that was the funniest thing anyone had ever said to him. Then when he'd finished laughing he said, "You do have a point."'

But with Jane Birkin, John's friends had noticed a change in him, although at first, she didn't seem his usual type. 'Jane was very school-girly, jolly hockeysticks and all that stuff,' says Michael Caine, 'which wasn't the normal par for the course with John. His usual women tended to be a bit more voluptuous and sensual, not that I'm saying Jane wasn't or isn't, but the outward appearance was wrong. The thing about her though, was that she was great fun. She was always ready for a laugh and I think that's what attracted John to her, 'cause he could be quite morose. He'd sometimes look very sad about something and you'd never quite know what it was. But Jane was bubbly, so although we thought she wasn't the right type, she turned out to be very good for him.'

1965 turned out to be rather good for John all round. He had continued the instrumental innovation he'd started in *Zulu* to great effect in his films for Forbes, and shown that his talent was definitely not limited to Bond films. As Forbes wrote in his sleeve-notes for *King Rat*: 'John Barry is a rare and unique talent. He manages to work in isolation with the minimum of fuss and understands the function of music in films better than anybody else I have come across. He is not a musical snob and welcomes every new challenge. One has only to contrast his scores for *Seance on a Wet Afternoon* and *The Knack* to realise that his range as a musician is quite out of the ordinary.'

And soon John would have to prove that range once again. Bond-mania showed no signs of abating. On the contrary, it had given birth to its own offshoot, and so the question now was whether John would be able to beat himself at his own game, and create an alternative spy sound.

10

SPYMANIA

'Give it size, give it style and give it class,' Fred Astaire once said. 'They're kind of simple rules, but that's hopefully what one did,' says John, referring to the Bond scores.

That was what he did. Throughout the Sixties his scores were about style, but they were also about innovation more than anything else. Yes, a lot of them had size too, but it was the other two factors that put them head and shoulders above the rest. The Bond scores were heavy on size, the Forbes' scores were heavy on innovation, and *The Knack* was big on style. Where style and innovation really got together, though, was in John's spy scores – most of all in *The Ipcress File*. With *Ipcress* John created the model that from then on practically all spy scores would follow. He invented the sound of the Cold War.

Just as 'The Bond Theme' mix of brass and twang had been the culmination of everything that John had been doing prior to that, *Ipcress* likewise brought together his pop sensibility with his striving for musical invention. It was his quest to find that one strange sound that could cut to the core of the character and underpin it. Then, having found it, his masterstroke was to put that sound in a context that made it contemporary and accessible, without diluting its impact.

'The Ipcress Theme' had an economy and starkness that fitted the central character Harry Palmer so well that it's impossible to imagine the film's images without John's music. As Michael Caine says: 'If you want to see an example of what music does for a movie, go and see *The Ipcress File*. Then you'll understand what John Barry's all about.'

John had done it with Bond; now he was about to create another sound that would become inextricably linked in the public imagination with the underworld of spy culture. It was the same with so many of John's scores: they were never just disposable accompanying music, but added something invaluable to the films so that it became impossible to imagine them without that vital element.

John was in an ideal position to respond to the spy challenge. He had been through the Army at a time when the Cold War was more than a vague, distant notion. For him, and his peers, it had been a tangible threat and part of their daily reality. With *Ipcress*, it was that fear, and that intensity that John managed to convey.

By 1965 Bondmania had spawned Spymania; the spy had become a ubiquitous figure in popular culture. The relaxing of the Cold War, and the lessening of tensions between East and West meant that fantasy could let rip without touching a public nerve. The popular spy could be as fantastical as he wanted, without so much as a nod to reality, and audiences couldn't get enough.

Suddenly every film company had at least one spy film on their schedule, and before you could say 'secret agent' there were spies in the cinema, spies on TV, spies on the radio and spy merchandise, from clothes to toys to lunchboxes.

In the wake of 007's success, Cary Grant had done his very best Bond impression in *Charade*, and now it seemed like every major actor in the business was desperate to have a go. Over the next few years, Paul Newman appeared in *Torn Curtain*, Gregory Peck in *Arabesque*, Dirk Bogarde in *Hot Enough for June* and David Niven in *Where the Spies Are*. And those were just some of the better ones.

There were variations on the spy theme as well. Some, like *The Manchurian Candidate* and *The Spy Who Came In From the Cold* were more sophisticated and actually questioned the ideology of the Cold War, while others, such as *Modesty Blaise* went for pure unadulterated op-art fun. There were even spies from outer space in *This Island Earth*. There were spies for every taste imaginable.

In fact, if you lived in the Western world, you couldn't fail to notice spy fever. One person who had definitely not failed to notice was Harry Saltzman. Keenly aware of the current mania, he had acquired the rights to Len Deighton's *The Ipcress File*, anxious that with all these alternative spies bursting forth from film and TV, 007 might lose his winning edge. The way things worked out, 007 didn't, of course – but Saltzman wasn't taking any chances.

The best way to be a spy without imitating Bond, Saltzman calculated, was to go to the other extreme – to be his antidote. And *The Ipcress File*'s Harry Palmer was the most perfect antidote you were ever going to find. Where Bond was a hero, Palmer was an anti-hero. Where Bond was the epitome of urbane sophistication, Palmer embraced the ordinary and the mundane. But that didn't make Palmer dull. He still managed to kill off his enemies and get his women into bed. What was different was how he went about it. 'Insubordinate, insolent . . . a trickster' – was how Palmer's report described him in the film, and instead of Bond's courteous civility, Palmer's attitude was cocky, blunt and to the point. What was more, he displayed a lack of concern for the class hierarchy, which at the time was still quite anarchic.

In spite of wanting Harry Palmer to be the opposite to Bond, Saltzman cleverly assembled the Bond team to work on *The Ipcress File*. He figured that you needed the people who knew the original inside out, in order to come up with something radically different. And so not only was John on board, but also set designer Ken Adam and editor Peter Hunt.

Finding the right actor to play Palmer was absolutely crucial. Bizarrely, Saltzman's first choice for the role was Christopher Plummer, but he was unavailable as he was already filming *The Sound of Music*. Not quite the same sort of film as *The Ipcress File*. Saltzman's next thought was the young actor he'd seen in *Zulu* – Michael Caine.

Saltzman had been impressed by Caine's performance, but as ever, he needed someone else's reassurance before making a decision. So knowing John had also worked on *Zulu*, he asked him what he thought.

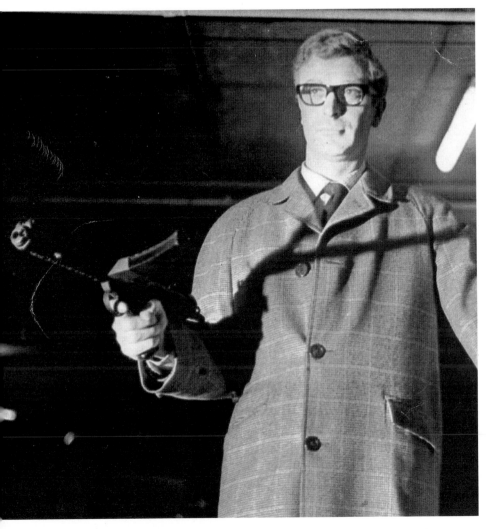

My name is . . . Harry Palmer. Michael Caine in *The Ipcress File*

Passion Flower Hotel's
swinging line up.
Left to right: Jane Birkin,
Francesca Annis, Karin
Fernald, Jean Muir,
Pauline Collins

John and Jane Birkin at
the premiere of *Born Free*

In Majorca on *Deadfall*, with Bryan Forbes and Nanette Newman

Recording John's 'Romance for Guitar and Orchestra'
with Bryan Forbes and Renata Tarrago

Getting that Bond brass – CTS Studios

John, 1969

With Louis Armstrong and Hal David

With Jane Sidey, 1969

John, 1997

'I think he's terrific,' said John. 'And I think he'd be great as Palmer.' With John and Caine, that was always part of their friendship. 'We were always very supportive of each other,' says Caine. 'Later on, if I was doing a movie, and the producers would be talking about who to get for the music, I'd always say, "Oh, John Barry's wonderful, you should get him in".'

Other people also agreed that Caine seemed to have potential, and gradually Saltzman began to realise he might have hit on something here. 'Harry Saltzman first saw me in the flesh in the Pickwick,' Caine recalls. I was in there having dinner with Terry Stamp and he sent a note over to me saying, "Would you come over and have a drink with me?". So I went over and he said, "I've just seen *Zulu* and I think you could be a big star. Do you know a book called *The Ipcress File?*" I said, "Yes, I do." "Well, I'm going to make a film of it," he told me. "How would you like to play the lead?" I'd just about managed a "Yes," when he said, "And would you like a seven-year contract with my company?" The answer to that was yes too, so he said, "Meet me for lunch tomorrow." And that was it!' *Ipcress* was to make Caine a star, but in the meantime, he was just pleased to have a lead role and, as John was already on *Ipcress*, to be working with his friend again.

As far as Saltzman was concerned, he had found his leading man. When it came to finding a director though, he wanted someone outside the Bond team and so he started looking around. He'd been impressed by a small British film made in 1963 called *The Leather Boys*, directed by a young Canadian director named Sidney J. Furie. *The Leather Boys* dealt with bike culture and homosexuality, but it was also a youth film, and Furie's direction had given the whole film a slightly malignant feel which Saltzman thought could come in handy. So Furie was hired.

But from day one, he and Saltzman didn't get on. Whether it was a clash of personal styles – Saltzman was a meticulous shirt and tie man, whereas Furie was decidedly jeans and leather jacket – or for some other unfathomable reason, Saltzman never really trusted Furie to deliver the goods. John remembers him telling people at the start: 'I'm gonna hold this guy's hand all the way through.' And saying to Furie himself: 'You just shoot the stuff. I've got Peter Hunt who'll put it all together.'

The choice of Furie proved a masterful stroke, however, as it was he who ended up giving the film its highly stylised visual feel. *Ipcress* looked different in every way. Basically it broke every rule in the film director's handbook. Conversations were shot across people's shoulders, dramatic moments through parking meters; there were close-ups on hands and feet, and the lighting was often a law unto itself.

But the whole look was almost an accident. According to Furie, once they had started filming, everyone on the set realised almost immediately that the script didn't do Deighton's book justice. 'It turned a unique book into garbage,' says Furie. And executive producer Charles Kasher agreed. 'You've got to save it,' he told Furie. And so a new scriptwriter was brought in.

By this time things were running behind schedule and so it was a case of rewriting day by day as they filmed. And in the absence of a strong script, the only option, Furie decided, was to give it style – lots of it. 'I just thought to myself, we don't have much of a script but let's give it ambience,' says Furie.

'The style and look of *Ipcress* happened because at that point we all thought it was so pathetic. We knew we had an incredible actor in Michael but we didn't believe in our story. We didn't think anything happened in the picture and it didn't. But way before music videos were around, I just said, "Well, let's give it style." I'd never seen it in any movie, but under the influence of putting Scotch in my coffee, I was free to create. That's what it was. I would just think, OK, let's put a big shoulder across the screen, why not? The Scotch was a godsend, because we were in such a mess in terms of not having a script and having an idiot producer who could only come on the set and upset people. At one point we even burned the script in front of Harry.

'Many a morning I would come in and the pages weren't ready yet, 'cause the writers had been up all night and they still weren't finished. So I would say to Otto Heller, the cameraman, "Listen, we need to kill time. We don't know what scene we're shooting today, but see that staircase – Michael will go up it at some point." So we'd sit there and spend two hours lighting that one staircase. That used to happen all the time.'

Meanwhile the relationship between director and producer was becoming increasingly strained as Saltzman couldn't get to grips with what Furie was trying to do. 'Sidney was breaking his ass to do things in a different way,' remembers John. 'But I was having to tell Harry Saltzman it was OK, because he kept complaining, saying: "How can they shoot that fight scene outside the Albert Hall in long shot? You need to get close in!" And I was explaining to him: "That's the way you do it with a Bond movie. The whole point of this is to do it *differently*. Otherwise everybody'll say it's just another Bond".'

Within a week's shooting though, Furie was at the end of his tether. 'We were filming in Shepherds Bush,' Caine remembers, 'and they had this huge row. Sidney suddenly just burst into tears, walked out and got on a number twelve bus to Marble Arch.' Even Saltzman realised at this point that it might be useful to have the director around, at least till they'd finished shooting, and so, dragging his crew with him, he headed off in pursuit. 'We all ended up getting in Harry's Phantom Six Rolls-Royce,' says Caine, 'and following the bus, with Harry leaning out the window yelling at the bus conductor, "Stop the bus! You've got our director on there!"'

Furie was coaxed back onto the film, but another week later, relations between him and Saltzman had hardly improved. Saltzman wanted to fire him. He was still completely baffled by what he considered the most bizarre camera angles he'd ever seen, but wanted to wait for editor Peter Hunt to get back from his holidays to reassure him he was doing the right thing. 'Peter ran the footage,' says Furie, 'and said to Harry, "You shouldn't fire him, you should kiss him, because this is the most brilliant stuff I've ever seen." All the really big problems were in the first two weeks when he didn't have Peter to tell him what was good, and what wasn't.'

By the time the actual shooting had finished, despite Peter Hunt's advice, Saltzman stuck to his original gameplan and threw Furie off the film. He was going to put the whole thing together with Hunt and that was that. What was more, nobody on the film was allowed to deal with Furie. Everything was to be done via Saltzman.

'Once the movie was put together and edited,' says Furie, 'but before the music, Harry Saltzman told John: "Do not meet with Sidney Furie. Only meet with me." That's how small-minded he was. And John Barry called me and he said, "Meet me at the Pickwick. I'm going to hum you the score." And there over dinner, against Harry's wishes, he went through every cue. He hummed the whole thing, told me what it would be like, told me the orchestration to get any reaction that I had in terms of where music went and all of that. It was one of the nicest gestures I've ever had done to me before or since. Just to bring me in on it was a great act of respect because *Ipcress* was my baby.'

John ended up meeting Furie several times more as the editing went on. 'I would see the film,' says John, 'and then two or three times a week I would have dinner with Sidney and tell him what was happening. And he'd say: "Did they keep that shot in? What about that other one?" It was crazy, but because it was an independent movie and not tied to the studio system, producers could get away with much more than they could have done otherwise.'

Although well aware of the tensions on the film, John had been very busy finding a musical identity for Palmer. With Bond he had concentrated on the action, but this time he built his score around the (anti)-hero. The way he saw it, Palmer was essentially a lonely man, and so what he needed for his theme was a lonely sound.

To John the whole thing was almost like a modern-day *Third Man*. Carol Reed's Orson Welles' classic was one of his favourite films, and Deighton's book conjured up much of the same feel. 'That score just used to kill me,' John reminisces. 'It's the most extraordinary score ever, played on one instrument – the ultimate lesson in simplicity and character. So *The Ipcress File* was like my homage to *The Third Man*. I knew that was how I wanted to do it from the start, but obviously I wasn't going to use a zither.' The zither had that Eastern European feel almost built into it, but the Hungarian cimbalom John had used on *King Rat* would be the ideal alternative.

The cimbalom was a type of dulcimer – a triangular box with strings that you hit with sticks, like an open piano without the keyboard, and it worked on a semi-Oriental scale of half-tones which gave it its melancholy sound. It had traditionally been played by Hungarian Jews or gypsies, but it had also since been discovered by various classical composers, including Stravinsky who had used it to compose. Until John's discovery of it on *King Rat*, however, it had remained unused in either pop or film music. But that would change with *The Ipcress File*.

'With *Ipcress* John really set a style,' says Sid Margo. 'My phone didn't stop ringing after that came out. Everyone in the business was on the line saying: "Sid, where did you get that cimbalom-player? Can you get him for our movie?"' But John's cimbalom sound was not that easily copied. John Leach had demonstrated the different types of sound the instrument could make, and John knew what he wanted. 'After I'd written the theme,' says John, 'I went back to John Leach and he played it, letting all the tones ring out. Sometimes when you play the cimbalom you deaden the tones, but I said, "Let them carry on," so it got that very distinctive sound which I wanted for the movie.'

London's film producers may have thought the cimbalom was key to John's *Ipcress* sound, and it was, to a certain extent. But there was a lot more to it as well. This wasn't just an odd-sounding instrument used to convey an eerie, sinister mood. It did that, but the same way that 'Goldfinger' mixed Bassey's merciless vocal with soaring melody, the warped twang of *Ipcress*'s cimbalom brought us the threat, while the melody itself and those plaintive, insistent flutes gave the whole thing heart. 'The Ipcress Theme' was titled 'A Man Alone', and that whole idea only worked because John's music made us sense that loneliness.

Having written his score, John now needed to make sure it worked with the film once it had all been edited and the sound effects added. 'I worked closely with the sound guys on this. I used to ask: "Is that coffee-grinder going to be whirring loudly through there? What sounds are we going to have?" I'd also check it with Peter Hunt who was editing, since he was in charge of the sound editor too. They'd either say, "Yes, that's gonna be in," or, "No, that's not." So you adjusted them so that we weren't all doing the same thing at the same time. We had to leave space for each other.'

The combination of sound effects with John's music was at its best in the film's brilliant title sequence. The sound of the door, curtains and coffee-grinder were expertly choreographed into the opening chords in a way that made them sound part of it. The way that coffee-grinder manages to grind its beans in key to John's theme has now become well and truly lodged in cult film history, but the machine's presence in the film was pure fluke. 'Charles Kasher, the executive producer, happened to own a mail-order company which sold those coffee-grinders,' says Furie. 'So that's why it was there.' This was product placement before its time. Thanks to John's music, that grinder ended up as one of the most pertinently placed kitchen appliances in film history.

In the beginning, everyone was nervous about the score. 'What people thought on *Ipcress*,' explains Caine, 'was that 'cause Harry Saltzman produced it, we were gonna make a tuppeny-hapenny Bond, and John was going to write tuppeny-hapenny Bond music for it. But what happened took everybody by surprise, 'cause the music was so very, very different to Bond and so clever. It was all Middle European, and so to Western ears it sounded a bit sinister. The unknown is always a bit frightening. And that was why it worked. John always went for the ethnicity of things. If you were to see that picture without the music, you'd realise how much John's score did for it.'

John's score for *Ipcress* was the antithesis of Bond, but as Harry Saltzman had correctly worked out, it was because as the author of the Bond style, John knew how to go the other way. 'We would never have done the whole thing the way we did, had we not come straight off a Bond movie,' says John. 'If I'd come off something else I'd probably have scored it totally differently. The music was kind of strange. It had nothing to do with action music at all. It was all slow arpeggios on the cimbalom and those strange chords.'

Although Caine liked John's music and so did the rest of the crew, Saltzman had different ideas. 'There were huge rows about the music,' says Caine, ''cause I think Harry literally wanted ersatz Bond, and when he heard all this foreign stuff he thought: "Christ! What's this?" But you could talk Harry round anything; his bark was very much worse than his bite and he loved John really. But he always hated everything when he first heard it. He used to wait for other people's approval.

That applied to everything, not just music. He hated what Sidney was doing with the picture as well and that was the cause of all the trouble.

'Harry was a very insensitive man. Whereas someone else would couch their criticism in language that would let you off lightly, Harry would start with: "This is crap!" And it went downhill from there. But John's very tough. He seems like a quiet, thin man, but there's a rod of steel going right up though him. He's very, very tough. And he'll *never* give in when it comes to the music.'

John wasn't prepared to give in on this occasion either. By the time *Ipcress* was completed, no one was quite sure whether the whole thing would work. 'When we saw the picture we didn't know what we'd got,' says Caine. 'We were in the middle of the whole Bond thing and there were cars with jets coming out with poison gas, and I'm coming along with a trolley in a supermarket buying mushrooms. And so it was a gamble. But it was our idea of trying to make a spy a bit more like a spy. Years later a woman came up to me at a function and said, "I used to be a spy, you know, and that film you made was the only one I ever saw which really showed what it was like. I spent more time sitting in cars waiting for people to come out of houses than anything else I ever did".'

But at the time, realism wasn't the producers' main worry. 'The main fear from the executives,' says Caine, 'was that there was this guy in the kitchen doing all this stuff and he would look gay. Because to cook a meal – an omelette – for them was seen as kind of faggy and certainly not something a hero would do. James Bond would never do it. We were at the height of this Bond macho thing and really Palmer was much more of a Nineties man.'

The producers needn't have worried. 'I remember the opening night of *Ipcress*,' says John. 'It didn't have a première, it just opened at the Leicester Square Theatre. Mike came over, and we went to the Pick-wick Club for dinner. On the way there we were in my car, in the E-type, and Mike said, "Look, the film starts soon. Can we just drive past the theatre?" We drove into Leicester Square and there were queues round the whole building. God knows how people get a nose for a movie. An unknown actor in a film with a weird title! But it was a massive hit. Then we went and had dinner, and afterwards, Michael said, "I want to see them coming out." So we phoned the theatre and said, "What time does the movie end tonight?", finished our dinner and got in the car again. We sat outside the theatre for ages watching everybody come out. It was thrilling and Michael was very excited. It was great for him – his first solo movie, first lead role, and it was a hit. Those are the good things that can happen in our business.'

John personally was not nervous at all. 'He was always confident,' says Caine. 'The rest of us were shitting ourselves every time one of our movies opened, but he wasn't. He was the calmest one of the lot. He was probably too tired most of the time!'

The Ipcress File was an instant success. It made Caine a star, leading to his next role – Alfie – and it established John beyond any doubt as the godfather of the spy-music genre. But it didn't end there. Having now created two different types of spy music, the action type for Bond, and the intellectual type for *Ipcress*, you could have been forgiven for thinking it might be difficult to come up with a third without being tempted to imitate or plagiarise himself. But for Michael Anderson's *The Quiller Memorandum* John did just that.

Most of the spy films that were made during this period of spy frenzy were pale Bond imitations or pastiches, but some, like *The Quiller Memorandum*, took a more thoughtful approach. Scripted in characteristically sparse style by Harold Pinter, it was the story of a neo-Nazi insurrection group and a lone British spy's quest to discover the whereabouts of their HQ. Starring George Segal, Alec Guinness and Senta Berger, it picked up on Harry Palmer's sense of isolation and continued the theme of misplaced loyalties.

But instead of returning to that isolation for musical stimulus, John approached this film as a completely new project, to be tackled according to its own requirements. The feel was still Eastern European, but the sentiment behind it was different. John could have centred on the darkness of the Nazi ethos, but instead he decided to come at it from the opposite direction.

And it was from Pinter that he got his inspiration. John and Pinter had actually met many years earlier, as the playwright reminded him.

'We've met before, you know,' he told John.

'Oh, really?' said John politely. 'When was that?' Thinking to himself that surely he would have remembered meeting the by now rather eminent playwright.

'Well,' said Pinter. 'Do you remember when you were with The John Barry Seven doing a season in Nottingham in 1961?'

'Yes,' said John, bemused.

'And do you remember at the digs you were all staying in, there was always one quiet bloke who used to come out to the pub with you all, but never really say anything?'

'Yes,' said John, by now even more confused.

'That was me,' Pinter announced. 'I was at the Nottingham Playhouse in rep. But I was called David Baron then.'

Pinter had obviously moved on quite significantly since his days in Nottingham rep, and with his script for *The Quiller Memorandum* he had strong ideas about the nature of the film. 'I'd spoken to Harold,' says John, 'and he threw me into doing this innocent childlike thing which goes totally against the picture. For him it was all about the indoctrination of youth – how you created young Nazis. And there were all those sequences in the film of lines of kids coming out of the school. So I said, "Let's play this innocence up against this possibly recurring nightmare," and I wrote that melody that was based on an eighteenth-century European lullaby.

'I just went right against the picture. Even when the guy's in the phone booth and gets shot, you still had this gentle melody running, and I think it worked beautifully. It gave the film a haunting, dramatic quality which kept it together.'

John had written a beautiful theme for *The Quiller Memorandum*, but neither the film nor the score were quite in the same league as *The Ipcress File*. With *Ipcress*, John had spawned the Cold War sound, although at the time he didn't realise it. 'I didn't really know that I had, I swear,' says John. 'I just thought we'd kicked into something that was very popular at the time, that had captured the public's imagination. But I didn't think of it as a major thing. I didn't feel there was any kind of profound shift of mood or anything. It just didn't occur to me.'

John's *Ipcress* score and the film stand as classic moments in film history, way beyond merely representing the Sixties' spy fad; unfortunately, the subsequent Harry Palmer films fared less well. With a view to making Palmer a permanent Bond rival, which was what he had always intended, Saltzman made two more Palmer films, *The Billion Dollar Brain* and *Funeral in Berlin*, but there was one fatal flaw in his calculations. He kept Caine, but he didn't keep the rest of the team, and consequently with a different director, different editor and different music, the continuity was lost.

John meanwhile had other projects to worry about. As the sleeve-notes to *The Ipcress File* soundtrack LP pointed out: '[John Barry] . . . is a young man who has already achieved great things in the world of music, and that he is going on to even greater success is beyond doubt.' John would have liked that greater success to take place in Hollywood, for that was still where he thought he needed to be. But changes in the British film industry were already afoot . . . And things weren't going to turn out quite as John had anticipated.

I I

HOLLYWOOD, ENGLAND

Hollywood doesn't generally move. But in the 1960s it did; it relocated to London. John had always believed that to really make it as a film composer, he would have to go to America, to the heart of the industry, but instead, Hollywood came to England.

'I kept thinking I'd have to go to the States,' says John, 'but the Americans started coming here. Because the government was trying to attract industry, they'd worked it out so that if you made money in the UK, you got subsidised. And so you got Bond, The Beatles, and *Born Free* – all over here. I soon started doing American movies in London.'

By 1965, London was irrefutably hip. It was where you went for fashion, where you went for music, and so it was only a matter of time before London became where you went for film too. 'Whatever picture you've got,' said *Time* magazine, 'it's going to shoot better in London.' The idea being that if a film was shot in the capital, it would surely benefit from the glamorous aura of everything else that was going on.

The success of *Goldfinger*, *A Hard Day's Night* and *Tom Jones* was a vital factor in the international belief that London, rather than Paris, Rome or Hollywood, was the most exciting place to be. It was also the most exciting place to make a film. American producers sent not only their own directors to London, but European ones as well, and

[177]

suddenly there was Truffaut making *Fahrenheit 451*, Polanski making *Repulsion* and Antonioni making *Blow-Up*.

London had become the capital of the film world and this meant that John had the chance to work with some of Hollywood's biggest names without venturing past his own front doorstep. On *Born Free*, there was legendary producer Carl Foreman, while on *The Chase*, the equally legendary Sam Spiegel was so keen to employ him that he agreed to pay a Hollywood orchestra thousands of dollars in compensation, so he could use John instead.

Working with people of this stature brought John into the world of serious Hollywood film-making. These men were the main movers and shakers at the heart of the industry, and John's standing benefited by association.

The film industry was finally beginning to understand how useful a hit song could be for a film. It had seen the benefits with The Seekers' 'Georgy Girl' and Cilla Black's haunting 'Alfie'. This new emphasis was good news for John. By the end of 1965, he had not only written 'Born Free', which would turn out to be one of the most successful songs of all time, but he had scored the most expensive Bond film so far – *Thunderball* – and had written another hit song of his own with the title theme.

Hollywood and Britain had been closely connected since the start of the film industry, as the little island across the Atlantic was an obvious market for American output and was also a good source of talent and cheap labour. What happened in the 1960s was merely the culmination of a trend that had been growing for some time.

By the end of World War Two the British film industry was well established and Britain was beginning to be very attractive to American film-makers. Lower labour costs meant that it was cheaper to make films in Britain than in Hollywood, and by 1956 one third of films made in Britain had some sort of American involvement.

The 1950s also brought a new influx of American talent to Britain, as significant figures from Hollywood were forced to flee the McCarthy purges. In Senator McCarthy's attempts to rid his country of Communist sympathisers, he was also unwittingly bolstering the British film industry, sending Joseph Losey, Carl Foreman and Sam Jaffe among others heading off across the Atlantic to London.

By the end of the decade there was an additional incentive for American backers and producers, apart from cheaper labour costs. This was the government's Eady Levy subsidy which offered a percentage return of box-office receipts on any film made in Britain, as long as the cast and crew were predominantly British. This, combined with the fact that London was now the epicentre of international youth culture, made the prospect of working in Britain that much more attractive.

Throughout the 1950s, America had been the source of inspiration for everything new, fashionable and exciting, and culturally Britain had followed its lead. Since the arrival of The Beatles, however, and the new 'swinging' age, the situation had steadily been reversed.

United Artists had led the way with their backing of the massively successful Bonds, Tom Jones and A Hard Day's Night, and by the middle of the 1960s, all the American majors had set up British production subsidiaries with offices in London. The boom had started.

The Hollywood-London fraternity soon became a recognisable social group. Lunches and dinners were invariably held at the White Elephant restaurant in Curzon Street, and when the new arrivals weren't hatching deals, they were playing baseball on Sunday mornings in Hyde Park.

One of the key figures on the scene was producer Carl Foreman who, after looking around for suitable projects, had got together with Columbia to film Joy Adamson's international bestseller Born Free. Since it had first been published in 1960, the tale of lions in captivity had already been translated into twenty-one languages and so it was an obvious choice for a sure-fire success family film.

When it came to the music for the film, though, Foreman and producer Sam Jaffe racked their brains to think who they could get. The film was a family picture, but it was also set in Africa, so the brief was in theory not that straightforward. But it was 'Africa' that provided the answer. Once they asked around, they were soon told about John Barry who had done the Bond films and who, most importantly for

[179]

them, had written for *Zulu*. *Zulu* was set in Africa, and that was all they needed to know.

'I thought *Born Free* was a very old-fashioned movie and I didn't really want to do it,' John says. 'I was asked to do it 'cause I'd just done *Zulu*, and in our business, if you've just done one movie that's set in Africa, they think, Oh, there's another African movie. The fact that one was a historical drama, and this was about a lion didn't make any difference. It didn't cross their minds that the two might actually have nothing to do with each other! It was like: "The whole of Africa's just one big movie location, like Africa's a real small place!'

John was no more convinced once he had seen the film. 'I didn't know anything about the book, and then I saw this movie and I said, "I really don't think I'm right for this. It's like a Disney movie."' He also thought the director's supposedly serious intentions with the film were misplaced. 'The director had really profound thoughts about the picture, but I felt it was just a big, sentimental family romp.' Director James Hill was equally lukewarm about John, but Foreman was adamant. 'We really want you to do it,' he assured John, and so John agreed.

Once he started playing around with some musical ideas, John found he still had major problems getting to grips with what was at best an overtly sentimental, how-hard-can-we-pull-at-those-heart-strings-style bonanza. Finally, he thought of a way he might get round it. 'If I can do it as a pastiche on a Disney-type movie and that whole sentimental thing,' he told them, 'then we're on. That's the only way I can find of doing it, and the only way I can have some fun with it. It'll be a lesson for me as well. I haven't scored a Disney movie before, so it'll be a challenge for me to do something in that vein. But if I can't do it that way, then you'd better find somebody else.'

Foreman duly reassured John that his approach was exactly what he'd had in mind, and so the project was on. The next hurdle, though, was once again over what would be used for the title song. By now, with the success of 'Goldfinger', soundtracks were widely recognised by the film companies as an important tool for selling a film. Producers were paying more attention to the whole notion of a film's theme.

Columbia wanted to get an American folk group to write and perform the title song, but John was insistent: either he wrote the whole thing, title song and all, or he didn't do the film. Foreman finally backed down, and John went off to write. After the days and nights he'd spent battling with 'Goldfinger', 'Born Free' proved a cinch. 'It just came,' he smiles. 'I think I wrote the whole thing from beginning to end in about ten minutes.'

Having written his melody, John needed some lyrics. Leslie Bricusse was by now spending most of his time in America, so John had to find someone new. Years earlier, he had met a song promoter or 'plugger' as they were called, at his music publishing company and had gradually got to know him. Their paths had crossed socially and by the time it came to *Born Free*, the plugger had mentioned to John that he had started writing lyrics. One of these – 'Walk Away' – had been a big hit for Matt Monro, and as John liked the record, he asked him if he'd like to have a go at 'Born Free'. The plugger's name was Don Black and their collaboration on 'Born Free' was the beginning of a long working association.

John had decided that the lyric should focus on the freedom theme, and he already had a couple of rough ideas for lyrics. So after a couple of meetings Black went off to write, and the fact that John knew what he needed made life easier. 'John's very word-conscious,' says Black, 'and that's unusual for most composers.'

Once Black had finished the lyric, John liked what he'd done and thought he was on course to get it recorded. The only problem was that Carl Foreman disliked it. 'There was tremendous controversy about it,' remembers Black. 'I'd made it more of a social comment kind of song, but he wanted a song about lions; I think he was hoping for lyrics about bars and cages.'

In spite of his doubts, John persuaded Foreman to stick with it and so now it was just the old question of who was going to sing it. John wanted his friends Nina and Frederick to do it. 'I thought they'd be ideal casting for it because they were like the offscreen equivalent to Virginia McKenna and Bill Travers and they were pretty successful at the time.' The producers wanted Matt Monro, however, and so, as

John liked Monro anyway, he was brought in to record it, and the song was put in the film.

The controversy wasn't quite over, though. James Hill, the director, and Sam Jaffe, the film's day-to-day producer, had their own thoughts about how the rest of John's score should fit in with the film. 'We need the music to come in really loud as the lions hit the screen,' Jaffe told him.

'Why would we want to do that?' asked John, dismayed. 'The last thing we want is everything happening at once.'

'No,' said Jaffe. 'That's *exactly* the way we need it.'

In despair, John got on the phone to Foreman. 'This whole thing's turning into a nightmare,' he said. 'You're the only one who understands what I'm trying to do here. Can you talk to these people and sort it out?'

Foreman did, and John's score was put in the film the way he'd written it.

It could be said that John's music actually turned out to be more interesting than the film. As with *Zulu*, he had delved deep into the percussion instrument repositories and dug up the best African sounds he could find. 'I wanted real African drums,' he says. 'Not those tom-toms you find in a bongo band.' And having found a huge variety of authentic instruments, John decided to use them on the main theme as well.

'John had a whole bank of tiny little sort of cowbells all tuned up,' says Eric Tomlinson, who engineered the session. 'And he played them along with the strings which gave a very, very interesting sound. The percussionist would just rattle them and follow the tune. It was a great live, open air sound. They were funny instruments, though. If you just struck them haphazardly, they sounded like a lot of budgerigars chirping away.'

John applied the same close attention to detail to the rest of the score. But despite his efforts, Hill remained decidedly unhappy – and wasted no words telling John so in a letter. John hadn't been his first choice as a composer, he wrote, he hated what he'd done, and what was more, he had serious doubts about how the Americans would receive it, once the film got to the States.

As it turned out, the Americans rather liked his score. Within a few months of its release, 'Born Free' – as covered by pianist Roger Williams in mock concerto form, complete with backing choir – was number one in the American charts. But the best was yet to come. In 1966 both the song and John's score were nominated for Academy Awards. His rival nominees were Burt Bacharach for 'Alfie' and Jim Dale for 'Georgy Girl', but John was too busy working in the studio in London to attend, or to pay the whole thing much attention. Besides, as this was long before the days of international satellite TV link-ups, it would be the middle of the night in London, and there was no way of knowing what was going on in Hollywood.

About four o'clock in the morning after the night of the Academy Awards, John's phone rang. Michael Crawford, who had by now become a good friend, was in a play on Broadway and was watching the Oscar ceremony on a telecast. 'John, John,' he said excitedly.

'What is it? What time is it?' asked John, sleepy-eyed.

'Never mind that,' said Crawford. 'You've won an Oscar! You've just won Best Song.'

'Oh,' said John, not quite taking it in. 'Is that right?'

'Yes,' said Crawford. 'Ooh, but hang on a minute . . . the ceremony's still going on . . . wait . . . wait . . . Oh my God, I can't believe it! You've just won another one! You've won Best Score too. It's incredible. You've just won *two* Oscars.'

At the age of thirty-three, John had achieved what many people in films work a lifetime to attain. And most of the time they never get there.

'Born Free' went on to become one of the most successful songs of the century; it was also latched onto by political and religious leaders worldwide. One African state adopted it as its national anthem, 1968 American presidential candidate Hubert Humphrey wanted to use it as his campaign song, preachers across America, according to Don Black, based sermons on its lyric and used it as a baptist hymn, and in 1992 the song was broadcast over the national airwaves during a state of emergency in Thailand.

But if you try to analyse the song's appeal, you keep coming back to John's highly crafted approach to songwriting and structure. By the time *Born Free* was released, pop music had broadened out since the early days of Merseybeat. Motown had happened, psychedelia had blown everyone's mind, and Roger Williams' fellow chart-toppers were the likes of The Four Tops, The Temptations, The Rolling Stones and The Electric Prunes. Yes, ballads were still doing well: Jimmy Ruffin was also in the Top Twenty with 'What Becomes of the Broken-Hearted?', and many of those other hits became pop classics, but 'Born Free' wasn't pop in that way. That was the point. It came from another tradition entirely, and that was its strength.

'I've always had huge successes with things that went completely against the grain,' says John. 'With "Born Free", that song was so old in terms of its concept. It was a thirty-two bar song based in the tradition that had started in the 1920s: first eight, second eight, bridge, last eight. Ninety per cent of all the Broadway tunes and all the popular songs were based on that.

'With "Born Free" the whole thing was very simple. It was a big, open, singable song, until you got to the end of the bridge and then it became kind of interesting. The release had a lovely strain back into the melody and that's the real key thing of how to get back into it with a bit of a surprise. The bridge is very important, and if you learn that early on, you're OK. It's quite an art to write a good bridge 'cause it lifts you into another area. It's got to be a variant on what you've done before but you have to come up with some surprise, so that when you get back to that last familiar strain it's almost like falling into something. I'm still pretty pleased with that bridge in "Born Free". I think that's the best part of it. It's the key to what makes the whole thing work.'

John's double Oscar win had set Fleet Street working overtime. But it wasn't just his Oscars. While the Academy Awards were being dished out in Hollywood, Jane Birkin had been in the London Clinic giving birth to John's third daughter, Kate. 'John Barry has two Oscars and a baby girl' ran the headlines. It had been a memorable week.

Prior to Kate's birth, Jane had been busy pursuing her own acting career. Since their marriage, she had not been content to be merely Mrs John Barry, and as her own professional status rose, she and John were fast becoming the Mick and Marianne of the film world. Over the next year, via a series of high-profile fashion shoots and film roles, she was starting to establish herself in her own right, and although she didn't technically need to work, she definitely wanted to. 'Naturally I don't need the money,' she told the *Daily Mirror*, 'and I could almost be persuaded to do a fantastic role for nothing, but I *need* to act for myself, and my husband knows that too.' Her husband did know, and was often on hand for the odd bit of career advice.

Cult Italian film director Michelangelo Antonioni, along with the rest of the international film community, was shooting his next film *Blow-Up*, in London. Like everyone else, he was intrigued by this 'new' London, and eager to capture it on film. 'This was big news,' says John. 'A huge Italian director deciding to come to London 'cause he was fascinated by what London was – what this society was about. *Blow-Up* was a revolutionary movie when it came out.'

Blow-Up is a darkly surreal tale of a shadowy murder set against the background of a Bailey-esque fashion photographer's 'swinging' lifestyle. Antonioni wanted Birkin to play one of two girls who end up in a nude romp with the photographer – played by David Hemmings. The scene caused a scandal when the film was released: and it is indicative of the values which still ruled that one of the most-talked about aspects of the whole thing was the fact that Jane's husband had allowed her to do it.

'I remember her phoning me,' says John, 'saying, "Antonioni wants me to do this movie, but I might have to take my clothes off. What do you think?" So we went and had dinner with him at Alvaro's in the Kings Road and we discussed the script. I remember him saying in his broken English: "I'm not going to do anything vulgar. I don't do vulgar things." So I told Jane to go ahead. I was protective in as much as I said, "If Michael Winner asks you to take your clothes off – don't do it. If Antonioni asks you to do it, you've gotta trust the guy." I didn't know a single movie Antonioni had made where the sexual activity hadn't been slightly intriguing.' So Jane made the film and took her first step to iconhood.

John's media profile was by now riding high too, and whether it was arriving back at airports from exotic holidays or out on the town, he was a regular fixture in the tabloids. 'Mr Barry wears his Barbados suntan like a success symbol, which is what it is,' wrote the *Daily Mail*. 'His E-type Jaguar is a symbol too, typifying his type of life – Chelsea house, beautiful actress wife, West Indian holidays etc.'

A few months later, *Variety* magazine ran a news story on John's latest composing instrument. The neighbours at Cadogan Square, they reported, were getting 'a bit touchy' about his unorthodox working schedule, and he was therefore having a clavichord hand-made for quiet late-night composing. Not so much had changed, then, since the days and nights of writing 'Goldfinger' when it had been Michael Caine who was trying to sleep, not the neighbours.

While London was enjoying its new status as the epicentre of the international film world, Bondmania remained the biggest filmic cult of the decade.

With the avalanche of spy films being made practically by the minute, you might have thought the whole craze would die off from over-saturation. But on the contrary, the success of *The Ipcress File* and *The Quiller Memorandum* had merely fuelled the public's appetite for spies of every description.

In the summer of 1965 United Artists re-released *Dr No* and *From Russia With Love* as a double feature at American drive-ins, while in Britain all the major newspaper colour supplements ran cover stories on Connery and location features on the making of the next Bond film – *Thunderball*.

Filming had started in France and the Bahamas in the spring of that year; from the start it was apparent that this Bond was going to be the biggest, and most expensive so far. 'Look up! Look down! Look out!' screeched the film posters. 'Here comes the biggest Bond of all! THUN-DERBALL!'

By the time Saltzman and Broccoli were planning *Thunderball*, John was the golden boy composer. 'Goldfinger' had spawned spy-music mania, and the only discussion this time was about what they should call the title song, not who should write it.

This Bond film was going to be bigger, louder and more elaborate than anything that had been seen before. Half of it was to be filmed underwater, and so now John had a new challenge. He'd tackled spy music and invented a style, now he had underwater music to deal with. 'As a lot of the action takes place underwater, I'm trying to create a special sound through the orchestration,' he told the papers that year.

'I can't emphasise enough how important it is to capture the mood of the film. It is not simply a matter of making the music fast when the action is fast, and slow when the pace slackens. But there is no room for half measures. You must go either with the action or against it.

'An example of what I mean will be seen in *Thunderball*. There is a particular scene in the film where the action is as fast as it can be because it takes place underwater. But instead of mirroring that, I went against it – and made the music slower. That way, the scene actually seems faster.'

By now, John was truly on board as part of the Bond team. That meant he was visiting location shoots as an essential preparation for writing a good score. So John flew out to Nassau in the Bahamas. The music and title song hadn't yet been talked about in any detail but sitting on the plane, he was already beginning to have misgivings about writing a song with a title like 'Thunderball'.

'On the plane out to Nassau I picked up a newspaper,' he recalls, 'and *Goldfinger* was everywhere. The Bond thing was in full stride by then and in one article it said that the Italians called Bond "Mr Kiss Kiss Bang Bang". All I knew was that "Thunderball" was the most horrendous title for a song, so I said to Cubby Broccoli, "Let's use Mr Kiss Kiss Bang Bang as the title for the song instead." And he said, "Yeah, go ahead."

'So I wrote this song which was very low-key. I was so far ahead in coolness with that song. It was a much more subtle approach to the whole thing.' And in need of some equally cool lyrics, John called in Leslie Bricusse again. Who duly delivered.

He's tall and he's dark
And like a shark, he looks for trouble
That's why the zero's double
Mr Kiss Kiss Bang Bang.

He's suave and he's smooth
And he can soothe you like vanilla
The gentleman's a killer
Mr Kiss Kiss Bang Bang.

Compared to the rest of John's Bond songs, 'Mr Kiss Kiss Bang Bang' stands alone. Instead of being about the villain, as the rest usually were, this one was about 007 himself, and both John's melody and Bricusse's lyrics had all the shaken–not–stirred sophistication of the man. This one wasn't high drama, this was seductive melodrama, with cocktails, and not pistols at dawn.

When it came to finding a singer, Leslie Bricusse suggested Shirley Bassey. After all, she'd done 'Goldfinger' so memorably, so why not let her do the next one? But Saltzman and Broccoli were keen to keep to their original plan. Each Bond song should be sung by whoever was hot news that year. And in 1965 that person was Dionne Warwick. She'd had a massive hit with her recording of Burt Bacharach's 'Walk On By' and her satiny smooth but chilly vocal style seemed just right for 'Mr Kiss Kiss Bang Bang'.

The song was recorded, but at the last minute United Artists got cold feet. 'We want the name *Thunderball* on the radio,' they said. 'We want it everywhere. *Goldfinger* worked brilliantly because it was the title of the song as well as the movie, so that's what we need with *Thunderball.*'

'But we hardly have any time,' John protested. 'We've got to wrap this thing next week, and *Thunderball* is so abstract to work with. At least with *Goldfinger* we had a villain.' But that was how the producers wanted it, so that was how it would have to be.

By this time Leslie Bricusse had gone off to America to record his own film project, *Dr Doolittle*, and so John was stuck with four days to write a new song, find a new lyricist, a new singer, and get the thing recorded. It was now Friday afternoon. Things had gone well with Don Black on *Born Free*, he thought, so he called him up.

'How do you feel about writing a song called "Thunderball" – *right now?*' said John.

'Fine,' said Black, 'but what does it mean?'

That was not a question John knew how to answer, and the whole thing was a complete last-minute panic. If John had had his doubts about 'Thunderball' as a song title, Black wasn't much the wiser. 'I remember going to my dictionary to look up the word,' he says. 'And of course it wasn't there. I thought, What does it mean? It doesn't mean anything!'

Having resigned himself to the fact that he was writing a song based around a completely meaningless word, Black sat down and came up with a lyric in suitably grandiose Bond style. He also came up with a singer who could give it everything it needed and then some.

'Let's get someone who can really go for a song,' John had urged.

'I think we can get Tom Jones,' said Black, who was still working at Brian Epstein's NEMS Management at the time, and knew people in the pop world.

'Great,' John enthused.

By Monday, Jones had been booked and arrived at Cadogan Square to rehearse. The trouble was, he was saying the same thing as everyone else.

'What does Thunderball mean?' he asked.

'Tom, just sing it – OK?' said John. 'Don't let's get deep. Deep's not what we're looking for here. Just be convincing. Take a note out of Shirley's book and don't worry about what it means. Just sing, and act like you mean it.'

'I can't do that,' Jones objected.

'You've got to,' said John. 'Just sing like hell.'

By the Wednesday he'd got it. 'In the studio', says John, 'he did the whole thing in one take. But when he hit that final note, he literally blacked out and fell off the podium. We went on and did other bits of the song again, but he could never do that bit again, so that was it.'

[189]

So from the producers saying, 'We need another song,' within a week 'Thunderball' had been written and recorded and put to bed. But as John says, 'That's the kind of pressure you get sometimes in a movie. And you have to go with it.'

What they came up with certainly delivered the *Thunderball* punchline and brought the whole concept home with at least one very loud bang. 'You have to be bombastic,' John declares. 'You just have to hit that audience with the idea: "We're in for a good show" – "We're in for an exciting evening".'

And true to his roots, when sitting down and thinking: How shall I do bombastic? it was to classical music that John looked. He didn't sit there and think: Drama? Yeah, that'll be Jerry Lee Lewis. He didn't think: That'll be 'Jailhouse Rock'. He thought: Who's the master of overblown drama? That'll be Wagner.

'"Mr Kiss Kiss Bang Bang" had been a saucy, tongue-in-cheek kind of thing,' says John, 'but "Thunderball" had these mock Wagner pretensions. Wagner was a complete master – those fantastic operas! – and so his style was very suitable for James Bond. Everything was over the top!'

This wasn't subtle. Was anything ever more literal than those alarm bell horns giving it their all every time Jones sang the word 'strikes'? This was Greek tragedy in the age of swing. It was a rollercoaster of anticipation and climax, eking out every inch of drama from every phrase and making it sound like the fight was 'worth it all'. We had romance and tenderness in the middle, then we had sex, revenge and death in the rest. What more could it need?

And when it came to the rest of the score, John's approach was far from half-hearted. 'From the outset,' he says, 'certain basic elements in the series became evident to me. The films put forth a kind of simple, almost endearing comic-strip attitude toward danger, intrigue and romance. The main thing is to carry it off with style; don't belittle the subject-matter or make it cheap. Just give it a whole lot of style and make it sound like a million dollars.'

And it did sound like a million dollars. It was alternately big and brash, and soft and languid in just the right places. John had followed his usual pattern of building the score around the title theme, but this time he had had two title themes to work with. And so although 'Mr Kiss Kiss Bang Bang' was never used as a song, it surfaced in various guises throughout the score, most memorably in the maraca-pulling, margarita-swigging cha cha version 'Death of Fiona' as well as the languorous, vibraphone-filled 'Cape Martinique'.

With 'Switching the Body' and 'Search for Vulcan' John had also created the atmospheric underwater sound he'd been looking for, and in his own inimitable style come up with what sounded like Debussy gone to Spyville. It was classic Bond, classic Barry and in a way it was to become classic underwater. Watch any Jacques Cousteau-style naturementary and see if the music doesn't sound like *Thunderball* somewhere along the line.

Although John's *Thunderball* score is vintage Bond, the film itself was not. *Thunderball* comes across as one of the least exciting of the Sixties' Bond films. It has neither the camp humour of *Goldfinger*, nor the style of *From Russia With Love*. It also includes an over-long underwater battle sequence at the end, which unless you're interested in diving techniques is more than a little tedious. But at the same time it did feature one of the best finales – although its allure may be assisted by sheer relief. Either way it was classic cinema, and once again it was John's use of 'The Bond Theme' brass that made it so. The final shots of Bond flying through the air with the decorative Domino clinging to him – Fay Wray style – as they're airlifted from the sea, are pure comic-strip Bond, and more importantly, pure entertainment.

Audiences at the time obviously agreed. In spite of tepid reviews from the critics, within months of its opening *Thunderball* was in *Variety*'s chart of Top Ten grossing films of all time and cinemas couldn't fit the crowds in. Even with twenty-four-hour screenings.

John's score was a success too. Jones had a minor hit with the title song, and within weeks there were two cover versions out – by Billy Strange and Sounds Orchestral. Jones' version continues to be the definitive recording, however, and has remained untouchable ever since.

★   ★   ★

While the Bond phenomenon raged on, John's profile among the American film-making community had continued to rise. *Born Free* had given him his first taste of working for big-time American producers, and in spite of the hassles along the way, the score itself had been more than successful. His next major American project was one which would give him his first experience of writing an 'American' score – a score set not in Africa or Singapore, but America itself – and consequently it had to have an American breadth that was different from anything he'd done before. It was also to prove an important precursor to what would become one of his most famous 'American' films of all – *Midnight Cowboy*.

In 1966 the famous American producer Sam Spiegel was in London. His credits included *On the Waterfront, Bridge on the River Kwai*, and *Lawrence of Arabia*, and his next venture was a dark, Tennessee Williams-style drama starring Marlon Brando called *The Chase*. Set in America's Deep South, it was shot in Technicolor, scripted by Lillian Hellman and co-starred Robert Redford and Jane Fonda. It was a brooding story of pent-up passions and frustrations in small-town America, and in theory should have been an entirely American production. But Spiegel's decision to use John for the music became the showbiz story of the month.

In 1966 the *Observer* wrote: '*Variety* magazine declares that it's now not only British dramatists, singers and pop groups that are big business in the United States. The sound that every composer is currently trying to recapture is made in England. It comes from John Barry . . . and geographically speaking, it comes from Cadogan Square, Chelsea.'

Spiegel had originally wanted Leonard Bernstein, who had memorably scored *On the Waterfront*, but by this time Bernstein had become a leading figure in the classical music world and was no longer interested in writing film scores. So John was called in to see Spiegel at his London office near Piccadilly.

Spiegel had loved *The Knack*, he told John, and that was why he'd called him in. 'I was very flattered,' says John, 'because *The Knack* was not at all similar to what Sam was looking for with *The Chase*, but he said he loved the style. He felt that I'd been able to pull everything together in a film that was very diverse and scattered. And that was the story with *The Chase*. Although it was set in the Deep South, there were several different layers of stories, and so that was the kind of function he needed.'

Spiegel sent over a print of *The Chase* for John to see, and John got down to work. But the American Musicians' Union was not happy. Not only was Spiegel using an English composer, they complained, but this composer planned to record the whole thing in London with an English orchestra. Spiegel knew he had a problem, but as one of the old school Hollywood mavericks, no way he was going to let a bunch of session-musicians tell him how to make a film.

His solution was masterful. Somehow he managed to persuade the studio to pay a full Hollywood orchestra the equivalent of their daily rates for what would have been the whole session, even though they wouldn't actually be playing a note. The Union, perhaps unsurprisingly, found this an acceptable compromise.

'Spiegel was something else,' smiles John. 'I mean, they really don't make them like that any more. He was wonderful and he had great taste, but he was a real operator and a most manipulative soul. But that's how you make movies. That was how those guys did it.'

When it was completed, the film featured a striking opening sequence designed by Bond title man Maurice Binder, and John's opening music burst forth with all the drama of a Bond film. And as the film unfolded, his stirring mix of plaintive harmonica, expansive wide-open-space orchestral sweeps and frenzied Hammond for the darker party scenes gave the whole thing the Big American feel it needed. *The Chase* may not stand up on its own quite as well as many of John's other scores, but its combination of styles was a foretaste of one that most definitely would: *Midnight Cowboy*.

With the Bonds and *Born Free*, John had proved beyond question that he was a versatile composer who could also write hit songs. There were people around who could do one, or the other – but few who could do both. With *Thunderball* and *Born Free*, John had created title songs and scores that were more memorable than the actual films themselves – and this didn't go unnoticed.

[193]

The success of the Bond films had propelled John to the upper echelons of the film-composing world, and that could easily have prompted him to leave London and emigrate to Hollywood which, after all, was still the industry's hub. But developments in London meant that he didn't have to. This would prove significant for his career over the next few years because London, as well as being the setting for some of the most glamorous and lavish films of the time, was also the source of some of the most daring ones artistically. The kind of films that were not frightened of taking risks – and needed music to match.

12

'CITIZEN BARRY'

In 1968 Hollywood still didn't really understand what John Barry could do. Even though he'd by now won two Oscars for *Born Free*, they saw that as a lucky fluke, and the success of the Bond films as merely a one-off craze. The Americans had long had an in-built scepticism towards their English colleagues and with John's pop music background, many had dismissed him as a young imposter.

The films John scored during the final two years of the Sixties would change all that. His scores for *Deadfall* and *The Lion in Winter* were greeted with respect and admiration, and from then on he was considered in a totally new light by the industry.

'I remember in Hollywood,' says Leslie Bricusse, 'the fraternity of film composers there being very condescending towards John, talking about him as this pop musician who'd been in a band. The top brass there were a bit like a Broadway boys' club who saw John as this kind of upstart. Even when *Born Free* happened, it was seen as a freak success movie which had only been successful 'cause there was nothing much else around that year. It wasn't till John had done *Lion in Winter* and *Midnight Cowboy* that he began to be taken seriously and given real credit.'

John invariably produced his best work when presented with a challenge. The greater the problem, the more daring his solution. He had proved it with *Ipcress* and the sound of the Cold War; he'd done it when presented with what for him was a new genre for *Born Free*, and it was to happen again with *Deadfall* and *The Lion in Winter*.

Deadfall was the culmination of all his work with Bryan Forbes. It was the sixth and final film they would do together, and it was the one that really counted. *Deadfall* is one of the great forgotten Barry scores; of all the films he and Forbes worked on, in many ways this is the best. The film's script required John to write something that could stand up as a bona fide piece of classical music. His 'Romance for Guitar and Orchestra' was a return to his classical music roots and a complete departure from anything he'd done before – and John knew it. 'He was really proud of that guitar concerto,' says Michael Caine, 'because that was the poshest thing he'd ever written. It was real musicians' music.'

With *Deadfall* John turned to the maestro of the Spanish classical guitar canon Rodrigo for inspiration, but with *The Lion in Winter*, he needed look no further than his own early musical training. The film was set in medieval England and John's years studying religious and choral music with Dr Jackson at York Minster really came into their own. But it was a challenge. If *Deadfall* had been ambitious, *The Lion in Winter* was even more so. The film had about twelve times *Deadfall*'s budget, and as well as featuring Peter O'Toole, who since playing Lawrence of Arabia was now a major name, it starred one of the greatest cinematic heroines of all time – Katharine Hepburn.

These films were unlike the stylised triumphs of the mid-Sixties – *The Knack*, *Ipcress* and the Bonds. They had a different level of emotional complexity, and almost without exception centred around darkness, loss and isolation – themes which would inspire John's greatest scores, allowing him to tap into a host of unresolved emotions and give them an outlet. As he had said with *The Knack*, he hated 'happy' music. That was never what he was about.

Anyone can master the ability to express conflict, tension and disharmony in their compositions, but what made John's music unique was the way he managed to do all of that, while giving it compassion too. His strength was the creation of melody, which meant that among the dissonance of his counter-melodies, there was always lyricism at the core.

Deadfall and *The Lion in Winter* were in a new league for John, but that didn't mean he had left his Bond days behind. Creating yet another Bond score could be considered a challenge of its own, for his style was by now so well established that it was almost a dare to keep on and remain fresh. But he did so – and thanks to his relentless perfectionism in the studio, 'You Only Live Twice' emerged as another consummate Bond score and another unforgettable Bond song.

While John had been busy expanding his musical horizons with the Americans in town, life in London had been changing. The 'swinging' London of Mary Quant, Courrèges boots and The Fab Four had given way to the newly psychedelic era. The Beatles had met the Maharishi, 'flower children' rather than Mods were the new sensation, and The Rolling Stones had been arrested on drugs charges. The chemical experience was never part of John's social scene, but the new look that went with it was all around: lapels were getting larger and hair was getting longer.

The Kings Road still raged strong as the centre of the social universe; it was just the trappings that had changed. 'Every Saturday lunchtime everybody you could ever imagine meeting would be in Alvaro's,' says Leslie Bricusse. 'It was just an incredible atmosphere, because we all lived along the same channels, so we'd always all end up in the same places. It'd take you two hours to get down the Kings Road, you just couldn't move down there. And the costumes – the whole street looked like Sergeant Pepper's Lonely Hearts Club Band. The clothes were amazing and excessive – all that Indian jewellery and outrageous fabrics, and that's when the long hair really came in.'

None of this had affected people's creative energy though, and the buzz on the streets and in the restaurants was still very much there. 'London was just one big club,' says antique dealer George Ciancimino. He and John had become firm friends since John had started picking up *objets* and pieces of furniture from his Kings Road gallery, and along with Michael Crawford, the three of them were regular features on the social scene. But the buzz wasn't just about parties. It was still about work too. 'It was different to the way it is now,' says Ciancimino. 'There was this incredible feeling all the time that we could all do anything we wanted to. And it wasn't competitive at all; it wasn't cut-throat. Everyone just got on with doing their thing and there was never any stress about it.'

London was awash with people hatching new projects and plans, and that included John. His idea was to write a stage musical based on Graham Greene's *Brighton Rock*. He approached virtuoso director Joseph Losey, hot from the success of his Sixties classic *The Servant*, and the not-so-classic *Modesty Blaise*, and asked him if he would direct it.

'I'd always loved the book, being a totally fucked-up Catholic myself,' says John. 'It was the most interesting thing in England. The horse-racing gangs in Brighton in the Thirties were the nearest we got to the Chicago gangsters. People were shooting each other, stabbing each other, and *Brighton Rock* dealt with that, with the character of Pinky as this Catholic boy stuck in the middle. But it was such a colourful idea. I met with Graham Greene several times and Wolf Mankowitz was going to do the scenario. Then Graham wanted to write words and he wrote some lyrics which weren't lyrics – they were just literature that rhymed, but he was the sweetest man you could ever wish to meet. My thinking was: America's done *West Side Story*. That was a musical about the gritty side of life. Why can't we do a musical about England in the Thirties, showing what that was about? But England wasn't ready for it.'

While the show was still in the planning stage, Broccoli and Saltzman were on the phone to John. They were preparing the next Bond film and were presuming that he'd want to be a part of it. For John, though, the novelty of the whole Bond concept was beginning to wear thin, and although *Thunderball*, *Ipcress* and *The Quiller Memorandum* had all been box-office and critical successes, he was doubtful about the artistic merit of his Bond scores and keen to tackle something new and more ambitious. When asked by the press at the time how he felt, he said: 'Yes, it's worked out, hasn't it? But I'd be daft to regard Bond as an

[198]

artistic achievement. The stuff which has been most successful is really million-dollar Mickey Mouse music. I'll call it an artistic triumph if my score for a stage musical of *Brighton Rock* comes off, or if I'm not too old to write a ballet.'

As it turned out, the musical didn't come off and John was enticed back into what would become the fifth Bond film. Fleming's twelfth novel *You Only Live Twice* was chosen as the follow-up to *Thunderball*, and if the underwater extravaganza had been lavish, this one was to be even more so. The budget for *You Only Live Twice* was an astronomical $9.5 million, nearly as much as for all four previous Bonds put together. Filmed almost entirely on location in Japan, it featured Ken Adam's most elaborate sets so far, and took the longest time to make. The media consequently went into overkill, sending reporters out to cover the minutiae of each day's filming while canny tour operators, eager to get in on Bondmania, organised bus tours out to locations. In spite of the media frenzy or perhaps because of it, Sean Connery, like John, was having doubts about doing yet another Bond film. He was getting seriously worried about being typecast and was hesitant about playing 007 yet again, but in the end he, too, gave in.

By this time, just as the Bond budgets had grown, so had Eon, the company originally set up by Saltzman and Broccoli to make *Dr No*. 'You'd go to see Harry,' recalls Lewis Gilbert, 'and he'd be getting his hair cut and having a suit made while he was talking to you. And there'd always be at least five people hanging around outside to see him, bringing him updates on hare-brained schemes that never came to anything. Harry was a man of intuition and he was always buying into new systems and ideas. Cubby was always much more conservative. He was very stable and great fun to be with. If people went to him with crazy projects, he just used to say "Look, I only know about film."'

Gradually though, mostly thanks to Saltzman, there were more and more people on the Eon payroll, and as Saltzman had always had a problem making decisions when it came to music, he decided to hire a Musical Supervisor. 'Harry had cloth ears,' says Guy Hamilton, 'and

[199]

somewhere along the line, he was probably shrewd enough to realise it.'

The unfortunate result was that John now had to put up with a third party making comments about his music. It was totally unnecessary. By this time John had proved himself more than capable of handling the music on his own. 'John's a very efficient guy,' says Gilbert. 'If he says he's going to do something, he does it. So there's no way he would have needed someone looking over his shoulder, checking on him.' Broccoli also doubted the necessity of the whole thing, saying to Saltzman: 'I don't think John needs a Musical Supervisor. I think he's fine on his own. Why does he need help?' But his partner was insistent.

So the Supervisor was brought in, and almost immediately there was trouble when it came to the eternal wrangle over the title song. John had written the heart-wrenchingly gorgeous 'You Only Live Twice' with Leslie Bricusse, and the question as usual was who to get to sing it. 'The Jiminy Cricket guy' as John called the Musical Supervisor, wanted to bring in a new young soul singer he'd heard called Aretha Franklin, but John didn't feel her vocal style was right for the song. As he says: 'Casting a song is terribly important. It's like casting a movie. You could have a good song, but if you get the wrong person doing it, you're dead.'

Broccoli and Saltzman had meanwhile looked around the charts and noticed that Nancy Sinatra had just had a major hit with 'These Boots are Made for Walking' and as Broccoli was an old friend of Sinatra Senior, and Ms Sinatra's godfather, they didn't have to look much further.

All did not go smoothly when it came to the studio, however. Sinatra may have just had a hit, and may have had an impeccable vocal pedigree, but when it came to the actual delivery, the fact that she was not in the league of a Bassey or Jones was evident. She was also very nervous in the studio. 'That was a scary experience,' she told the papers. 'Cubby Broccoli has known my mother and father for years. Then the London Philharmonic were playing on the session, so it was real pressure.'

And the fact that the song itself was quite demanding vocally didn't make her life any easier. ' "You Only Live Twice" was a real stretch for Nancy,' says John. 'As a song it's kind of all over the place, and the bridge is particularly difficult, so all in all it was a bit of a reach for her. What's now in the movie was made up of about twenty-four takes. It was a real masterpiece of editing. There was just no way that we'd ever have got it in one take. She'd get one bit right the first time, but then she'd get another bit wrong. So that was what we call "a glue job" – the whole thing.' But Sinatra at least was aware of her limitations. 'She knew,' says John. 'She'd say: "That's a good bit there, you can cut that in, John, can't you?" She didn't have any illusions about it.'

After some adept editing the whole thing was put together, and it sounded good as new. John's approach to the song had been softer than his previous Bonds, because this time the plot was more romantic than usual. 007 actually gets married, albeit in the service of his country, and it was a change, so John set out to reflect the softer, more lyrical style in his score. Bricusse had similarly picked up on the poignancy of John's melody and come up with the gloriously existential, 'And love is a stranger/Who beckons you on. Don't think of the danger/Or the stranger is gone.' It was as classy as John's music.

From a lyricist's point of view, John was great to work with. He automatically understood a song's requirements – melodically, lyrically and structurally. 'John's a very stylish fellow,' says Leslie Bricusse. 'That always affected everything, from his home furnishings and his clothes to his music. He always had very good taste, and I never once needed him to change anything to suit a lyric. He was instinctively a very good architect of a song.'

You Only Live Twice and the next Bond film *On Her Majesty's Secret Service* together became the most romantic of John's Bond scores. In both films Bond gets married, the second time for love, and the scores reflect that. When it came to orchestration on *You Only Live Twice* therefore, John's score was characteristically lush. Throughout his career, particularly in his post-Sixties work, strings would become an instantly identifiable element of the Barry style. They had been there from the start with the 'stringbeat' style, but it was how he used them later on that made his scores unique. In spite of having studied brass himself, strings had always appealed to him as the ultimate means of conveying emotion.

'Strings are the most expressive instrument in the world and I love them,' says John. 'They carry such a weight with them, they're the definitive thing. They touch you. The whole string section of an orchestra is quite the most phenomenal group that you could ever use. The vividness and variety of expression that you can get out of the strings is quite astonishing. Next to the human voice it's the most expressive instrument; that's why I use them.'

When it came to going into the studio, John's fixer Sid Margo had by now built up a regular cast of top session players who knew the score in more ways than one. 'We always knew,' says Don Lusher, trombonist. 'If we got a booking for a Bond session with John, it'd be, "Oh yes. That'll be another week of F minor then." It was always F minor. You could bet on it!'

But in spite of a certain predictability, John was respected and popular with both his musicians and his engineers. 'We always admired John's writing,' says CTS engineer Eric Tomlinson. 'He tended to write in a certain key and it was so effective. It hit that colour right on the nose every time and it was different to the run-of-the-mill things we'd been doing up till then. It created a totally different approach to writing for that type of film.'

John's scores always sound as if they've been honed and perfected ad infinitum, and that's because they usually have. 'John was always very meticulous on the sessions,' continues Tomlinson, 'to the point of absolute frustration from everybody else's point of view. He couldn't make up his mind. He'd say, "Well, we'd better do another one just in case," and I think we did twenty-one takes on the main titles. Take three was normally more than adequate for the director of the film, the producer and the musicians, but it was never right for John. In the end we'd usually wind up using a bit of the last take and a bit of the third one. We'd nearly always end up chopping a few things together.

'In those days before the advent of multi-tracking recording, it had to be right when it was played. When he came in for the playback, that was the finished soundtrack. There was no messing about saying we can fix it later, redo it tomorrow. It had to be right, so we did do a lot of takes, but that was par for the course.'

Although *You Only Live Twice* featured an unforgettable title song, as well as 'Capsule in Space' – later to become better known as 'The Space March' – the score itself didn't reach the heights of John's subsequent *On Her Majesty's Secret Service*, and in some ways neither did the film. In spite of direction by *Alfie*'s Lewis Gilbert, and a script by Roald Dahl, Connery's dwindling enthusiasm for the role was becoming apparent on screen and the gadgetry was becoming more and more fantastical. But as far as the public were concerned, that was half the fun of it, and they didn't seem remotely put off. Spy fever was clearly still raging hard, and despite the simultaneous release of rival Bond extravaganza *Casino Royale*, audiences opted firmly in favour of the real thing. The alternative had been made as an elaborate, twelve-million-dollar spoof, but misfired badly on all cylinders. To create a memorable pastiche you need to home in on the core element of the original, and with *Casino Royale*, they didn't even come close. Burt Bacharach's wacky caper score, apart from featuring one classic song called 'The Look of Love', had literally nothing to do with Bondness, and the whole thing quickly descended into an over-elaborate bore. The genuine Bond article had definitely won the spy game.

While John had been busy being the musical arm of James Bond, he had also continued his other long-term partnership with Bryan Forbes. Since doing *King Rat*, John had worked on another two films for Forbes, *The Whisperers* and *The Wrong Box*. *The Whisperers* was a small, black and white drama starring Edith Evans as a lonely, elderly woman who hears 'whispers' around her. There was pathos in this story, with malevolence creeping around in the shadows, but the whole thing was a marvel of restraint. Typically of Forbes' style, it managed to say a great deal without labouring its subtext, and that was really what Forbes had always done. It was also the essence of John's music and maybe that's why the partnership worked so well. But although Edith Evans was nominated for an Academy Award, the film itself did very little.

The Wrong Box was completely different – a lavish, colour comedy bonanza, set in supposedly Victorian London, featuring a Who's Who of Sixties' British comedy, from Peter Cook and Dudley Moore to Peter Sellers and Tony Hancock. It also starred Michael Caine, who since doing *The Ipcress File* had played Alfie, and thereby become a major-league star. But even this wasn't enough to save it. In theory it had every reason to be hilarious, but instead ended up being a kind of pale forerunner to Monty Python-type farce which just never really quite worked. In Britain it was consequently a disaster at the box office, although abroad its caricature *Quality Street* Englishness ensured it reasonable success.

Deadfall was a different story, though. Set entirely in Majorca, it again starred Michael Caine, this time as a jewel thief who gets emotionally ensnared in a complex three-way partnership. It was shot in colour, and was heavy on visual style, but instead of merely reflecting that style, this time Forbes' requirements for the music were more demanding.

'*Deadfall* posed a major problem for both John Barry and me,' says Forbes. 'I had written into the screenplay a long robbery sequence running some seventeen minutes without benefit of dialogue, and the actual robbery had to be timed against a concert performance. The music for the concert performance had to do two things: firstly it had to underline, dramatically, the action and at the same time it had to stand alone as a major piece of music, capable of being performed by a renowned symphony orchestra and a star soloist. In addition, since the concert was to be cross-cut with the robbery, I had to film a complete musical performance.'

John and Forbes discussed the form the concert music would take and finally agreed on guitar as the solo instrument. The London Philharmonic Orchestra and Spanish classical guitarist Renata Tarrago were booked, and John now just had to sit down and write. He felt inspired, not daunted, by the challenge. This was the first time he'd been commissioned to write a piece of music that was actually intended to stand up in its own right. His scores had usually done that anyway, once they'd been adapted for soundtrack albums, but this one had to do that from the start.

John shied away from calling the piece anything too grandiose. 'He felt that it would be too pretentious to to call his work a concerto,' says Forbes, 'so instead he elected to write what he termed "A Romance for Guitar and Orchestra".'

Calling it that at least made it easier in John's mind, but really he needn't have worried. After six or seven weeks' writing, what he came up with was probably the most ambitious single piece of 'serious' music he'd written so far, and what's more, it met Forbes' requirements beautifully. It worked with the action, but it still stands up as a dramatic, atmospheric work for guitar and orchestra.

Writing the piece was a triumph for John, but recording it was a thrill too. John once said that there were two things in life that gave him the biggest kicks – sex and conducting his own music. The buzz he got from conducting an orchestra was enormous. For his close friends it seemed as if he almost changed personality as soon as he mounted a podium.

'I remember going down to the studio,' says Michael Caine, 'and it was quite amazing. There he was like Leopold Stokowsky conducting this great big orchestra, doing it beautifully and absolutely loving it. It wasn't like the guy I knew. It was some kind of mirage. But then he went back to being John again immediately afterwards.'

The 'mirage' ended up being captured on film as the concert performance had to be filmed to playback, and so John, feeling nervous once again, came to make his extended cameo appearance conducting the orchestra. The concert was beautifully shot, John generating cool from every pore, while Renata Tarrago, elegant, poised and attractive, lent further glamour to the scene. Some critics felt that the way Forbes intercut between Caine's jewel heist and the concert slowed down the action, but in fact it works rather well, doing what it was supposed to – adding to the tension.

Deadfall was a stylish film. It looked great all the way through, featured a strong central performance from Caine, and the end sequence, although it owed a lot to Hitchcock's *Vertigo*, provided an equally stylish conclusion. But in spite of all that, and maybe due to a flaccid performance by Giovanna Ralli as the central love interest, the public were not enthusiastic. Not about the film at any rate. 'When the film came out,' says Michael Caine, 'people talked more about the music than the film. It was often like that with John. He never did any duff music, even for a duff movie. 'Cause *Deadfall was* a duff movie – with great music in it. I think the LP made more money than the picture.'

The *Deadfall* soundtrack probably did, as it featured not only the 'Romance for Guitar', but also John's own Spanish symphonic pop track, 'Statue Dance'. For the party sequence in the film itself, John had ended up trawling through his own back catalogue, and lo and behold, what did we have but wealthy Majorcan sophisticates grooving in fancy-dress to 'Beat Girl'. The reason was technical rather than humorous, though. 'We recorded a band out of Majorca,' says John, 'and thought they had clearance for the tunes to be used in the film, but later found out they didn't. So we had to find some music in a hurry which was owned by the publishers. In the end, 'cause it was a last-minute thing, the only piece I could think of was "Beat Girl", so that's what we ended up with.'

More interestingly though, *Deadfall* also included a stupendous title theme sung by Shirley Bassey called 'My Love Has Two Faces'. On first hearing it, your immediate thought is, Oh yes, another Bond song, but maybe that's just because Barry plus Bassey spells Bond. But this was Bond on an Awayday – there was the sensuality and ache, but this time John had left the action at home. It had a melody to literally die for, and lyrics by old-school Sinatra writer Jack Lawrence. Then on top of that there were *From Russia With Love*-style strings encasing Bassey's yearning, pent-up-passion-and-despair vocal; the combination was hotter than Madrid in August. As Bryan Forbes memorably said in his sleeve-notes for the soundtrack album: 'It was snowing in London when we recorded Shirley's vocal, but as always, she raised the temperature the moment she started to sing.'

The theme song was recorded in London, but while scoring the film, John had gone out to Majorca with Forbes and the rest of the crew, and had been enchanted by the countryside. Near the Bay of Alcudia, they had met the local Count, an English-educated, urbane Frenchman, who lived in a vast, crumbling *parador*. According to John's friend Pete Varley, the Count bore more than a passing resemblance to the old

Hollywood actor Fernando Lamas. He provided a lavish open house, frequented by a mêlée of passing adventurers, models, actors and jetset travellers. John was soon smitten by the Majorcan life, and when the Count mentioned that the land on the next hill was up for sale, he lost no time in buying it. In true maverick style he later built his own fantasy lair there, and 'Casa Barry' would be the perfect getaway from the London frenzy.

Set in three and a half acres, amid almond and orange trees, John designed the house in mock-Alhambra high style, with four Moorish towers, an interior cloistered courtyard and a sixty-foot drawing room overlooking the Bay of Alcudia. 'We called it the Majorca Hilton,' says Leslie Bricusse. 'When we first went there, it just had these two enormous twin towers completed and one wing, but it was already the full Don Quixote folly. Never mind Citizen Kane – this was Citizen Barry. It was going to be the greatest pleasure palace on earth, that was John's dream. He just had this wonderful fantasy of how it was all going to be.' John and Jane began to fly out to Majorca whenever they could, but John's frantic working schedule meant that visits weren't that frequent. There was work to be done, and the work was in London.

Although John's most interesting films were for British directors, it was still American money that was funding them all. And his next and most ambitious project so far was to come via yet another American producer. It was 1968, and Joseph E. Levine was in London planning a film with Peter O'Toole; he wanted John to write the music. The film was called *Ski Bum* and was about a ski instructor, but to John, the script looked far from promising.

'It was the worst script I've ever read in my life,' says John, 'about this awful romance in the Swiss Alps. I couldn't understand why Peter O'Toole would be interested in doing a picture like that and finally he declared he wasn't going to.' This left Joseph Levine and his producer Martin Poll with a budget, a lead actor and a composer, but no script. But at that point, Poll suddenly remembered a script he had been given, based on a play called *The Lion in Winter*.

Set in the twelfth-century English court of Henry II and Eleanor of

Aquitaine, it was a verbal tour de force in which the Royal couple and their children battled out a complex web of power struggles, political intrigues and incestuous family feuds. It was riveting, and Peter O'Toole liked it so much that he immediately decided Levine and Poll should film this instead. He would play King Henry and for his Queen, he would call in the first lady of razor-sharp dialogue – Katharine Hepburn. Now all they needed was a director. And it was John who would suggest the ideal person for the job.

The previous year John had worked on a one-hour, tiny-budgeted British film called *The Dutchman*. John had scored this low-key, black and white tale of racism on the New York subway for virtually no money as a favour to the director – Anthony Harvey. Harvey was well known in the British film industry as a top-class editor and had worked extensively with both the Boulting Brothers and Bryan Forbes, and that was how he'd met John.

Although in subject-matter *The Dutchman* was worlds away from *The Lion in Winter*, John had been impressed, and recommended the film to O'Toole, Hepburn and the producers, saying: 'Look at this. I think this guy could be just perfect for our film.'

'I hoped they would see what the director was capable of doing, and they did,' says John. 'They thought *The Dutchman* was terrific.' And so Harvey was on board.

For John, the prospect of writing a score for an international-scale, big-budget film set in medieval England was the biggest challenge faced so far, but as he'd done with Bond before, he found the solution by going back to his roots.

'When *The Lion in Winter* came along after the Bond movies,' says John, 'everyone thought that was a strange departure for me. Actually, the Bond movies were a departure for me. Writing *The Lion in Winter* was a labour of love.'

As the composer, John had to pick out one central aspect of the film on which to base his score, and then another which would give him the style. With *The Lion in Winter*, the core was obviously discord and conflict, and for the style John drew on the power of the Church of Rome. Even though in terms of the script, this only became evident briefly towards the end of the film, it was a powerful notion and gave his score a strong extra dimension.

Drawing on those years as a teenager with Dr Francis Jackson at York Minster, John unearthed everything he had learned about religious and choral music. 'I loved the chance to do a choral score,' he says, 'because I'd studied choral music, but rarely is there an opportunity to write that kind of material. It was a great experience. The Bond pictures are technically very difficult because they're right down to split-second timing, whereas something like the score for *The Lion in Winter* is much broader, not so technical; it's more or less an overall dramatic feel, rather than a specific picture, music and action feel, as the Bond pictures are.'

What John came up with was a complete departure from anything he'd done before. The score showed a maturity and refinement far beyond his previous work, from its driving *Carmina Burana*-style main title to the sombre, melancholy male voices of 'To Rome'. John's triumph, as with his earlier work, was to create a score that added something of its own to the images on the screen, without distracting from them. The music did everything the script demanded – it evoked strife and struggle, but it also held a mirror up to the castle where human warmth had long been shut out.

Taking the purist approach to medieval music would almost certainly have alienated audiences, so what John did was to combine what he'd learned at York Minster with the modern instrumentation and recording techniques that he knew would give him the driving sound he wanted. The opening title had an emphasis on rhythm that had only been glimpsed at in some of John's Bond cues, and he achieved this by his arrangement and by the use of a Moog synthesiser to weld it all together.

'I used a Moog on the bassline to that driving opening to give it a ruthlessness. You can use timpani and bass on that traditionally, but the synth gave it that ballsy kind of thing. It was just back enough so you wouldn't say "that's electronic", but it gave an edge to the pulse. I'd been listening a lot to this album which was one of the best-selling albums in America at the time – *Switched-on Bach* – which was that whole synthesiser interpretation of Bach's music. And I thought that was fantastic – the force of those Bach basses on that were amazing. So I used it, but not all the way through. Only in select places where it was right.'

Once John's score was completed, Katharine Hepburn loved it, and more importantly, so did director Anthony Harvey. 'So few composers write melody,' says Harvey, 'and John always had this wonderful feeling for the film without showing off, and that's what he did for *The Lion in Winter*.' Harvey was thrilled with the music, but he was also thrilled, as Bryan Forbes had been before, with John's flexibility and professionalism. 'He was wonderful for a director,' says Harvey, 'because he would come to a music session and if a bit didn't work, he would say, "fine", fly off to the piano and *make* it work. He was just a joy to work with because he had this enormous generosity, and so often whenever I've done music sessions with other people you invariably end up being stuck with something you don't like. John was always such a wonderfully sensitive fellow, and nothing was ever a problem with him.'

The Lion in Winter won John his third Oscar for Best Score as well as the British Film Academy's Anthony Asquith Award, and the score finally made the Hollywood top brass sit up and take notice. This would eventually have significant repercussions on his future career, but for the time being, there were other changes on the home front.

By the end of 1968, John's marriage to Jane was over. He had been keen for Jane to take time out from acting and go to drama school. 'I'm a composer,' he told her. 'I'm earning terrific money, so you don't need to work. Learn how to be an actress, learn how to do it right. If you can be Katharine Hepburn or Audrey Hepburn, that's class, and I think you can be that, but you have to learn what that is.' But Jane had other ideas.

John had also by this time bought another flat in Cadogan Square to work from, and that proved the death knell to the relationship. His frantic working schedule and equally frantic social life meant that he was very rarely around, and finally their marriage buckled under the strain.

Jane Birkin eventually went to France with young Kate, where she soon met Serge Gainsbourg and began a new life. Back in London, by spring of the following year, John had moved out of Cadogan Square and into a vast penthouse-style apartment overlooking the Thames on the south side of the river. The flat was on the eleventh floor of Alembic House and had panoramic views across London from just about every corner. John eventually sold it to Jeffrey Archer, who still lives there, but at the time it had become a minor film-world colony. Stanley Baker lived in the flat above, while Richard Harris lived in the one below, so even though the Kings Road was no longer on John's doorstep, he didn't have to look too far for drinking partners. Along with the new flat, John also had a new girlfriend – Jane's friend, Ingrid Boulting, the nineteen-year-old adopted daughter of film director Roy Boulting, and the model who would later adorn a thousand teenage bedrooms as the Biba girl.

John now had a new home, a new relationship and there were still more changes ahead. There were new projects to discuss practically every day, each one posing a different creative problem. Musically, John had risen to all the challenges that had been set him, and had done so each time in his own singular way. The prevailing sound of sitars and psychedelia had virtually no impact on him; apart from his days with The John Barry Seven and Adam Faith, John had carried on in his own filmic universe, writing timeless songs and classic melodies which drew on traditions which were far older than contemporary pop styles. But he hadn't left his pop sensibility completely behind. Not yet. It was still to serve him rather well in his final films of the Sixties.

13

WE HAVE ALL THE TIME IN
THE WORLD

Try watching *Midnight Cowboy* without John's music and you'll lose a vital part of what the film's about. From Bond onwards, John delved into the essence of each film he tackled to give it another dimension. So much so, that all the way along, his music became inextricably linked in the audience's minds with the images it related to. He'd created an audio-visual language all of its own which people the world over instinctively understood: Bond brass meant car chases and danger, cimbaloms – the Cold War . . . the list went on.

What John had done went directly against the old adage that film music shouldn't be noticeable. On the contrary, John always believed that it had a specific function and could become an intrinsic element of a film in its own right. 'This old wives' tale that if you notice the music it's bad is wrong,' says John. 'There are whole areas of *Midnight Cowboy* where the director decided to go with the music, and it's part of the framework of the entire picture. The same with Tony Harvey in *The Lion in Winter*. There are moments of, if you like – repose, when a sequence shot that way with music gave you a complete, added dramatic tension that otherwise wouldn't have been there.'

John's ability to add significantly to a film had become one of his major selling points as far as directors were concerned. They also saw that what you got from a Barry score was never standardised or predictable. John's enthusiasm for film meant that he tackled each project afresh, and consequently each score sounded different and tailor-made for its film. It was this versatile approach that set him apart from his contemporaries.

'John cornered the market,' says Lewis Gilbert, 'because there just wasn't anyone else around like him. Everyone wanted John, because they knew that whatever the film was, you could call on him and get what you needed, and that he'd make a definite contribution as well. The other composers who were around just didn't have the same attitude. I remember going to see Michel Legrand about a film, and he pulled six themes out of a drawer and said, "You can have something like this, this or this." John would never do that. He'd never talk about music till he'd seen the film.'

By the end of the Sixties, the diversity and strength of John's work had made his reputation unshakeable, and this meant that there was an ever greater choice of projects for him to work on. The end of the decade saw a great flowering of all the promise and opportunity that it had offered up. It also – inevitably – signalled change, and as the American film industry began to fall into decline, it was only a matter of time before London, its biggest financial beneficiary and outpost, would feel the effects. Soon Hollywood, America was once more the home of film.

On a personal front, the end of the decade for John meant the final culmination of everything he'd been working towards. *On Her Majesty's Secret Service* was the last Bond film of the Sixties; with his score for it, John reached the pinnacle of the musical style he himself had created. But apart from Bond there were other ventures – some successful, like John's move into TV themes with *The Persuaders*, others less so, like his ditched attempts at musicals and film producing. But it was his very last film of the decade that proved not only one of his most monumental, but also the one which would point him in an entirely new direction.

Midnight Cowboy continued the core themes of loneliness and isolation which had by now established themselves as key to John's best work, but it also pointed to America, which within a few years would become John's new home.

★   ★   ★

[213]

John's Oscar-winning success had given him a phenomenal sense of achievement, of having finally arrived, in every sense of the word. He had proved he had a lot more to him than just another Bond score, and he was ready to branch out, not just in tackling new film challenges, but in the role he played as well. Along with the idea of doing musicals and ballets, John by now knew so much about the working process of film-making, that if he wasn't going to direct a film, producing one made sense. He had toyed with the idea of directing, but had decided that his nature was not rumbustious enough, gregarious enough, or even diplomatic enough to juggle the demands of cast, crew and producer. Producing, on the other hand, could be creative but less demanding.

He had chanced upon a short story by the Argentinian fantasist and original *Blow-Up* writer Julio Cortazar called *On The Speedway* and thought it would make a great feature. It was about the scenarios that develop in the traffic jam to end all traffic jams, and its working title was therefore 'The Jam'. He brought in director Anthony Simmons to direct it, his old *Goldfinger* title pal Robert Brownjohn to design it, and literary legend William Golding to write the script. There were even plans for Jane Birkin to act in it. And the music wouldn't exactly be a problem. John had talked to Golding and together they had begun hatching plans to do something based on the *Switched-on Bach* John had been so impressed by in America. The whole thing was an exciting move for John and a new departure, and he and Simmons set off around Britain researching possible speedway locations. They even talked about going to Brasilia to film there, but all this needed money. John had already sunk a large amount of his own finances into the project, but he needed a distributor and backer to fund the bulk of it. Film companies, however, were not as enthusiastic as John and as nobody was ready to finance it, the project was shelved, although the germ of the story later surfaced as Jean Luc Godard's *Weekend*.

There were other projects on the go for John which weren't shelved, although perhaps with hindsight they should have been. First was *Boom*, which seemed to defy all odds and end up being catastrophically bad. Joseph Losey directed it, Tennessee Williams wrote the script, it starred Elizabeth Taylor and Richard Burton, as well as a cameo by Noël

Coward, and had a John Barry score. Somewhere along the line something went drastically awry, and the result was a pretentious bore, with Burton declaiming, 'Boom! – the shock of each moment of still being alive' as waves crash thunderously against rocks. Musically, there were only about five minutes of John's score throughout the whole thing anyway, and its barrel-organ motif sounded as if the score had lost its way and wandered in from a neighbouring film set. All in all, *Boom* was a disaster from start to finish.

Next was Sidney Lumet's *The Appointment*, which this time was a case of a great theme in search of a film. Omar Sharif was at his dewy-eyed, simpering worst, while Anouk Aimée mooched around for two hours trying to look mysterious in a sub *Belle de Jour* plot. John's haunting Mozartian score spent the whole film waiting in vain for something to happen to justify it. Once the film was completed, the producers had the wisdom to realise something was amiss. Thinking maybe they could solve their problems by replacing the score, they commissioned the American Stu Phillips to write an alternative.

'You know, when in doubt, when a movie doesn't play too well, the first thing they do is rush to the music,' says John, 'which is of course the *last* thing they should do. It's like, "Oh yeah, the music is going to make *all* the difference." You should go back to the original script and find out why you bought it in the first place. But they always think your music is the problem, because it's about the only thing they *can* change. By that time, everything else is a lock.' The film subsequently died a death anyway, but there are still two prints in circulation, both of which credit Stu Phillips as composer, but one of which features John's score.

By this time in his career, John was reaping the rewards for all his hard work. Along with the luxury flat with the luxury antique furniture, John now had the luxury car to match. He'd bought a Citroën Maserati – one of the fastest cars in the world. Not that he was interested in racing it anywhere, or even attempting to tear around London in it. On the contrary, friends of the time don't seem to remember him ever driving anywhere. It was just fun.

'John would never have bought a Rolls-Royce or a Bentley, even though he could have done so easily,' says George Ciancimino. 'You see, that wouldn't have been fun, and the Citroën was. That's what it was all about.'

His personal celebrity status continued to attract media attention, with the papers eagerly photographing 'Britain's most successful composer of film music' at airports, arriving back from Majorca with girlfriends. The press were fascinated by his lively personal life, and even John's outings with his by now seven-year-old-daughter Susie from his first marriage to Barbara Pickard, were considered newsworthy. 'Susie,' they reported, 'is taken out to the sort of London restaurants which are always full of actors, photographers, models and similar "today" folk, and treated to steak, followed by strawberries and cream.' One journalist who was obviously rather impressed by John described him saying: 'Mr Barry is treacherously likeable. He can look like a nineteenth-century poet – smokey, steel-framed specs, ruffled shirt, high-buttoned waistcoat . . . an aura of inscrutable romance calculated to make any girl feel like Jane Austen. He is dreamy, secretive and curious . . . and dismisses his private life as "just one of those things".'

But John's life wasn't all wine, women and film song. There were also quieter, darker times when John just stayed in. He had always been an avid reader, and Ciancimino remembers him going through a long phase of reading nothing but biographies of the great composers. 'It struck me as an act of great humility,' says Ciancimino. 'There he was, having written all this wonderful stuff, but he was still so keen to learn everything he could about how the great masters worked and what made them tick.'

At the end of 1969, John gave the press something worth writing about when they found out that he'd got married again. John had recently broken up with Ingrid Boulting, and it was thanks to Ciancimino that he met his next leading lady. Ciancimino was going out with a model at the time, and seeing that his friend was feeling low, he suggested to his girlfriend that she bring a friend along for dinner. 'So she brought this friend – Jane Sidey,' says Ciancimino, 'and the next thing we knew, three months later, they were getting married.' The

[216]

couple were wed at Lambeth Register Office, and the press were not invited. Later a friend commented: 'I have a feeling it was a private thing with no one there.'

John's marriage was not to be long-lived. But in a way it was almost like just another of those Sixties schemes that seemed like an awfully good idea at the start, and then less so, soon after the event.

As far as Bondmania was concerned, as the 1960s drew to a close, neither audiences nor the media showed any sign of waning interest. On the contrary, the biggest film news of the year was the hunt for the actor who would be the new James Bond. Sean Connery had been hesitant about doing *You Only Live Twice*, but this time he was adamant. He'd had enough, he told Saltzman and Broccoli. He really didn't want to spend the rest of his career just playing 007, so they'd just have to find someone else. What followed was the biggest media sensation since the search in 1939 for Scarlett O'Hara.

'I tested about a hundred,' says Peter Hunt, who had been promoted from editor to director, but still there was no sign of the new Bond. The selection process was made more complicated because the decision had to be taken by committee. There were now three separate parties who had to agree: United Artists – the distributors, Saltzman and Broccoli – the producers, and the Fleming Trust – administrators of Fleming's estate. And the decision consequently proved far from straightforward. It wasn't just a case of who looked and seemed right; first they had to make up their minds what they were looking for.

'At that time the whole style in England had changed – the hippies or long-hairs had arrived,' says Hunt, 'so it was: "Shall we go with somebody young and in the fashion of today? Or shall we make it a completely different character and do something else?" We went through at least half a dozen different characterisations, and in the end we said, "No, let's find somebody like Sean Connery." But it took two weeks just to get there.'

Having decided what they were looking for, now it was just a question of finding it. 'We went through a lot of actors who were like Sean,' Hunt recalls. 'I shot test after test after test after test. I even shot

[217]

sequences of fights and love scenes and cut them together and we still didn't find anybody that all three different groups could agree upon.'

Enter the young Australian actor, model and car salesman George Lazenby. Lazenby had recently had a cult hit as the Fry's chocolate man, hauling a crate of chocolates in a TV ad; unawed by the prospect of taking on practically every other actor in showbusiness, he set about perfecting the Connery look. He got kitted out by his Savile Row tailor, and bought himself a Rolex watch, but it was while getting his hair cut in the Connery style that he got his break. There in the chair next to him at Trumper's hair salon in Curzon Street was none other than Cubby Broccoli.

Lazenby immediately switched into his best 007 routine, and the next thing he knew, he had a screen-test with Hunt. 'As far as I was concerned, he certainly looked the right physical type,' says Hunt. 'He was the sort of guy the girls would go for. So I tested him and tested him. He was seen with clothes on, with clothes off by everybody you could possibly think of, but we still weren't quite sure. But by then time was beginning to run out. I'd found the locations and everything else, and we still hadn't got a James Bond. Cubby was getting adamant and saying, "I think he really could be very good," so for want of finding anyone else, I said, "OK, we'd better go with him. Everybody likes him, so let's do it." And that was it.'

Hunt was also reassured by the knowledge that even though they had a new 007 actor, the Bond team regulars would be there as ever, so with all that back-up, surely there couldn't be too much room for disaster. 'Even though I wasn't quite sure,' says Hunt, 'I thought, Well, everything'll turn out all right, 'cause whatever happened I knew I had the right crew and they all knew me.' Hunt was also well aware just how crucial John's music was to the success of each Bond film and how much it could contribute. And he relied on him accordingly. 'Even if things didn't work out with Lazenby', says Hunt, 'I knew that come what may, John Barry would deliver the goods. 'Cause otherwise, if he didn't, I told him I would kill him! It was my first film as a director and I was so determined it was going to be a great film. So I took him by the throat and threatened him with his life, and I said,

"You had better write me the *best* Bond score ever." And he did.'

What John came up with was indeed probably the best Bond score there's ever been. In *On Her Majesty's Secret Service* everything was at least doubled: there was twice as much drama, twice as much tension, and about four times as much romance.

'What I felt was: Well, we've lost Sean, and we've got this turkey in here instead,' says John. 'And so I have to stick my oar in the musical area double strong to make the audience try and forget that they don't have Sean. You could have gone either way. You could have said: "We've got a new Bond, let's try to go a new way," but what I did instead was to over-emphasise everything that I'd done in the first few movies, and just go over the top to try and make the soundtrack strong. To do Bondian beyond Bondian.'

It was just as well John had taken that approach, for as it turned out, the film would need every second of extra help. Luckily, Hunt knew the capacity of music to transform a film from the start and was adept at using it. 'In my opinion,' he says, 'film-making is a mixture of elements, and every element should really be there to help the other elements along, to tell the story. The scriptwriter writes all these wonderful descriptions about the sun shining and the moon coming up, and then when you get there it's pissing with rain or it's snowing. And you've got no money, and you've got to shoot it today, because tomorrow you haven't got any time. And I think that from then onwards it's up to the editing and the sound effects and the music and the colour to make it look the way the scriptwriter intended. That's really what film-making is all about. Each thing helps the other. But the music shouldn't be dominating it. As a member of the audience you should be relaxed and not even notice it. But as a film-maker I know that something here requires a little underlining perhaps or whatever. That's where I would work closely with John, to get the right effects.'

On Her Majesty's Secret Service was John's fifth full Bond score, and his sixth collaboration with Hunt. Since his early days on *Dr No* and *From Russia With Love*, where Hunt had still been showing him the ropes in some ways, John was now a master of his craft. 'Over the years John progressed enormously,' Hunt acknowledges, 'and by the time we were doing *On Her Majesty's* I didn't treat him with kid gloves any more. I just expected him to know it all.'

But that didn't mean John had completely free rein. Hunt told him clearly what he wanted for the different parts of the film. 'As a film-maker you have certain quirks and ideas, but by then we were friendly, and so it was of no consequence. He could say whatever he liked to me, and I could say whatever I liked to him. So we'd go through it and I'd say. "Do you think that's all right? Don't you think we ought to have something to help that poor old actor along?" Or "I wanted to make a point here and I didn't get it properly – let's have more of that."

'Sometimes I used to do things to him that he hated, like I would take a piece of music he'd written for one section and put it somewhere else. He never liked that. He used to say, "What did you go and do that for?" And I used to say: "Well, it fits there very well, doesn't it?" And he'd say: "Hmmm." But we used to argue as well, 'cause I used to say: "We can't have this lovely orchestration over a chase, because you're going to slow my movie down, and we can't have that. We've got to keep it moving." And sometimes he'd say: "OK," but that's all part of making the music fit the film. You can't just have music plonking along. The thing with me, though, was that at least I could read music and I didn't do anything that wasn't complimentary, so John respected my opinion. Later on he used to have such fights with them all, 'cos they put his music in all over the place and they didn't know what I'd done and see how I'd done it. They were nine-to-five jobbers and technicians. I was a fan.

'I'd had certain ideas from the start, though, as to what kind of thing I wanted. I told John: "I want beautiful, lush, nightclub-sounding music here, I want saxophones there." I just said: "I want the whole film to sound lush, big and beautiful".'

And that's what Hunt got – mostly – from the Prokofiev-and-brass angularity of 'This Never Happened to the Other Feller' to the sub-limely languid, long, slow smooch of 'Try'.

One of the staple ingredients of the Bond style which John had established was the one which galled him the most – the use of the original 'Bond Theme'. Since Hunt had used it so effectively throughout *Dr No*, he'd consigned John to weaving it into his own scores for ever after, and so John was stuck with the one Bond element for which he got no official credit. 'Do we have to have that "Bond Theme" in there again?' John used to ask. 'But at the same time it was his version that sounded so good,' says Hunt. 'So it was his own fault – he should have ruined it. But that's the genius of inexperience. I never deliberately told him to include it in a particular way, he just knew he had to.'

To get round the problem, John had already written his own alternative '007 Theme' which he'd been using since *From Russia With Love*, but with *On Her Majesty's Secret Service*, he'd end up with another one as well. It was obvious from the start that they weren't going to have a song called 'On Her Majesty's Secret Service' and so Cubby Broccoli came up with the idea of using the last line of Fleming's novel: 'We have all the time in the world'. Being the close of the story meant, however, that it couldn't really be used at the top of the film.

'The reason that we used an instrumental over the titles', says John, 'was because "We have all the time in the world" is the last line in Fleming's book. It's the only time that Bond ever gets married for real, so to start the movie off with that would have been dramatically inaccurate, so I said, "Let's do the instrumental for the opening, and then we bring in the song halfway through the movie as the love theme, and go from there".'

And so that's what he did. The Moog-fuelled 'OHMSS Theme' is the great John Barry TV Theme that never was. Had it been written for a *Persuaders*, or *Avengers*, it would have long ago ranked alongside the all-time classics, but it wasn't. And consequently it's long been lost amid John's other work of the time, swamped by competition from its own author.

As far as the rest of the score went, Peter Hunt had said he wanted 'lush, big and beautiful'. He'd got big on 'OHMSS', he'd got lush on 'Try', but where he really got beautiful was on the song John wrote with legendary lyricist Hal David – 'We Have All the Time in the World'.

John had homed in on the emotional final scene in the film, where

Bond is with the woman he truly loves, planning their future together, just before she's murdered. 'I harked back to "September Song" from the film *September Affair*, by Walter Huston – John Huston's father,' says John, 'singing about the autumn of his years in a reflective vein.'

In order to give the song the same poignancy, John needed a singer with a voice that could convey years of experience, whilst at the same time giving it heart. His brainwave was to call in Louis Armstrong, although Armstrong had by then been seriously ill in hospital for some time. John knew that if the old maestro could make it to the studio and sing it, he would be perfect. Peter Hunt agreed, but they still had to persuade the producers.

'John had this idea to have Satchmo do the song,' says Hunt, 'and I thought it was great, but then someone phoned Harry and said, "Well, we can get him, but he's going to cost five thousand dollars, and we can't have the rights." So Harry said, "OK, forget it." When he told me, though, I said, "No way." I just screamed at him down the phone and said, "We're going to have this man do it, come what may!" and I made him so frightened that he said, "OK, hold on."' And so they got the deal. 'I was just so determined 'cause I thought it was such a marvellous song, but it was John who had had the idea to start with.'

The session itself proved difficult as by now Armstrong was really gravely ill, but in spite of it all, he behaved like the true professional and gentleman he was, and John was not only moved by his performance but thrilled to have met one of his all-time heroes and to have worked with him. 'He was the sweetest man you could ever meet,' says John, 'but because he'd been laid up ill for so long, he had very little energy left. He couldn't even play his trumpet, but he managed to sing our song, even if it was just one verse at a time. What I couldn't believe, though, was that at the end of the session, he came up to me and said, "Thank you for this job. Thank you for using me." I couldn't believe it. *I* should have been thanking *him*, and there he was, my hero, thanking *me*.'

It was the last song that Armstrong ever recorded, and although it wasn't a hit at the time, it became one nearly thirty years later in Britain when it was used in a Guinness TV ad. The film was not a box-office smash, although it didn't do badly. Lazenby had played Bond with confidence, but perhaps never had the charisma or panache to really carry it off. He had also proved a media liability from the word go, boasting to the press how he was looking forward to being Bond, 'mainly for the broads and the bread'. As he started to believe his own hype even before filming had started, he wasn't endearing himself to anyone else either, particularly not John.

'I remember George Lazenby came down to one of the sessions,' says John. 'He stood at the back and listened to the score for one of his scenes. Then he came up to me and said, "It fits!" as if it was the greatest compliment I could ever have hoped for. I thought, Christ, we've got a real brain going here. What do you think I do for a living?'

For the last few years, there had no longer been any question as to what John did for a living. His days of dividing his time between a pop group, arranging and film-work were long gone, and even though he was still scoring TV ads intermittently, generally the whole idea of TV themes was something he'd left behind. So it came as a surprise when he was contacted by Geoffrey Heath at ATV music publishers and asked if he'd like to write the music for a new TV show. ATV was the music publishing arm of TV company ITC, and Heath was responsible for commissioning music. They had a new TV series in the pipeline and decided they wanted to raise the calibre of the music as much as possible.

John was initially sceptical, but agreed to see Heath to find out more. Heath came to Alembic House and started to explain. 'It's called *The Persuaders*,' he told John, 'and it's got Tony Curtis and Roger Moore in it.'

'Hmm,' said John. 'I don't really do TV, you know.' John had, after all, won three Academy Awards by this time, and was an established film composer.

'Sure,' said Heath, 'but this is a quality programme. It's got big-name stars, and also it's been pre-sold to America already, so the royalty potential is considerable.'

John said he'd think about it; he'd drive down to Elstree Studios with Heath to see the filming and talk some more. In the end, Roger Moore persuaded John to do it. 'He found it quite novel – the idea of doing a TV show again,' says Heath, 'but because he was a commercially minded guy, he understood the show's potential too.'

John's title theme ended up being one of his biggest hit singles when it made the Top Twenty in 1972. It also marked the beginning of a successful working relationship with ATV, for whom John wrote two more monumental themes over the next couple of years – for *The Adventurers* and *Orson Welles' Great Mysteries* – each of them similar in mood, but unique in melody.

With his theme for *The Persuaders*, John confirmed his reputation for versatility and innovation. Although he was dealing with a scenario that was highly derivative of Bond, he yet again created something that was distinctive, new and highly memorable. To find the right sound, he went back to John Leach, who devised a way of overdubbing a cimbalom with the zither-like Egyptian instrument – the kantele. He then worked out the melody from there, because only certain notes could be played on the cimbalom. 'The way it was, you were very restricted and had much fewer notes,' says John, 'but because I'd done the music by maths years earlier, I knew exactly what you could do, and what you couldn't.'

Once he'd worked out the hypnotic melody line, he used the Moog to bind it all together. He'd discovered the driving dynamism of the Moog sound on *The Lion in Winter* and *On Her Majesty's Secret Service*, and he drew on it again for *The Persuaders*. As with *The Ipcress File* before, John managed to blend all these elements in a way that sounded contemporary, whilst using a traditional format.

'The thing about "The Persuaders",' says John, 'is that it's in three/four, while practically the whole of rock and roll is four/four. I always remember reading somewhere that Richard Rodgers had said, "When in doubt, go with three/four, because it has a natural energy that carries it along."

'The Persuaders' was perfect pop – the ultimate three-minute melody that once heard, never quite leaves you. In this, as in so much of his work, John's pop sensibility was paramount – an important factor in his final film of the Sixties.

British director John Schlesinger had been approached by United Artists to make a film for them, and after much dispute had finally persuaded them to let him film *Midnight Cowboy* in New York. He had initially had major doubts about UA's commitment to the project. After all, the subject was not exactly upbeat, and Schlesinger worried that the Americans would never really get behind it. But they did, and so the director flew to New York.

The next thing was to find a musical director to tackle the score. With the film's various locations in New York, as well as Texas and Miami, a contemporary score was required – one that used different pop tracks to reflect what was going on in the film. *The Graduate*, made by *The Lion in Winter* producer Joe Levine, had recently been a big hit; it had shown that pop music could be used throughout a film to good effect, and not necessarily just over the titles. So what Schlesinger wanted was someone who understood pop, could source suitable material and then pull it all together.

'What we were looking for when we first started,' he says, 'was a co-ordinator of popular songs – someone who wasn't necessarily going to compose. But we also wanted a totally different-sounding score from the usual things at the time. We'd decided that the clue to the image of the film was neon, so we needed a score that was rhythmically pretty hip and could embrace the various aspects of the New York scene. John was already known as a very versatile composer, but he'd also had his own pop group, so we knew he would understand what we were after.'

Fortuitously, John happened to be in New York anyway at the time. He'd been there for six months working on plans for a musical of F. Scott Fitzgerald's *The Great Gatsby*. The producer was John's old hero, the jazz clarinettist and band-leader Artie Shaw, who had optioned the rights to the book, and John had started working with lyricist Carolyn Lee. Then, out of the blue he got a call from Jerome Hellman, Schlesinger's producer. 'John Schlesinger's in town,' he said, 'and he's making a movie called *Midnight Cowboy*. Why don't you come and have a meeting?' And so, sensing that things might not completely work out on the Gatsby project, John agreed.

Schlesinger had provisionally laid Harry Nilsson's 'Everybody's Talkin'' over the title sequence, but United Artists were reluctant to use it as they wanted to own the copyright to whatever track was used. Schlesinger tried to persuade them, explaining that he thought both the rhythm and the lyric of Nilsson's song worked brilliantly with the film and that it would be difficult to find a replacement, but United Artists stood their ground. 'Anybody can write a song like that,' said the Head of Music. 'Like who?' asked Schlesinger, as UA went off to commission something of their own. 'They came back with somebody quite hopeless, who'd written music for The Monkees,' says Schlesinger, 'and it was *absolutely* inadequate.'

Plan B was for John, who was now on board as Musical Supervisor, to sit down with Nilsson and write a new alternative theme. Which they did. 'It was called "Child, You are Yourself",' says Schlesinger. 'It had a similar rhythm to "Everybody's Talkin'"', but it didn't really satisfy me as well as Harry's original recording, because lyrically it wasn't as good. In the end we showed the film to the distributors again with "Everybody's Talkin'"' back on it, and the music guy jumped out of his chair at the end of it and said, "My God! Where d'you get that music from? That number's just perfect!" And we said, "Well, we showed it to you six months ago and you said, 'Anybody could write it'." So in the end they finally bit the bullet, and "Everybody's Talkin'"' was in.'

Re-recording the song for the film, however, proved an insight for Schlesinger, for Nilsson's schedule was not quite what the director was used to. 'It was my first introduction to this awful business of "Shall we start at two in the morning?",' says Schlesinger, 'which is what Nilsson preferred. It was always the dead of night and John worked very closely with him, re-recording the title in various forms and lengths so that it fitted the different places it cropped up in the film.'

As well as re-recording Nilsson, John's role on the film ended up being much more than merely that of Musical Supervisor. 'I did all the underscore,' says John, 'the actual score, plus the *Midnight Cowboy* harmonica theme. I also supervised everything else – all the other songs. I worked closely with Jerry Hellman and John Schlesinger and we took a lot of time choosing those songs very carefully, going out to gigs and sourcing bands. And except for "Everybody's Talkin'" and "Elephant's Memory" which had already been done, we recorded all the rest in New York. It was really like scoring, but with songs. The tempo, the feel, the lyric content – everything was very carefully selected, and it was very fresh at the time to see a movie scored like that.'

The songs that were used were indeed well chosen, and give the whole score a unity that shows the skill of its Supervisor. Since then countless scores have been constructed on the same principle of using different pop tracks, but what makes *Midnight Cowboy* stand out is that John did it with not only sensitivity, but supremely good taste.

His most memorable contribution to the film was his own theme; the ache of that yearning harmonica over that out-on-the-prairie clip-clop bass made a direct line for your heart. 'Just sing it,' John had told Shirley Bassey with 'Goldfinger', and she gave it all she'd got; in the same way, virtuoso harmonica player Toots Thielman made that instrument sing as never before, coaxing out John's melody and defying you not to be moved.

'Everybody's Talkin'' expressed the sense of exploration and optimism at the start of the film, while John's theme captured the essence of everything else the film was about. It would have been easy and obvious to emphasise the darkness and despair, the seediness and wretchedness, but John always looked beyond the surface and sought out the emotion underneath.

'You drive through New York City's bad streets and you see these guys walking around, and there's this terrific sadness in the air,' says John. 'That's what life is like there, and it's not going any place. That harmonica theme was the soul of that character in New York. I wrote the whole thing in an apartment on Fifth Avenue, in twenty minutes, counter-melody and all. That's how it's done. You think about it a lot, clear your mind – and then that's it.'

With his theme to *Midnight Cowboy* John had again created something

[227]

uniquely appropriate for its subject and diverse from his other work of the period. He'd also achieved a long-held ambition: he'd written a theme that would convey a deep sense of America. During the course of the Sixties, his understanding of country and his musical capability had developed to the extent that he could bring the two together to create the ultimate theme that wasn't just about a lonely city, it was about lonely America.

'I remember going to a party with Al Bart who's a big producer and agent over there,' says John. 'They handle all the big composers and he said: "How come *you* did *Midnight Cowboy*? There were about four writers up for that, so how come a goddamn limey ended up doing it?" I said: "Because a 'limey' directed it and decided to use a 'limey' composer. Because a 'limey' knows how to look at New York. New York doesn't know how to look at itself, and Yorkshire doesn't know how to look at itself, but John Schlesinger knew how to look at New York and he wanted me to do it because I knew how to look at it too. And *that's* why it was a success.'

Since childhood, America had been the source of all the most exciting things in John's life. During the war there had been American soldiers in York bringing with them an affluence unseen at home, and then later, while England was still stuck in the austerity of the postwar years, America represented a whole new style of life. It was where the cinema came from. It was where jazz came from, the Hollywood Musical and rock and roll. In fact, everything that was new, exciting and glamorous came from America. For John's generation, America was the land of their pop mythology. Their male icons were the Hollywood Rat Pack – Frank Sinatra, Dean Martin *et al* – and it was that culture that inspired them.

Since he'd first visited there in the early 1960s, John had been using American slang, way before it was commonplace. 'He used to say, "right on" in that American way,' recalls Trevor Peacock, 'and I remember thinking, What does he mean? Is he getting on a horse or something?' In his dealings with the American film moguls in London, John had also related to their verve, dynamism and energy. He had inherited a similarly ballsy, no-nonsense approach from his father, and

[228]

so, in a way, his working style had more in common with the Americans than the more traditionally indolent English.

With *Midnight Cowboy*, John had finally tackled America musically, but this was an America which had changed significantly since the relatively innocent optimism of the Kennedy era. The end of the decade had brought change with it once again, and the change wasn't only in America.

The Sixties' bubble was finally beginning to burst both in England and abroad. There were anti-Vietnam demonstrations on London's streets, Enoch Powell had given his 'Rivers of Blood' speech and the break-up of The Beatles seemed symbolic of Britain's malaise. 'When The Beatles split up in 1969 it kind of drew the curtains on the era,' says Leslie Bricusse, 'and it was over. It was as if all that energy could only be sustained for a certain time.'

Changes were afoot in the film world too. It was inevitable really that London would in the end be weighed down by its own hype. For every great film made at the peak of the London boom, there was a handful of flops, near-flops and out-and-out disasters. Some of them, like *The Battle of Britain, Cromwell* and *Goodbye, Mr Chips* had been expensive disasters. In the scramble to make the best, biggest and most lavish English film, some efforts had misfired badly and the money men were soon keeping a tighter rein on the budget-strings.

'When you have big successful films like the Bonds and *Tom Jones*,' says David Picker, Head of United Artists' London Production Office from 1961 to 1972, 'everyone starts to copycat, and costs start to escalate. That changes the market-place. We were very, very successful for a long time over there, but the fact is that things change and directors who make successful movies move on and change their attitudes and their demands. Everything is always evolving and the challenge everybody has is to try and stay ahead of the curve if you can, as opposed to producing more of the same.'

American money had fuelled the British film industry for much of the decade, but by 1970, almost all the major American backers had over-spent on investments which hadn't paid off, and were now heavily in debt. Having less money all round, it was only natural that they would look to keep their own industry afloat before worrying about anyone else's. Besides, Britain was no longer 'swinging', and it was now America itself which was producing its own vibrant 'new' cinema. Films like *The Graduate*, *Easy Rider* and *Woodstock* had captured the spirit of young America, and just as Britain had at the start of the decade, America suddenly had its own new generation of directors – Coppola, Altman, Nichols and so on – and actors like Dustin Hoffman, Jack Nicholson and Jon Voight, and what was coming out of England seemed suddenly remote and irrelevant by comparison.

The knock-on effect was that suddenly the financial backbone of the British film industry had disappeared. The talent was still there; there just weren't any funds. But the withdrawal of American backing had only worsened an already slackening situation. The magic really seemed to have gone out of British film. Good films were made, such as *Performance* and *The Go-Between*, but those were the notable exceptions. Generally the industry appeared to have lost its way. Even Saltzman and Broccoli had both individually had flops with the Ken Russell-directed Harry Palmer film *Billion Dollar Brain*, and the ill-fated *Chitty Chitty Bang Bang* respectively.

But although the Americans were no longer putting large-scale finance into British film, they were still decidedly interested in British talent. And British talent needed an outlet. So we got Schlesinger's *Midnight Cowboy*, and Richard Lester's *Petulia*, which John also scored – both made in America. Likewise there was Peter Yates' *Bullitt* and John Boorman's *Point Blank*, and so gradually, the creative energy that had propelled the British film industry along throughout the 1960s began to move to America, back to where the money and the work was. And that creative energy included John. Within a few years, he would have left London for good and America would become his new home.

From seeing a black and white Mickey Mouse on the big screen at his father's cinema, John had risen to the top of the film-composing world. As well as his three Oscars, he had just won a Grammy for *Midnight*

Cowboy, and he was widely admired as one of the most talented and versatile composers in the industry. It had been an unusual route, but either by chance or design each step along the way had contributed to the Barry sound. His exposure to film and classical music throughout his childhood had developed in him an in-built sense of the dynamic between music and drama, whilst the brass-heavy sound of big-band jazz would form a vital part of John's Bond sound. But it was his pop sojourn that would have the broadest effect. The ability to construct a concise, yet unforgettable melody is the essence of pop, and John's understanding of it and talent for it made his scores unique.

During the Sixties, John's scores – like the films – came served up with large helpings of style, but from the Seventies onwards that was no longer the case – or at least not to the same extent. *Midnight Cowboy* had marked a turning point in John's career. Just as *Dr No* had been a bridge between his pop career and film music, so *Midnight Cowboy* was a link between his Sixties' scores and what would follow. It gave a nod back in the style direction, but it also looked forward to the more emotive, sweeping scores of the Seventies, Eighties and Nineties. John wasn't turning his back on stylisation for good, it was just that it would no longer play such a vital part.

The Sixties' scores did have emotion, but it was repressed. The music reflected the man and John used musical discipline to keep emotions tastefully in check. Those scores had refinement and elegance, but also the intensity of burning passions simmering just below the surface. And that's what gave them their impact. The way a present that comes gift-wrapped in twelve layers of perfectly patterned, hand-made tissue paper is always so much more enticing than the one in the cellophane bag. With music, what's memorable is the mystery that takes time to unravel. The emotion was there; it was just kept under wraps. Maybe that's why John's Sixties' scores have a greater appeal in England, whilst in America, it's generally his later work which excites the most interest. After all, despite the social changes of the last thirty years, we're still essentially a nation who prefer to keep our emotions hidden, rather than wearing them on our chests.

The term 'Barryesque' has come to mean a liberal, lush use of strings, which is of course a major feature of John's work, but those same strings have also come to be associated with so-called 'easy listening'. None of John's music was ever 'easy' though. Easy doesn't even come close. There is too much pain, loss and darkness in there by far. Loss is the essence of the human experience, common to us all. What John Barry has always done is to reach to the centre of that loss, and bring it back to us in a multitude of ways that reflect not only the pain, but the diversity of life itself: the joy, the romance, the sex and the laughter. And that's what makes his music special. That savouring and delight in the melancholy of life which is, after all, the hallmark of the true romantic.

EPILOGUE

HOLLYWOOD AND BEYOND

In the 1960s, John was at the heart of new music, new film and the new London. But what happened afterwards, once the Sixties euphoria had evaporated? What did America hold in store for him?

America became not only John's new home, but the continuing inspiration for some of his best work. The move from England also brought with it a change of style musically for John, and a new, slower pace of life. During the Eighties and Nineties, in scores such as his Oscar-winning *Out of Africa* and *Dances with Wolves*, John's music took on a different colour to his earlier work – characterised by a new, more outwardly emotive style and more traditional orchestration. But it didn't happen overnight. The Seventies were the transition period, a time of musical and geographical change, in which John made the gradual move from London to Long Island, New York.

The Seventies and Eighties also saw the culmination of John's epic musical contribution to the James Bond films. John had seen 007 through the different guises of Connery, Lazenby, Moore and Dalton, and incorporated the changing face of music and technology into his scores. But after composing for more than ten Bond films, it was time to move on.

★　　★　　★

[233]

Before making the final move to America, John spent the first few years of the Seventies between London and Majorca. As the Sixties faded, most of the London film industry found itself in the grips of a strange hangover period, but in spite of the less than buoyant mood, Bond, as ever, was still going strong.

Between 1970 and 1974 John scored two Bond films: *Diamonds are Forever* and *The Man with the Golden Gun*, but the job was already beginning to lose its lustre for him. 'John had a loyalty to Bond,' says director of *Goldfinger* and *Diamonds are Forever* Guy Hamilton, 'but it was also becoming a chore, because there were other things that John wanted to be doing, and was doing. Really a lot of the excitement had gone out of it.'

Despite John's lack of enthusiasm, he still wrote two very good scores and one and a half classic title songs for *Diamonds are Forever* and *The Man with the Golden Gun* respectively. The *Diamonds'* song was vintage Bond, and became one of the all-time Bond favourites, but was also the cause of yet another rumpus between John and Harry Saltzman. Saltzman hated Don Black's lyrics, considering them too vulgar and obvious, but John refused to accommodate any changes. In the end, the song was of course kept in the film, but thanks to the severely cooled relationship between producer and composer, and the fact that John had committed to other projects, he didn't score the next Bond film *Live and Let Die* and it was written by Paul McCartney's Wings and George Martin instead.

John was coaxed back to Bond for *The Man with the Golden Gun* in 1974, but it was a hurried affair, with John doing the whole score in under two weeks. The title song recorded by Lulu hasn't lasted too badly but is dismissed by John as one of his lesser moments, and on release neither the song nor the film were big hits with the public.

While British film in general seemed to have lost its way, many people in the industry, who hadn't left for America, were looking for alternative ways out. John thought he'd found his own temporary respite when the chance came to write a stage musical. Ever since *Passion Flower Hotel* he'd been wanting to try his hand again, but neither *The Great Gatsby* nor *Brighton Rock* had materialised. In 1970, however, the opportunity arose to work with his all-time hero – lyricist Alan Jay Lerner on a musical adaptation of one of his favourite books: Nabokov's *Lolita*. It was a dream-project come true.

The show was an American production and the pair spent a happy few months writing in Majorca, before moving on to New York for further writing and rehearsals. As a try-out for Broadway, the show opened initially in Philadelphia, but closed within several weeks due to poor reviews and even poorer attendance. After reworking and re-rehearsing it, they tried again in Boston a few months later, but had no more success, and the show closed for a second time. Director Mike Nichols saw the show there and thought he could make it work. 'I know what this show needs,' he said. 'I think I can make it work'. He suggested that he'd like to direct it on Broadway in a year's time, once he'd finished editing his film *Carnal Knowledge*. But Lerner was not prepared to wait. He had other projects scheduled and so the show was shelved.

Not one to give up though, even after the third less than successful stage musical attempt, John persevered and scored the well-received film musical of *Alice's Adventures in Wonderland* in 1972. The following year he set to work on a musical again, with lyricist Don Black. The subject was another favourite of John's – *Billy Liar*. He had loved Keith Waterhouse and Willis Hall's original play and recognised the central character from his own North of England youth, and so *Billy – The Musical* was born. Starring John's old friend Michael Crawford in the title role, *Billy* turned into one of the most successful British shows of the Seventies and established Crawford as a major star. The songs were classics of the old-school sing-along musical kind and 'Some of Us Belong to the Stars', the show's big hit song, was soon being whistled at bus stops across the country.

In between scoring the musicals and the Bond films, and while still officially based in London, John also managed to work on various film projects including Anthony Harvey's cult oddity *They Might Be Giants* and John Schlesinger's *Day of the Locust*. Following on from his work on *The Lion in Winter*, there were also two more historical films – the turgid *The Last Valley* which starred Michael Caine as a medieval mercenary warrior, and was another case of, as Caine put it, 'a great score for a duff movie'. The second was the infinitely more successful *Mary Queen of Scots* starring Vanessa Redgrave, Glenda Jackson and a young Timothy Dalton. This time John's haunting theme and Oscar-nominated score complemented what was also a very good film, and included the song 'Vivre et Mourir', masterfully sung by Vanessa Redgrave with original lyrics by Mary Queen of Scots.

The other high point of the early Seventies film-wise was John's beautifully evocative score for Nicolas Roeg's equally beautiful *Walk-about* in which John picked up on the film's unspoken central theme of loss of innocence and self and brought it to life in his music. Less memorable, at least filmically, was another oddity, *Follow Me*, starring Mia Farrow and Topol. But it was directed by Carol Reed, and so for John, the chance to work with his *Third Man* hero mattered more than the quality of the script, and he turned out a lovely, wistful score. Also falling into the 'music more interesting than the film' category, were Patrick Garland's film of Ibsen's *A Doll's House*, and the offbeat Western *Monte Walsh* for which John rejoined forces with Hal David and the sublimely-voiced Cass Elliot for the song 'The Good Times Are Coming'.

In 1975, tax problems forced John to leave England and he spent the year in Majorca. It was to be his year out, his getaway time from the whole industry and everything to do with home. But never one to do absolutely nothing, John occupied himself writing a non-film-related instrumental jazz album for Polydor – *The Americans*. It was the first non-soundtrack album he'd done since *Stringbeat* with The John Barry Seven. But whilst the earlier album was subject to the musical requirements of a pop LP, this time John had carte blanche. The result was a homage to jazz, and harked back in particular to the American jazz film scores of the 1940s. 'In a strange way,' says John, 'it was about the superficiality of American life, but it was also done with a lot of love.'

John flew to Los Angeles to record the album, and while he was there, he was offered the score for an American TV special on the Roosevelts called *Eleanor and Franklin*. Thankful for the opportunity to be back working in Hollywood, John accepted. The idea was to stay in America six weeks. Six weeks turned into over twenty years.

On the strength of *Eleanor and Franklin*, John was offered the score to Dino de Laurentiis's remake of *King Kong*. Trumpeted at the time as the most expensive film ever made, the project also featured one of the most bizarre filming schedules. Terrified of competition from a rival production, Laurentiis decided to shoot the film in sequence, and John, alongside the cast and crew was consigned to work for months without any idea of the film's ending. 'I was flying by the seat of my pants,' says John. 'It was mad.'

John's score once again gained more recognition than the film, and he was subsequently offered another TV special – *Young Joe: The Forgotten Kennedy*, as well as Richard Lester's film *Robin and Marian* and Peter Yates' *The Deep*. Here again, although the film was only reasonably successful, the score yielded a hit single for Donna Summer with John's theme.

The last few years of the Seventies were not a creative high point for John, however. Tired of the frenzy of Los Angeles life, John bought land on a deserted mountain top in the foothills of the Sierras and decamped there for several months. The film industry's attitude to music had changed dramatically with the runaway success of both *Saturday Night Fever* and *Grease*, and John's style of score was no longer particularly fashionable. 'You couldn't get arrested,' says John.

The scarcity of decent offers ended up working to John's advantage, though, when a Hong Kong producer contacted him to score Bruce Lee's *Game of Death*. The Lee cult was at its height at the time, but as it had never held any particular attraction for John, he decided to avoid any involvement with the project. Eager to achieve this as politely as possible, John suggested the most outlandish fee he could think of, presuming it would be instantly refused. To his complete surprise the producer agreed, and a precedent was set. John's going rate in Hollywood suddenly went up.

From then on, getting a good fee was never a problem. Getting a stimulating film to work on was not always so easy. Bond, however, was still going strong, albeit by this time in the shape of Roger Moore. John had been unable to work on *The Spy Who Loved Me* because of his tax situation in the UK. The Inland Revenue had declared all his royalties frozen in 1977, in a dispute over unpaid tax, and as the situation was not yet resolved, John had to decline. However, 1979's *Moonraker* was partly filmed in France and so John was able to go to the location and liaise with the director without coming to England.

For the title song, John reunited with lyricist Hal David and wrote 'Moonraker' in what had by this time become recognisable Bondian style. It was originally recorded by Johnny Mathis, but John felt his version didn't quite capture the spirit of the song, and so the hunt began for another vocalist. Around the same time, John happened to be in the Beverly Hills Hotel one day when he heard a familiar voice coming from the hotel's Polo Lounge. 'John, John,' cried his old friend Shirley Bassey. 'Are you here for a while?' John asked her. The answer was 'yes' and within days, Bassey was in a Los Angeles studio recording 'Moonraker'.

At the beginning of the Eighties, John decamped from Hollywood and set up home in Oyster Bay, Long Island, just outside New York, with his fourth wife Laurie, who he had married in 1978. During the course of the decade John wrote three of his most famous later scores: *Somewhere in Time*, *Body Heat* and *Out of Africa*.

Somewhere in Time was a time-travel romance starring Christopher Reeve and Jane Seymour. Although it was a critical and commercial flop on release, it has since gone on to inspire an official fan club of devotees, all of whom are equally devoted to John's highly romantic score. The soundtrack has now gone platinum.

Body Heat meanwhile was a temporary return to more natural Barry territory. Its film noir subtext took John back to his cinematic jazz roots, and echoing his sultry treatment of *The Human Jungle* years earlier, John picked up on the sexual charge and malevolence of the Kathleen Turner character and used his favourite West-Coast jazz style alto sax to give it heat, tension and sex in equal measures.

Sidney Pollack's *Out of Africa* won John his fourth Oscar and established the broad, sweeping style of score that was to become his signature from then on. It was about Africa, but from a Western perspective. As John says: 'It was a romantic score about two people who love that country more than life itself. That's where the whole score lay – in that observation.' It was also about loss – that key Barry subject – and John's score reflected his own bereavement after the death of his elder brother Patrick in a car crash some months earlier.

The Eighties also saw the conclusion of John's role as the musical arm of James Bond. His tax situation had prevented him working on *For Your Eyes Only*, but by the time *Octopussy* was being filmed in 1983, it had been settled and John was once again free to work in England. He came back to London to write the score and also wrote the theme song 'All Time High' with lyricist Tim Rice. At the same time he bought himself a flat in his much-loved Cadogan Square. John once again had a home in London.

His last two Bond films, *A View to A Kill* and *The Living Daylights*, featured pop collaborations for their title themes with Duran Duran and A-ha respectively and both topped the charts. Working with British popsters Duran Duran was a happy experience for John, as the band's guitarist and songwriter John Taylor was an avid Barry fan, and surprised John daily with his encyclopaedic knowledge of his work. The band were thrilled to be working with their hero and to be part of the Bond film-making process, and the result was one of the best of the later Bond themes.

John's involvement in *The Living Daylights* was an altogether less happy affair. The shortlived Norwegian pop sensation A-ha were brought in by the producers, on the basis that the Duran Duran collaboration had spawned a hit, and so another pop act might do the same. On that count, they were right, the band's title theme got to number five in the UK charts, but in terms of artistic compatability the partnership between the band and John was less successful. In contrast to Duran Duran's enthusiasm, A-ha declined to visit any of the film shoots, and avoided all sessions except those which were strictly imperative. John was unimpressed, but nevertheless wrote a convincing, contemporary and varied score.

John's experience of working on *The Living Daylights* sounded the

[239]

final death knell to his enthusiasm for Bond, and although Cubby Broccoli tried to entice him back for *A License To Kill* a year later, John had had enough. John had created the musical identity for what had become the longest-running and most successful film series in the history of the cinema. He had been with Bond, virtually since the beginning and by the Eighties, apart from Cubby Broccoli, was the only remaining member of the original Bond production team. But his interest was beginning to wear thin. 'It lost its natural energy,' says John. 'It started to be just formula, and once that happens, the work gets really hard. The spontaneity and excitement of the original scores is gone, so you move on.'

It was the close of a chapter for John. As much as he had contributed something integral to Bond's screen identity, equally the films had become a significant part of John's musical persona. It was a link that was here to stay, but while John could have looked on the whole thing as an ending for him, instead he saw it as a means of having more time for other projects. As it turned out, over the next year, there were to be no other projects at all.

In 1988, John was rushed to hospital with a ruptured oesophagus and underwent major surgery. Doctors considered his survival miraculous, but after months on the critical list, John was discharged, although it was to be some time yet before he could return to normal life.

Once back home, the last thing anyone expected John to do was to get straight back into film-writing. They certainly didn't expect him to write another Oscar-winning score. But that was exactly what John did. His music for Kevin Costner's epic tale of the Native American West – *Dances with Wolves* – was to become John's most famous score of recent years.

As is often the case, though, the film was not seen as a likely hit at the start. 'At that time in Hollywood, there wasn't a big buzz on it,' says John. 'It was seen as an ego-maniac's three hour Western.' But the screenplay appealed to John nevertheless. 'I loved the script, and then when I saw half an hour of footage I could tell right away it was something special. You look at it and see if it's right, if it's fulfilling its potential on the page, and then if it is, you say "fine". Then you know what you're writing about and as a composer you have a real clarity of how you're going to approach it.'

In *Dances with Wolves*, as he had done in *Out of Africa*, John veered away from the indigenous musical styles the script may have suggested. He loved the music of the native Americans, but for him, the film was more about John Dunbar's perception of those people. 'I approached the whole score from John Dunbar's viewpoint,' says John. 'It was about the way he observed the Sioux tribe. Musically it was his assessment of the graciousness and dignity of other people.'

The 'John Dunbar Theme' was in a way a return to John's old, cherished themes of Americana and the West, but this time also infused with the core idea of one man's solitary quest to find something beyond his normal daily experience. It was a notion that had particular resonance for John. His recent illness had brought him face to face with his own mortality, and Dunbar's venture into the unknown was something he related to.

Over the next decade John scored Richard Attenborough's *Chaplin*, Adrian Lyne's *Indecent Proposal*, the ill-fated period drama *The Scarlet Letter* starring Demi Moore as well as Michael Apted's 2001 wartime code-breaking drama *Enigma*. All these scores bore the hallmark of what has now become the recognisable, and much-imitated, Barry romantic style. But, according to John, the change in direction from his earlier more stylised scores of the Sixties was not a deliberate move. 'It wasn't a conscious shift on my part,' says John. 'It was just that the scripts I was offered required a different kind of approach.'

But although his early Nineties work often contained strong, powerful themes, it was his 1998 non-film album *The Beyondness of Things* that proved the next landmark. Here, for the first time since his jazz album *The Americans* in the Seventies, John was given free rein by his record label Polygram to follow his musical heart, unhampered by the constraints of a film. The album became an autobiographical journey in which John traced his life from York to New York. It was a natural move for John to return to the themes of self-exploration and America, and it allowed him to not only further explore a symphonic style, but also to rediscover his Sixties pop jazz roots on the gutsy 'Dance with

Reality', with its echoes of *The Knack*, and the *Midnight Cowboy*-ish mournful harmonica of 'Kissably Close'. It was a look back for John, but it also looked forward. The album was dedicated to the bright new beacon in John's life – his son Jonpatrick, who was born in 1994 – and as much as it was about reflection, it was also about hope for the future.

John continued to explore his new-found musical freedom with the follow-up non-film score album, *Eternal Echoes*. Partly inspired by the best-selling book by Irish poet and philosopher John O'Donohue, John also continued the autobiographical themes of *The Beyondness of Things* and the album became an even more personal reflection of some of the deeper experiences of his life.

The success of *The Beyondness of Things* and *Eternal Echoes* has shown the continuing popularity of John's music, regardless of whether it accompanies a film or not. And that popularity is testimony to the fact that although over the course of forty years, the outward style may have changed, there is almost always a plaintive, vivid melody at the heart of all John's music which is essentially, uniquely John Barry.

AUTHOR'S JOHN BARRY TOP TEN THEMES

(In order of chronology, not priority)

1. *Goldfinger*
2. *The Knack*
3. *The Ipcress File*
4. *Deadfall*
5. *You Only Live Twice*
6. *We Have All the Time in the World*
7. *Midnight Cowboy*
8. *The Persuaders*
9. *Orson Welles' Great Mysteries*
10. *The Good Times Are Coming*
11. *Walkabout*
12. *Monte Walsh*
13. *Mary Queen of Scots*
14. *Follow Me*
15. *The Dove*
16. *Body Heat*
17. *Out of Africa*
18. *Dances with Wolves*
19. *Cry The Beloved Country*
20. *The Beyondness of Things*

[243]

Recommended compilations
The Very Best of John Barry (Polydor)
Themeology (Sony)
John Barry – The EMI Years – Vols 2 and 3
Ready When You Are J.B. (deleted)
John Barry – The Persuaders (deleted)

DISCOGRAPHY

FILM

1958	*6.5 Special*	GB 45 Parlophone R4294
1959	*Beat Girl* (US *Wild for Kicks*) (d. E. T. Greville)	GB CD Play 001
1960	*Never Let Go* (d. John Guillermin)	GB CD EMI 7 894162
1962	*The Cool Mikado* (d. Michael Winner)	GB LP Parlophone PMC119
1962	*Dr No* (arranged theme only, d. Terence Young)	GB CD EMI CDP7 962102
1962	*The Amorous Prawn* (d. Anthony Simmons)	GB CD EMI 350462
1962	*The L-Shaped Room* (d. Bryan Forbes)	
1963	*Zulu* (d. Cy Endfield)	GB CD FILMCD 022
1963	*The Party's Over* (d. Guy Hamilton)	GB CD EMI 350462
1963	*From Russia With Love* (d. Terence Young)	GB CD EMI CDP7 953442
1963	*It's All Happening* (d. Don Sharp)	GB LP COL SCX 3486
1964	*Goldfinger* (d. Guy Hamilton)	GB CD EMI CDP7 953452
1964	*A Jolly Bad Fellow* (d. Don Chaffey)	GB CD EMI 350462

1964	*Seance on a Wet Afternoon* (d. Bryan Forbes)	GB CD EMI 350462
1964	*Man In The Middle* (d. Guy Hamilton)	GB LP TFM 3128
1965	*The Ipcress File* (d. Sydney J. Furie)	JA CD MCA MVCM 22046
1965	*Mister Moses* (d. Ronald Neame)	
1965	*King Rat* (d. Bryan Forbes)	US CD COL JK 57894
1965	*The Knack . . . and How to Get It* (d. Richard Lester)	GB CD RYKO RCD 1071
1965	*Four in The Morning* (d. Anthony Simmons)	GB CD Play 002
1965	*Thunderball* (d. Terence Young)	GB CD EMI CDP 79062
1966	*The Wrong Box* (d. Bryan Forbes)	GB LP Mainstream S6088
1966	*The Chase* (d. Arthur Penn)	US CD PEG A 33530
1966	*Born Free* (d. James Hill)	GB LP MGM 2315031
1966	*The Quiller Memorandum* (d. Michael Anderson)	US CD Varese VSD 5218
1967	*You Only Live Twice* (d. Lewis Gilbert)	GB CD EMI CDP 790626
1967	*Dutchman* (d. Anthony Harvey)	GB 45 CBS SS63038
1967	*The Whisperers* (d. Bryan Forbes)	GB CD RYKO RCD 10720
1968	*Deadfall* (d. Bryan Forbes)	US CD RETROGRADE FSM 801242
1968	*Petulia* (d. Richard Lester)	US LP Warner Bros WS 1755
1968	*Boom!* (d. Joseph Losey)	GB LP MCA MUPS 360
1968	*The Lion in Winter* (d. Anthony Harvey)	US CD COL CK 66133
1969	*On Her Majesty's Secret Service* (d. Peter Hunt)	GB CD EMI CDP 790618
1969	*The Appointment* (d. Sydney Lumet)	FR 45 MGM 61629
1969	*Midnight Cowboy* (d. John Schlesinger)	GB CD EMI CDP 748409
1970	*The Last Valley* (d. James Clavell)	GB LP Probe SPB 1027
1970	*Monte Walsh* (d. William A. Fraker)	
1970	*Walkabout* (d. Nicolas Roeg)	
1971	*Murphy's War* (d. Peter Yates)	
1971	*Diamonds Are Forever* (d. Guy Hamilton)	GB CD EMI CDP 796209
1971	*Follow Me* (d. Carol Reed)	JA LP MCA MUPS 5137

1971	*They Might Be Giants* (d. Anthony Harvey)	
1971	*Mary Queen Of Scots* (d. Charles Jarrott)	GB LP MCA MUPS 441
1972	*Alice's Adventures in Wonderland* (d. William Sterling)	GB LP WB WK 56009
1973	*A Doll's House* (d. Patrick Garland)	GB CD Polydor 2383462
1974	*The Dove* (d. Charles Jarrott)	US LP ABC ABD R852
1974	*The Man with the Golden Gun* (d. Guy Hamilton)	GB CD EMI CDP790619
1974	*The Tamarind Seed* (d. Blake Edwards)	
1974	*The Day of the Locust* (d. John Schlesinger)	GB LP Decca PFS 4339
1976	*Robin and Marian* (d. Richard Lester)	
1976	*King Kong* (d. John Guillermin)	GB LP Reprise MS 4090
1977	*The Deep* (d. Peter Yates)	GB LP Casablanca CAL2018
1977	*The White Buffalo* (d. J. Lee Thompson)	
1978	*Game Of Death* (d. Robert Clouse)	GB CD FILMCD 123
1978	*The Betsy* (d. Daniel Petrie)	
1978	*Star Crash* (d. Lewis Coates)	GB CD FILMCD 085
1979	*Night Games* (d. Roger Vadim)	GB CD FILMCD 123
1979	*Hanover Street* (d. Peter Hyams)	
1979	*Moonraker* (d. Lewis Gilbert)	GB CD EMI CDP790620
1979	*The Black Hole* (d. Gary Nelson)	GB LP Pickwick SHM301
1980	*Somewhere in Time* (d. Jeannot Szwarc)	GB CD MCA DMCF 3333
1980	*Inside Moves* (d. Richard Donner)	US LP WB FMH 3506
1980	*Raise the Titanic* (d. Jerry Jameson)	
1981	*The Legend of the Lone Ranger* (d. William A. Fraker)	US LP MCA 5212
1981	*Body Heat* (d. Laurence Kasdan)	US CD SCSE CD 1
1981	*Bells* (d. J. Lee Thompson)	
1982	*Hammett* (d. Wim Wenders)	
1982	*Frances* (d. Graeme Clifford)	US CD SCSE CD 5-G
1983	*The Golden Seal* (d. Frank Zuniga)	US LP Compleat CST R–600

1983	*High Road To China* (d. Brian G. Hutton)	US CD SCSE CD 2
1983	*Octopussy* (d. John Glen)	GB CD RYKO RCD 10705
1984	*Until September* (d. Richard Marquand)	GB CD FILMCD 085
1984	*Mike's Murder* (d. James Bridges)	
1984	*The Cotton Club* (d. Francis Coppola)	GB CD GEFFEN GEFD 24062
1985	*Out of Africa* (d. Sydney Pollack)	GB CD MCA DMCF 3316
1985	*Jagged Edge* (d. Richard Marquand)	US CD Varese BCL 6001
1985	*A Killing Affair* (d. David Saperstein)	
1985	*A View to A Kill* (d. John Glen)	JA CD EMI CP 325076
1986	*Peggy Sue Got Married* (d. Francis Coppola)	US CD Varese VCD 47275
1986	*Howard the Duck* (d. William Huyuk, Gloria Katz)	US LP MCA 6173
1987	*The Living Daylights* (d. John Glen)	GB CD RYKO RCD 10725
1987	*Hearts of Fire* (d. Richard Marquand)	
1988	*Masquerade* (d. Bob Swain)	
1990	*Dances with Wolves* (d. Kevin Costner)	GB CD EPIC ZK 46982
1992	*Witness* (short film)	
1992	*Chaplin* (d. Richard Attenborough)	GB CD EPIC 4726022
1993	*Ruby Cairo* (d. Graeme Clifford)	JA CD SONY SRCS 6618
1993	*My Life* (d. Bruce Joel Rubin)	US CD PIC EK 57683
1993	*Indecent Proposal* (d. Adrian Lyne)	GB CD MCA MCD 10863
1994	*The Specialist* (d. Luis Llosa)	GB CD EPIC EK 66370
1995	*Across the Sea Of Time* (d. Stephen Low, IMAX 3-D Film)	US CD EPIC EK 67355
1995	*The Scarlet Letter* (d. Roland Joffe)	US CD EPIC EK 67431
1995	*Cry, the Beloved Country* (d. Darrell James Roodt)	US CD EPIC EK 67354
1997	*Swept From the Sea* (aka *Amy Foster*, d. Beeban Kidron)	GB CD LONDON 458 7932
1998	*Mercury Rising* (d. Harold Becker)	GB CD Varese VSD 5925
1999	*Playing By Heart* (d. Willard Carroll)	GB CD 466275
2001	*Enigma* (d. Michael Apted)	GB CD Decca 467864

TELEVISION

1957	*6.5 Special* (wrote arrangements & appeared)	GB LP PARLOPHONE PMCJ 1047
1958	*Oh Boy!* (wrote arrangements & appeared)	GB LP Parlophone PMCL 1072
1959	*Drumbeat* (wrote arrangements & appeared)	GB 45 Parlophone PMC 1072
1960	*Juke Box Jury* (theme only, recorded as 'Hit and Miss')	GB CD EMI 7894162
1962	*Dateline London* (theme only, recorded as 'Cutty Sark')	GB CD EMI 8350462
1963	*Elizabeth Taylor in London* (complete score)	GB CD PLAY 002
1963	*The Human Jungle* (arranged theme only)	GB CD EMI 8350462
1965	*Sophia Loren in Rome* (complete score)	US CD PEGO 23
1965	*The Newcomers* (theme only, recorded as 'Fancy Dance')	GB CD FILMCD 022
1966	*Vendetta* (themes 'Vendetta' & 'Danny Scipio' only)	GB CD COL 488582
1971	*The Persuaders* (theme only)	GB CD COL 488582
1972	*The Adventurers* (theme only)	GB CD Polydor 8490952
1973	*Orson Welles' Great Mysteries* (theme only)	GB CD Polydor 8490952
1973	*The Glass Menagerie* (complete score)	
1976	*Eleanor and Franklin* (complete score)	
1977	*The White House Years* (complete score)	
1975	*Love Among the Ruins* (complete score)	
1977	*The War Between the Tates* (complete score)	
1977	*The Gathering* (complete score)	
1977	*Young Joe, The Forgotten Kennedy* (complete score)	
1978	*The Corn Is Green* (complete score)	

1979   *Willa* (aka *Willa, Texas*, complete
       score)
1983   *Svengali* (complete score)

MUSICAL THEATRE

1965   *Passion Flower Hotel* (lyrics by   GB CD SONY SMK66175
       Trevor Peacock)
1971   *Lolita, My Love* (lyrics by Alan Jay
       Lerner)
1974   *Billy* (lyrics by Don Black)   GB CD COL 4728182

CONCEPT ALBUMS

1961   *Stringbeat*   GB CD PLAY 001
1975   *The Americans*   GB LP Polydor 2383405
1998   *The Beyondness Of Things*   GB CD LONDON 460 0092
2001   *Eternal Echoes*   GB CD Decca 470238

TELEVISION COMMERCIALS (A selected list)

Ariel, Austin Cars, Ballito Stockings, Castrol, Chivers Jelly, Dulux Paints, Izal,
Ingersoll watches, Kraft Sauce, Morris Cars, Nestlés Milk, Players Bachelor
Cigarettes, Pro-Plus, Rowntrees Black Magic, Silvikrin Shampoo, White Horse
Whisky, Wool, Yardley's.
(US) White Owl Cigars, Eastern Airlines (Second Summer), Kodak.

FILM PERFORMANCES

1958   *6.5 Special* (appeared as himself)
1961   *A Matter of Who* (appeared as himself)
1962   *The Cool Mikado* (appeared as himself)
1963   *It's All Happening* (appeared as himself)
1968   *Deadfall* (appeared as the Symphony Conductor)
1987   *The Living Daylights* (appeared as the Symphony Conductor)

Discography compiled by Robert Wood of Movie Boulevard, Leeds.

INDEX